HOME GROWN

Food Champions
of England's Northwest

© 2008

Published by The Bluecoat Press, Liverpool

Book design by March Graphic Design Studio,
Hope Street, Liverpool

Printed by Grafilur

ISBN 1 904438 70 9

Acknowledgments

The idea of a high quality hard backed book featuring the best of local and regional
foods was championed in 2006 by all the members of the Northwest Fantastic Foods
Partnership which included Made in Cheshire, Made in Cumbria, Made in Lancashire,
North West Fine Foods, Local Food First Manchester and Local Food First Merseyside.
The book was to provide a follow on to the successful *Food Lovers Guide to the North West*
developed in partnership with The Bluecoat Press and published in 2004. Independently
Paul Askew, chef patron of London Carriage Works, Hope Street and local food
champion Anne Benson were promoting the development of a book featuring the best of
Merseyside chefs and producers. It made sense for everyone to combine their efforts and
produce a book featuring chefs, producers and suppliers from across the Northwest. This
has been made possible by working in partnership with The Bluecoat Press and with
support from NWDA, Food Northwest and the Culture Company. Myerscough College
has provided the project and contract management.

*Any views or opinions expressed in this book are solely the interpretation of the author and do not
necessarily represent those of the Northwest Regional Development Agency or the Culture Company.*

This book has been part-funded by the Northwest Regional
Development Agency and the Culture Company.

HOME GROWN
Food Champions
of England's Northwest

Deirdre Morley

Additional text by Anne Benson and Liz Wilkinson

Photography by Colin McPherson

The Bluecoat Press

Contents

8

Introduction

Good restaurants with talented chefs, backed by an army of outstanding producers, are now a defining characteristic of England's Northwest. Working together, these two groups have set in motion nothing short of a food renaissance in the region, and one so dynamic that its products have penetrated right to the centre of the nation's capital. Today, you can find Mrs Kirkham's Lancashire cheese in Harrods food hall; eat Reg Johnson's corn-fed Goosnargh chicken at Fortnum's; buy Cumbrian Herdwick mutton and Galloway beef from Farmer Sharp on Borough Market.

Yet twenty years ago and less, regional cheeses made by hand at the farmhouse, using inherited recipes and traditional techniques, were close to extinction in the Northwest. The situation was similar with native breeds of sheep and cattle: thrifty beasts, attuned to the climate, raised to thrive outdoors on grass and forage, and yielding richly flavoured meat with not a trace of growth promoters or intensive rearing in sight. Nevertheless, those who farmed them struggled and often failed. As for mutton, no-one wanted that.

Today they are back, along with black pudding, rhubarb, damsons, potted shrimps and other honest-to-goodness favourites. Great-tasting new specialities have joined them: Cumbrian air-dried ham; Wirral asparagus; vegetarian black pudding – and those Goosnargh corn-fed chickens. They were bred at the instigation of a chef, the celebrated Paul Heathcote. After moving back to his native Lancashire from Le Manoir aux Quat'Saisons, he discovered that he couldn't get the kind of top-quality, local produce he needed for his distinctively British style of haute cuisine. So he began educating suppliers and working closely with producers, while bringing together like-minded chefs across the region who would buy their products.

The benefits were life-changing. The quality of produce rose sharply, the local rural economy looked up, diversity and innovation increased with the promise of a profitable market. Michelin stars began to twinkle in the north-country, and two of them were Paul Heathcote's.

The synergy from those partnerships has radiated across the region. Strong regional food bodies have provided vigorous support. Creative collaborations between chefs and producers have multiplied. Local produce and regional specialities of superb quality are now abundant. Through a new wave of small-scale retailers, particularly farmshops and farmers' markets, they are increasingly accessible to the mounting numbers of Northwest shoppers who want to buy them.

In this book we explore the Northwest food phenomenon through the people who are powering it. More than fifty of them let us into their lives, opening up their intriguing worlds of work with great candour and generosity. Chefs from twelve of the region's leading restaurants tell their personal stories, talk about their attitudes to food, share their recipes and the realities of this demanding profession. Their culinary styles are as different as their personalities, but what unites them is an unwavering commitment to using the best-quality, best-tasting ingredients for their dishes. Their shared preference is for the fresh, seasonal foods of the region, as little-travelled as possible, and produced to the highest standards by people they know and trust.

The chefs have personally chosen all the producers on that basis and feature their products in their recipes. We meet them on their daily rounds: hard-working farmers who take time to explain about their crops and livestock, who show respect for the land and living creatures, and cherish both. Together we walk orchard, field, fell and moor, whether in sunshine, mist or relentless rain. We are up with the lark to go shrimping, and out before dawn to join market traders; we watch the magical transformation of milk into cheese, of blood into black pudding, hear about hanging meat, and witness the alchemy of brewery and smokehouse, while practitioners unfold the secrets of their ancient crafts.

They are a remarkable band of people: ordinary and extraordinary at the same time. Their work is hard and repetitive, sometimes dangerous, but the zest with which they do it, the care they take, the light in their eyes as they talk of it, lift the spirit time after time. Of course, they must make a profit to live – and that's not so easy in the food line. But it's not money that drives them. It's love of what they do and faith in its value. They all believe in the intrinsic importance of food in the scheme of things: that it should be honest and wholesome, be accorded time in our lives and bring us joy. Its place should be at the centre of the home and family life, introducing children to the pleasure of good eating and mannerly give and take around the dinner-table, easing them into adulthood. Many of the chefs are active in education programmes with schools, and so are producers, eager to pass on the delight of growing and cooking.

The knowledge that millions of us don't know the origins of our food, or how to cook with raw ingredients, worries them deeply. The chefs are concerned that culinary skills are disappearing from the profession too, and are responding through educational bodies, and with training schemes in their own kitchens. A leading proponent is Liverpool chef, Paul Askew, and at his suggestion a royalty from this book will go to sponsor a scholarship for the winner of Northwest Young Chef of the Year.

At present, global food security is high on the agenda yet, in Britain, we produce barely 60% of the food we eat. Land is continually going out of production, and the number of British farmers is dwindling at an alarming rate. The people in this book are succeeding despite the odds. Guardians of our land and our culinary heritage, they are true champions. Let's support their endeavours and join with them. After all, it is in our very best interests.

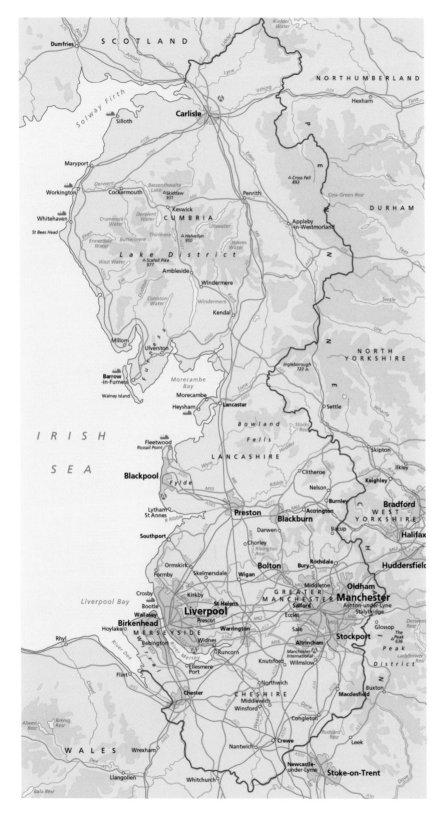

The journey to meet our Food Champions spans the five counties which make up England's Northwest: from Cumbria in the north, through Lancashire, Greater Manchester and Merseyside, to Cheshire in the south.

Paul Askew

The London Carriage Works

Hope Street Hotel, Liverpool

A RESTAURANT REVOLUTION has been taking place in
Liverpool. Hope Street is the nerve centre; Paul Askew the
dedicated standard-bearer, and officially designated Food Sector
Champion for Merseyside. His acclaimed restaurant sits
midway down this famous thoroughfare. It is part of the smart,
new, award-winning Hope Street Hotel in the heart of the
university district, flanked by theatres, surrounded by elegant
Georgian terraces, and provided with a spectacular cathedral at
either end. Despite the architectural competition, this stylish
establishment habitually turns heads. The attraction is not so
much the handsome Venetian palazzo that houses it, as the
street-level view of restaurant, bar and brasserie, revealed
through a grand sequence of plate-glass windows. These
exercise a filmic allure on passers-by, framing relaxed diners,
exquisite food, crisp white linen and chic modern design, in an
atmosphere of warm hospitality. The diners look out in their
turn, both actors and audience in the life of this sociable street.
Above all, they celebrate the superlative cooking of chef-patron,
Paul Askew. Under his direction, The London Carriage Works
has become a lodestar of fine dining and host to many celebrated
figures. The cuisine is modern international with influences
from around the world but, as the menu attests, the inspiration
is the fresh, local, seasonal produce of England's Northwest. In
the heyday of Victorian Liverpool, the discerning came here for
fine carriages; today they come for fine food.

"ANY REGION, ANY GREAT CITY, NEEDS A CULTURE OF GOOD FOOD. In
Liverpool, and throughout Merseyside, we have a restaurant scene that is
developing at an incredible rate of knots. Food festivals are going from strength to
strength, and farmers' markets are growing too – we even have one here on Hope
Street every month.

15

Of course, we're very lucky in the Northwest of England: top quality produce is right on our doorstep. Meat, fish, game, fruit, vegetables, dairy produce – they're all here in profusion and the range of products is immense. It's great for the chefs and, even better, it's great for the public because good eating is all about good ingredients. The integrity of what you buy, how far it's travelled and how long it's been kept: that's what determines the taste, the texture, the quality of food.

At The London Carriage Works we spend almost as much time and care sourcing ingredients as preparing them! Whether it's Bowland beef from Lancashire, pork from Cheshire, venison from the Lake District or sea bass from Liverpool Bay, we want the best. Not every ingredient is homegrown, of course. We have charcuterie from Spain, for instance, and olives from Italy and Greece. On the other hand, a lot of our produce is very local indeed. Our fruit and vegetables from Claremont Farm on the Wirral peninsula, travel just thirteen miles door to door. They can be picked in the morning, whisked through the Mersey Tunnel and served by lunchtime.

We have a few foreign chefs in our kitchen and they have been astounded at the sheer quality of the regional produce coming in. They're also genuinely impressed by the food renaissance in the UK as a whole, and by the high standards of cuisine being achieved now.

When your ingredients are first-rate, cooking can be such a joy. It's therapeutic too, for me. The kitchen is my fortress and my sanctuary. Although it's the engine room of the business, I can relax there.

Every morning I greet the staff, check that all the sections have what they need and solve any problems. Mine is not a combative style of management. I think you should lead by example. When things are going well, everything is quiet. When they're not – that's a different story. You need to be able to empathise with each person from having done their job yourself, and know when to put your arm round their shoulders, or give them a kick!

The brigade all know that if they come up with a good idea for the menu, it will go on. Instead of being dictated to, the way I was in my early career, and craving the day when I could have some creative freedom, we encourage them to have input. Everybody takes ownership of the menu. We're like a football team: we have different needs and strengths; we're only as good as the last meal we cooked and we have to keep improving!

Don't let's forget the people who serve the food either. They are key players. We rely on them to be well informed, to understand customers, to gauge their preferences and the different levels of service required. They have to work with a certain style, a certain sense of humour and develop that all important atmosphere of conviviality. We want to give people a great time, here. If we can do it for Condoleezza Rice, Ewan McGregor, or the Barcelona football team, then we can do it for everybody!

For years, I'd dreamed of opening a restaurant of my own in Liverpool; somewhere I could offer diners ambitious cooking, shaped by superb produce from the surrounding region. In 2003, my chance came. I was working here in Hope Street, in the glorious art deco Philharmonic Concert Hall, where I'd been executive chef for about seven years. Across the road was A. J. Buckingham's Furniture Repository, a really striking nineteenth-century building. Every morning I would drive past and think: 'That's got hotel and restaurant written all over it …'

No sooner had I started imagining the possibilities than I discovered it had been sold to a property developer. My heart sank. Then I found out that the buyer was a local businessman, David Brewitt. He wanted to create – and run – the city's first boutique hotel. The emphasis was to be on style, quality, thoughtful service and a personal approach. My spirits rose – we shared the same vision. Before long, we'd teamed up as partners.

We began the task of transforming what was essentially a run-down 1860s warehouse into a state-of-the art, modern hotel. Basia Chlebik was our lead architect and interior designer. She was the one who took our aspirations and turned them into wonderful reality. She restored the outside of the building to its Victorian grandeur and gave us superb contemporary interiors filled with natural light. And she did it in such a way that the original structure was preserved and exposed to view: beams, brickwork, and slender cast-iron columns (they're one of my favourite features).

We spent hours together debating everything, from the wood for the floors to the styling of the bedrooms, to the spectacular shards of glass that she designed to run, like rays of light, from ceiling to floor in the restaurant. Then tragically, Basia died before seeing the completed concept in operation. This is her legacy to us: a wonderful stage where we can perform each day for the pleasure of the public.

A lot of people ask about the name of the restaurant. Originally, we had chosen an entirely different one, but when Basia's renovation work uncovered 'The London Carriage Works' carved into the stone over the main doorway, we just had to call it that. In December 2003, we were ready to welcome our first customers.

Until you actually open the doors of a place like this, you don't know if the people will come. It's real 'Field of Dreams' stuff! Then, when they do come, you wonder anxiously if they'll like your food.

I knew the kind of menu I wanted to create: a true 'market' menu, one dictated to us by nature. So, if a dish sells out on a particular day and you can't get the fresh ingredients next day, you change the dish. There is nothing new in that. It's what has characterized French, Italian, Spanish cuisine forever. But we Brits, we'd bring food in from anywhere, anytime, regardless of the sacrifice in freshness and flavour. So would my concept be too radical? How would customers' react?

We had two years of utter experimentation to get it right for our clientele. Thankfully, the market menu was embraced and we've stuck to our guns! The people have come, and now we hope they'll continue on the journey with us, to the culinary heights which we hope to achieve. You have to progress all the time, and we are constantly innovating. But you must always remember that you are cooking for your customers, not for a Michelin star – although every chef would love one.

I'll come out and talk to customers at the end of the night, and I encourage our waiters to give me feedback too. Chefs have to be prepared to take constructive criticism and real food lovers will give that to you. You're a fool if you don't open your mind to what people think about your food. After all, your euphoria may be someone else's nightmare. We cook for our guests, not for ourselves.

I'd describe our cuisine as modern international. There are clean, crisp, contemporary flavours and old favourites re-invented. Molecular gastronomy à la Blumenthal is not my thing – I prefer to maintain the mystique! Although it's true to say our food has become more european as it has developed, those are not the only influences. I've lived in the Middle East, South East Asia, and New York and they've all made their mark on my cooking.

The first two go right back to my childhood. My father was a ship's captain in the merchant navy. Very appropriate for Liverpool you might say, but in fact our family came from Sunderland. We moved here when I was four, after he joined the Blue Star Line. It was part of the Vestey Group, owners of Dewhurst Butchers, a company that was founded in Liverpool in the 1890s to import food for Britain's growing cities. So, in his own way, my father was in food too.

He was at sea for forty years, finally becoming director for South East Asia and Australia. So, as a family, we travelled a lot when I was young. Between the ages of eight and fourteen I went to eight different schools. One was in Dubai and I think that's where I began to fall in love with food. I got taken to good restaurants because my father would be showing people around, but it was the food markets,

with their incredible displays of fish, fruit, and vegetables, that fascinated me.

Children love markets. I can still smell the first spice market I ever walked through. I'd have been about eleven. It was in Dubai's Old Souk: the narrow lanes concentrated the aromas. Cinnamon, saffron, cloves, nutmeg, cardamom, ginger, all the spices you could think of were there – and scores more you'd never seen or heard of – sold straight from open sacks and chests, a fantastic kaleidoscope of colours.

Two years later we moved to Singapore – an even bigger culinary centre! Four and a half million people live there, in an area about the size of the Isle of Man; they love food and have an incredible variety of different cuisines – Chinese, Indian, Malaysian, Sri Lankan, to name just four. I still remember the first food I ever tasted on Singapore's famous Newton Circus. It was beef satay off a tiny grill at a hawker's stand … and it was to die for!

Although I still went out there in the vacations, by the time I was fifteen or sixteen, I was back here and studying for my exams at Wirral Grammar School. A turning point in my life came when I decided to take a holiday job as a porter in a hotel kitchen. I got to see how chefs worked and how kitchens operated. I was gutting fish, peeling veg, washing dishes, cleaning floors – and I loved it! The restaurant wanted me to stay on and become a commis chef. My father said: 'What are you doing in the galley?' He despised the work.

I rebelled. I was doing A levels and I simply decided not to work for them. Instead, at eighteen I went straight to catering college. I'd inherited my father's

grit and determination so, despite his objections, I got my way. I don't think he realised just how passionate I was about the job.

To appease him, I did a management course, but I made sure I specialised in the culinary side. Now, I'm very glad that I did, because I learnt what's involved in running a restaurant – when, for example, you should change the linen; why a waiter should spend an hour polishing glassware before dinner, how cooks and waiters must work together. I got some French classical training too, which sparks off other ideas about food. You start researching Escoffier and really appreciating the great French classical tradition.

My first proper job was with De Vere Hotels as a chef tournand, moving around all the sections in the kitchen, gaining useful experience. I worked my way up to sous chef, but the way things were done in the UK then – the traditional roasts and grills, the general absence of innovation, the lack of creative input allowed to staff, the production-line feel – was depressing me. The Roux brothers, who started the culinary revolution in this country, had published their inspiring *New Classic Cuisine* – one of the first cookery books I ever bought – but I was was being asked to prepare prawn cocktail, steak chasseur and Black Forest gateau. And that was about the culinary peak. I asked for the freedom to do my own thing. When I was refused, I left and went to America.

Eighteen months in upstate New York with Herberts Restaurant and Banqueting Company taught me a lot in a very short time – about life and about cuisine. One time you'd be cooking in a busy restaurant, then for the Jockey Club at Saratoga, next a dinner for ten in a private home, then a barbecue for two-and-a-half thousand! I worked in a massive team, a brigade of all nationalities: Bolivian, Mexican, Polish, French, German – all, that is, except American. Only

'Chef' was American. His name was Joe Maloney and he encouraged us to put forward our national dishes, gave us creative licence and input into the menus. Joe made it feel as if every dish was a part of you.

I felt liberated, but then visa problems kicked in. I came home and, at 25, got my first job as a head chef, at Wincham Hall Hotel in Cheshire. That's when I realised what running a kitchen is all about – staff management and chasing suppliers!

I was ambitious, hungry for success. But you need luck, too. 1995 brought me a wonderful stroke of it. The Liverpool Philharmonic Hall, here in Hope Street, was completing a £10m refurbishment and seeking an executive chef for the new restaurant. I was recommended to them and duly recruited. With no suppliers and no crockery, we had two weeks before the Royal Gala Opening and the arrival of the Queen. It seemed like mission impossible – but we did it!

I have twice had the pleasure of cooking for the Queen. Over the years at the Philharmonic, the team and myself had the opportunity to serve a host of marvellous musicians: among them Joan Baez, Elton John, and the original Buena Vista Social Club. Great times! I think of the Phil as my spiritual home. It gave me the platform for what I'm doing now. Our business is only a few years old but, in many ways, it feels as if we've always been here.

My dream has come true, and currently we are expanding into the building next door. However, I'm very conscious of how much still needs to be done on the wider food front, in terms of public and professional education. I'm a member of our national Academy of Culinary Arts, which holds a brief for this work, and one of their initiatives, that has proved very effective, is the Adopt a School scheme. This helps member chefs to team up with their local schools, throughout the country, to get kids tasting and cooking food, finding out where it comes from, and learning what's good for us. I've met seven and eight-year-olds in suburbia who don't know how to use a knife and fork and whose packed lunches consist solely of chocolate, biscuits and a bag of crisps. There's a lot to be done!

On the professional front, there is a skills shortage in the industry that we need to address by improving professional training. A lot of the old methods are disappearing. I'm passionate about keeping the best from the past. If we're not careful, much of the knowledge and the craft of cuisine could be lost within another generation.

Promoting the highest standards of ingredients and cooking is vital too. I was doing a demonstration with the School Food Trust for 300 school cooks recently. Their response was really encouraging, but 50p per day to spend on a child's lunch is the problem, not the people cooking it.

At the end of the day, this is a British cultural problem. We only allow ourselves as long as it takes to put fuel in our bodies instead of giving time to what is one of the true pleasures of life. Mealtimes are when families and friends can come together and communicate with one another. It's a fundamental way of giving and sharing love. If only we can embrace this as a nation, we can have something truly worthwhile."

Paul Askew, The London Carriage Works **21**

Claremont Farm Asparagus with Gazpacho, Citrus Hollandaise and Summer Cress

SERVES 4

For the Asparagus

12 spears of jumbo size Claremont Farm asparagus, peeled and trimmed.

1 bunch of watercress

For the Hollandaise Sauce

2 large shallots

300ml white wine

10 black peppercorns

1 bay leaf

1 sprig thyme

2 egg yolks

250g butter

A squeeze of lemon juice and zest of lemon to taste

Maldon sea salt

For the Gazpacho

1 punnet of purple cress (or red chard)

5 vine tomatoes (ripe)

$^1/_2$ cucumber peeled and diced

Juice of half a lemon

2 shallots

1 clove of garlic, peeled and crushed

100ml tomato juice

50ml olive oil

Fresh basil and parsley to taste

Extra virgin olive oil for dressing

Cracked black pepper to taste

Maldon sea salt to taste

Pinch of pimento (smoked paprika) for seasoning

2 slices of stale bread

250ml water

Gazpacho (make in advance up to a day before and serve chilled) **[1]** Cut the vine tomatoes into chunks, peel the cucumber and cut into chunks, tear 2 slices of stale bread into pieces and place into blender with the olive oil, lemon juice, shallots, tomato juice, 1 clove of garlic, 250ml water and a couple of ice cubes. **[2]** Process until smooth, adding water or straining if necessary. **[3]** Season then refrigerate. **[4]** Garnish with olive oil and cress before serving.

Asparagus **[1]** In a pan bring some water to the boil with 2 tbsp of Maldon salt. **[2]** Once boiling, drop into it the washed and peeled asparagus, for no more than 2 minutes and refresh in a bowl of iced water.

Hollandaise Sauce **[1]** Peel and chop the shallots, put them in a pan with the white wine, lemon zest and juice, black peppercorns, bay leaf and sprig of thyme, reduce by half, pass through a conical sieve to create a liquor. **[2]** Melt the butter and carefully remove the opaque film that has formed on top, to clarify. **[3]** Put a pan of boiling water on the hob with a glass basin on top (taking care not to over-heat) add the egg yolks to the liquor and hand whisk to emulsify to a 'ribbon' or custard consistency, adding the butter in small quantities until it is all incorporated. **[4]** When at the required consistency, season.

To Serve Spoon the sauce over the asparagus, and arrange as in the photograph with fresh salad cress.

Pan roasted fillet of John Dory with New Season Leeks, Potatoes, Dry Cured Bacon & Granny Smith Apples

SERVES 4

4 fillets John Dory 200g each

2 large Victoria potatoes peeled washed, diced and blanched (cook the trimmings in a little cream and fish stock to make a sauce)

8 baby leeks, peeled washed and chopped

4 rashers dry cured bacon, finely shredded

1 bunch chives

100g unsalted butter

Vegetable oil for pan roasting

3 Granny Smith apples, peeled and diced

1 vanilla pod

100g caster sugar

Purple cress for garnish

Olive oil for garnish

Maldon salt and freshly milled white pepper to taste

1 Take the apple, most of the sugar and scraped vanilla pod with a little water and cook until a purée, blitz with a stick blender. Adjust the taste of the purée so that it isn't too sweet allowing a little of the acidity to remain. Cool and put the purée into a plastic bottle for dressing. **2** Heat a small sauté pan with a splash of vegetable oil and add the bacon, cook lightly then add the potato cubes, leeks, a knob of butter, white pepper and chives and cook for 2 minutes. **3** While this is cooking heat a splash of vegetable oil in a non-stick frying pan. When hot add the seasoned fillets of John Dory, skin side down and fry until the colour of autumn leaves. **4** Turn down the heat and add some butter. Allow to finish cooking in the pan for 2 more minutes and then plate as in the photograph. **5** The potato cream and fish stock just needs seasoning and blitzing before use as a loose, sauce-like, purée. **6** Dress as shown in the photograph.

Assiette of Claremont Farm English Strawberries, to include Sorbet, Soup, Panna Cotta, and Champagne Jelly

This is complex but good fun and many of the elements can be done in advance.

For the White Chocolate Crunch
(to form a base for the sorbet and sprinkle on the plate)
80g white fondant
120g glucose
80g white chocolate

For the Strawberry Sorbet
200ml water
200g sugar
80g strawberry purée
Shortbread biscuit for the dressing

White Chocolate Crunch [1] Place fondant and glucose in a small pan on a moderate heat until it reaches 155°C. Take off heat and add chocolate. [2] Stir until chocolate is melted then spread on greaseproof paper, wait until it sets, then blitz (use a stick blender or liquidizer).

Strawberry Sorbet [1] Place the water and sugar into a pan on the heat, and boil, without stirring, until thickened but not coloured. [2] Pour the thickened syrup onto purée then place into ice cream machine to churn, or freeze in a flat dish, stirring every 30 minutes until set. Store in the freezer. [3] Place in a ball shape on a shortbread biscuit as shown in the photograph.

For the Strawberry and White Chocolate Panna Cotta
200ml double cream
40g sugar
White chocolate to taste
1 leaf gelatine
50g strawberry purée

For the Strawberry Soup
200g fresh strawberries
20g sugar
30ml rosé wine
20g basil
Pinch of cracked black pepper
Shortbread biscuit for the dressing

For the Champagne and Strawberry Jelly
100ml strawberry jus
100ml champagne
2½ leaves gelatine

Strawberry and White Chocolate Panna Cotta [1] Place the cream and sugar on the heat to boil. While this is happening your gelatine should be soaking in a little warm water (drain water before use). [2] Once the cream has boiled stir in the white chocolate until smooth and then add the soaked gelatine, pass through a fine sieve and place strawberry purée in the bottom of ramekin with the panna cotta mix on top.

Champagne and Strawberry Jelly [1] Heat the strawberry jus in a pan and once heated through add the gelatine that has been soaking in water. [2] Place in container to set. Once nearly set whisk in the champagne. This will make a light foam on top of the jelly and will set accordingly. [3] For the garnish use slightly sweetened vanilla mascarpone and plate as in the photograph.

Strawberry Soup [1] Place all ingredients in a perforated tray then place another tray underneath to catch all the juice as this will become your soup; make sure you pass it through a sieve before serving. [2] Finish with chopped fresh mint and serve in a shot glass, with a shortbread biscuit.

Andrew Pimbley

Farming with flair
Wirral, Merseyside

IN THIS TINY, CROWDED ISLAND where land is under mounting pressure, a lot of us still picture farms as remote rural places, rather than just-off-the-pavement operations on the urban fringe. But that's where you'll find Claremont Farm's 250 acres: hemmed in by suburban housing on one side, a hospital on the other, and bisected by a motorway in between.

A sorry situation for a farm run by the same, environmentally conscious family for over a hundred years? Not a bit of it. An opportunity for conservation and dynamic diversification is how the Pimbleys see it. That's Ian and Pauline and their sons, Guy and Andrew. They grow cereals on most of the land, but since road schemes and housing sprawl put them within such easy reach of the public, they've developed Pick Your Own fruit, a fishery for anglers, a superbly stocked farmshop, the hugely popular, annual Wirral Food Festival and, now, a thriving new business marketing their own fresh produce straight into the kitchens of local restaurants. Asparagus is their big speciality and its quality has been taking Merseyside chefs by storm.

The idea of tuning in to dining out came from elder son, Andrew. Now it's easy to chart the short chronology of his career – from farm-boy, to agricultural student, to globe-trotting farmer to horticulturalist – and it's easy to recognise that he grows good stuff. But before you can fully understand his remarkable rate of success, you need to appreciate the man. Quite simply, Andy Pimbley sparkles. With energy, ideas, good humour – and good looks (they call him Farmer Handsome in Liverpool's best known bistro). He has the sort of enthusiasm that leads straight to action, the determination to sustain it, and the sense to research a new enterprise thoroughly before he starts. Add to that, he's a natural adventurer, a friendly, outgoing kind of guy who really cares about what he does, and you begin to get a feel for the personal momentum behind his enterprise.

It was 2004, when he started, aged 27 and just back from Venezuela where he'd spent three years as an assistant ranch manager. 'It was very dangerous there, a lot of kidnappings and cattle thieves: time to come home. My mum and dad were glad to have me back, but finding that extra wage placed a strain on the family farm. One of the reasons I went away was the poor state of UK agriculture. So I had to forge my own job to justify my existence on the payroll.'

He began to do just that by selling farm-fresh, seasonal fruit and vegetables to local restaurants on the Wirral. The following year, after a few fortuitous

introductions at a restaurateurs' party, he started to attract some pretty impressive customers in Liverpool, especially in the restaurant-rich Hope Street area. Among them was Paul Askew, chef-patron of the London Carriage Works. In no time at all, chef and grower gelled to form a particularly close working relationship.

'In the first year we were sort of testing each other out, weren't we', says Paul to Andy, over a mug of coffee in the Claremont Farm kitchen. 'We started with root vegetables and red cabbages ...'. He pauses, ruminates and then, with a glint in his eye and a smile on his lips: 'But the second year was when it got a bit more exciting, wasn't it?' And like runners at the crack of the starting pistol, they're off – lamenting the rain that shortened their first fruit season, mooting new crop options, rhapsodising over the taste and quality of fruit and vegetables, past, present and to come. The thought of Claremont's berry selection has Paul reciting the names, lingeringly (and Andy echoing each one in turn). 'Redcurrants, blackcurrants, tayberries, strawberries, raspberries.' Paul sighs, 'For us it's summer pudding on one farm!' These are two men conjoined by true professional passion.

Before they met, unbeknownst to them, their lives were already tenuously linked. Paul's house is just two miles from the farm, and every summer, he and his wife Helen and their son Harry would pop along for a spot of Pick Your Own fruit. In Venezuela, Andy worked for the Vestey Group, the same company as Paul's father. Both their mothers sing in the same choir and turn out to have been friends for years.

Their sons are a well-matched pair in character and objectives. Both have drive, stamina and a marvellous capacity for hard work. Both are perceptive, imaginative, sunny personalities, and peals of hearty laughter permeate their

nonetheless serious deliberations. Paul is delighted to have discovered top-quality produce within half-an-hour's reach of his restaurant, and a grower who will respond to his culinary needs. 'You can't beat it. Having this quality of fruit and vegetables, knowing it's just been picked and come straight to you, not PYO but PTM – picked this morning!'

Andy can't get over finding people who actually appreciate what the Pimbleys have been doing for so long. 'It's great for the family, especially my dad, the true farmer here. He's well chuffed, after all the years of hard work, and then suddenly to see Claremont Farm mentioned on the front page of The London Carriage Works menu.'

Andy recalls the response when he first started deliveries at the restaurant: 'I used to walk into the kitchen and everybody would be looking to see what I'd got. They'd all come over because they'd never seen stuff straight out of the ground. It hadn't been refrigerated, so it hadn't lost that initial taste or scent. The chefs were all coming up and saying, "Wow, you can really smell it", and then they'd be tasting it.'

Their enthusiasm hasn't diminished. It's not just the top three or four chefs, it's the commis too, all firing questions at him: 'They'll say, "What's growing now Andy? Have you got any in?"

"No, you'll have to wait, it's early yet."

"Alright, okay. Well, let us know, let us know". Not even I quite realised the passion behind the food.'

He's impressed that they want him to taste their dishes, to know about the finished product, what they are seeking to do and what they succeed in achieving.

Andrew Pimbley, Claremont Farm. Paul Askew's supplier **31**

'Working with the chefs, I've understood more about the product and the harvesting. Just closing that gap between chef and producer has been good for me and, I think, good for you as well, Paul.'

No disgreement there. 'We know our product has improved since we've been using your ingredients. It's just a case of moving things on towards that holy grail ...'

That's why they keep experimenting with new crops. Paul's a great one for 'baby' veg. On that score, they've done baby parsnips together, baby beets ('phenomenal but a pain to prepare – the guys have to use tiny little paring knives') and now they're pondering baby fennel. Their outstanding success has been with baby carrots, although it took three or four goes to get them to the right size.

When Mr Pimbley senior saw the result he was less than charmed: 'You can't be serious, Andrew? Are you going to take those in to the restaurant?'

'We've got an old-school farmer here', explains his son. 'They love it, I'd tell him, they fit on the plate. The world's gone bonkers, he'd say. He couldn't understand it. But then he'd never tasted them. When you taste them you see.'

Paul takes up the theme: 'To capture that baby taste! It's like when you've just nipped the feathery green top off the carrot and you smell it – that's exactly what you taste. It's like essence of carrot, precisely the intensity of flavour that we're looking for.'

Flavour is high on Andy's agenda too and he hates the way it has been forfeited to appearance and uniformity. 'There seemed to be so much more choice when supermarkets began shipping fresh produce in from all over the world, but everything became bland. It was all about how it looked on the shelf, not about how it tasted. We ended up with uniform rubbish. There was no real passion about growing the food.'

The Pimbleys have that passion and have always striven for quality in everything they grow but – and it's a defining 'but' – quality has additional nuances when you are dealing with the upper echelons of the restaurant trade. Take the asparagus. Claremont has been cropping it successfully since 1995. Their farmshop customers have long been in the know, and each new season finds them poised, ready to snap up the first, fresh-cut bundles. However, to satisfy top chefs it does have to be absolutely perfect. In the early days, Andy used get it in the neck a bit from his dad because he'd be sifting through, almost double-grading it.

'What do you think you're doing? That's perfectly good asparagus.'

'Actually, it's not quite good enough for what I need.'

'Are you serious?'

Well, he was, he is, and that commitment, along with ideal soil and climate, is why Claremont asparagus has risen to vie with the area's famous Formby variety which is grown just up the coast, north of Liverpool, near Southport.

The season is short, from late April to mid-June, and it's a demanding crop. 'Asparagus takes up a lot of space. Of the 25 acres we've got given over to fruit and veg, 14 are taken up by asparagus. Plus it's got to be down two years before you can start harvesting. You've got to be very patient. It takes a lot of tender loving care does asparagus.'

Since the restaurants have discovered the quality and proximity of the Claremont crop, they can't get enough of it. Asparagus is a fragile, easily damaged vegetable, its delicate flavour fading from the moment of harvest. So any good cook wants it as fresh as possible, as little handled as possible, as little travelled as possible. That makes Claremont's crop a true object of desire.

Rhubarb, potatoes, broccoli, courgettes, courgette flowers, and other produce from the farm, offer similar attractions. Nothing is done that diminishes the flavour, changes the texture or the way they will react when cooked. There's no washing in diluted chlorine, treating with preservative gases, or refrigerating. They don't use sprout-suppressant to prolong the life of stored potatoes either.

A proportion of their carrots, parsnips and potatoes will be hosed down with water, because a lot of kitchens aren't used to handling dirty vegetables. Some, like The London Carriage Works prefer them dirty – 'that way we know they're the genuine article'. Root vegetables last better if the earth is left on. 'The thing I say most often to Andy when I'm phoning is, whatever's coming out of the ground, tell us and we'll build it into our menu. For us, the more natural the product the better', says Paul.

In fact, 'natural' is an epithet that can be aptly applied to Claremont's whole approach. It starts with their growing methods. They practise traditional crop rotation which helps to avoid the build-up of pests and diseases, and nurtures the soil, rather than depleting it. The farm is also a member of the government's

Environmental Stewardship scheme, designed to protect wildlife, without affecting farm production. As a result, creatures now rarely seen by most of us enjoy a haven here.

Buffer strips, left at the field-edges, provide habitat for wildflowers and beneficial insects, along with daytime resting places for brown hares. They attract small rodents too, which provide food for visiting buzzards and the farm's resident barn owls. Lapwings love the bare ground where the asparagus and strawberries grow; partridge and pheasants come into the strawberry fields, even into the polytunnels, and control weevils. Ladybirds deal with aphids on the asparagus.

'We try to take environmental methods and the science of commercial farming and mix them to get the best, the most harmonious way of working for this particular farm.'

For Andy, striking the right balance is as important in business development as it is in cultivation methods. Claremont has its base in agriculture – wheat, barley and oil-seed rape – rather than horticulture and that must continue, even as they try to forge a new market in horticultural produce for restaurants. 'The chefs tell me they'd like this, that and the other, and we'd love to accommodate them, but although the market is expanding, it's still limited. Growing small quantities of different crops is time-consuming and costly, and if we start spreading ourselves too thinly we risk losing the quality of our current produce. So, little by little.'

The gradualist approach has served him well. Before leaving for Venezuela, he developed the farm's shop. 'I had a back-problem, so I couldn't work on the farm, but I really felt I wanted to give something back to my parents for all they'd done for me. I thought: I've got the ability; I know what I want; I've learnt about diversification at college; we're in a prime location; let's get it sorted!'

He did his market research, then set about sourcing a wide stock, including interesting new products that would differentiate Claremont from other farmshops. 'We try and ensure you can get all your shopping with us, if you want to – bread, milk, fruit, veg, fish, meat, game, sauces, olives, home-made cakes – even a bottle of wine. I've kind of handed it over to my mum to run now. She does a lot of the sourcing and testing of new products.'

It was while he was setting up the farmshop that he first started learning about local produce. 'It opened up a whole new world to me and a whole new set of people – so many great personalities down little country lanes.' They inspired another initiative: what about a food festival for the Wirral? 'I'd been to a few food festivals and thought they were a great idea but not quite fulfilling the expectations of either producers or consumers. Yet again, I was a little bit big-headed and thought I've got a beautiful venue, I could do one and I could do it better.'

The result was the first Wirral Food and Drink Festival in 2006. A big success. The second, in 2007, was an even bigger one. Under blazing August sunshine, over a hundred stalls, and chef demonstrations galore, attracted three times as many people on the first day as had its precursor's entire run. When the crowds

tired, they could refresh themselves in a world food court or a cheese and wine marquee, try specialist beers in a spectacular tepee, or recline on hay bales to enjoy a sublime panorama of the distant Welsh hills.

Not surprisingly perhaps, he's been invited to set up another food festival on Merseyside and he's helping to put a bit more oomph into a local farmers' market too. He's spurred on by fellow feeling for small, quality producers, beavering away unknown and unregarded. 'A lot have gone out of business in recent years. Now there's definitely a resurgence. We just need to get ourselves organised and publicised a bit more ...'

With no money to be made on the wholesale market for small producers of fruit and veg, the restaurant business developed at just the right time for Claremont. Now Andy's nurturing new projects. The latest involve setting up a farm kitchen to produce jams and coulis from their own fruit, and a discovery centre where children can learn all about food. 'Education is something I'm quite passionate about', says this young farmer who calls himself 'not particularly academic'.

It was failure to get the grades to go into teaching that led Andy to agricultural college. It was the downturn in British agriculture that led him to gather wider farming knowledge and experience in Australia, Zimbabwe and South America. It was economic constraints on the family farm that led him to develop new businesses. If you want a study in plucking success from adversity, look no further than Andy Pimbley and Claremont Farm.

Oh, and they're pretty good for fruit and veg too.

Peter Jones
Wirral Watercress

WATERCRESS: it conjures up images of riverbanks, lush and cool; of floating down rivers in a rowboat, plucking the peppery green leaves from the banks and enjoying them, then and there. For this is where you would expect to find watercress: by fast-flowing streams where its growth can be fuelled by the fresh water.

However Wirral Watercress is different. No scenic views here, just an exceptional product. Sitting in a polytunnel supping tea from his 'Wirral Watercress' mug, is grower Peter Jones, a typical down-to-earth farmer. But one with a secret skill.

Stretching before us in long rows of gravel-filled troughs on raised tables, are thousands and thousands of watercress plants. They are constantly fed by water, running down hoses to recreate a river environment. But don't ask exactly how the system works – Peter keeps that a closely guarded secret. However, the effect is crystal clear: it gives Wirral Watercress a palpable freshness due to the fact that these plants are picked, delivered and put on your plate within a few short hours.

People love watercress for its piquant tang, but from earliest times it has been valued for its health-giving properties too. In ancient Greece, Xenophon is said to have fed it to his soldiers to give them vigour for the battle ahead, while Hippocrates, who revolutionised medicine in the fifth century BC, is reputed to have used watercress to treat his patients. Restoring health, promoting intellect, preventing baldness, cleansing the blood, stopping hangovers, maintaining youthfulness – all these powers have been attributed to the plant. It has even been thought of as an aphrodisiac.

What is certain is that it contains a host of vitamins and minerals including, gram for gram, more vitamin C than oranges, more calcium than milk, more iron than spinach. A recent study by the University of Ulster showed that watercress appears to raise levels of beneficial compounds, and cut levels of harmful compounds in the blood.

The very first watercress farm in Britain was opened two hundred years ago in 1808 in Kent. Then the coming of the railways, nearly thirty years later, brought this highly perishable plant within the reach of city-dwellers. As a result, it would be sold in the streets to eat on the move or bought to go in a breakfast sandwich. Victorian workers knew it by such names as scurvy grass and poor man's bread.

Peter believes that watercress fell out of favour with the general public when centralised distribution systems came in, rendering the product four or five days old before people got to eat it, by which time it had lost its tang and taste. He says: 'It was popular in the 1960s but I think interest declined when people couldn't get it fresh.'

More recently, when he spotted a niche in the market, this third generation grower who has worked as a market gardener across the country, took his 30 years experience in farming, and studies at university, to create his own system for growing watercress on the Wirral. His business has grown rapidly and he now produces around 1,500 bunches of watercress a week. Not only selling to chefs, but also to the public at farmers' markets, farmshops, food festivals and other selected retail outlets across the area.

People love watercress for its piquant tang, but from earliest times it has been valued for its health-giving properties too.

Encouraged by the interest shown by local chefs, Peter has developed his business in new directions. As well as growing tomatoes, courgettes and other vegetables and fruit, he is diversifying into micro-salads. For these he grows a variety of plants such as peas, radish, beetroot and coriander, but only to the stage where they have just sprouted. The tiny young seedlings are very popular with leading chefs.

This versatility and willingness to experiment has stood Peter in good stead. His business seems set to thrive as healthily as his watercress.

Peter Jones, Wirral Watercress. Paul Askew's supplier 39

Paddy Byrne
& Tom Gill

The Everyman Bistro

Hope Street, Liverpool

THINK FOOD FULL OF MEDITERRANEAN COLOUR, fresh ingredients, beguiling aromas, good cooking, irresistible desserts. All set out on a counter, calling to you. Think three big basement rooms and a bar; conviviality, warmth and laughter: late hours, easy-going atmosphere, a buzzing cross-section of society. Think all of that, and you have a sense of Liverpool's oldest, best-loved bistro, the legendary Everyman. You'll find it under the famous theatre of the same name, a landmark establishment in what might well be called Liverpool's Latin quarter. Its neighbours include a couple of universities, and cathedrals; its clientele, actors and academics, writers and artists, locals and tourists; ladies who lunch and students who forget to. It's a place to meet and to talk. In many languages. About everything and anything: from Premier League to Proust. A little bit of the Left Bank in Liverpool – and completely authentic. It was founded in 1970 by a couple of young, self-taught cooks who cared about good, affordable food. They liked the place so much that, later, they bought the entire building. Their principles remain unchanged but they've handed over the cooking to kindred spirits of a younger generation. Whoever you are, wherever you come from, this establishment will wrap you in a warm embrace. Everyman by name and by nature.

Patron: Paddy Byrne

"IT WAS SHEER CHANCE GOT ME INTO THIS. I was a young teacher, trained in chemistry, working in the east end of London and coming back home to Liverpool at weekends for the social life. It was a kind of artistic village round here in the late '60s – painters, poets, musicians, actors. My friends knew lots of interesting people and I'd just tag along.

To keep in touch with everyone, I used to have parties. The unusual thing about them was I actually did food. To me it seemed natural. I didn't think I was doing anything particularly novel or enterprising, but it got me a bit of a reputation. So when the Everyman Theatre was looking for someone to take over their faltering bar, they thought of me.

I wasn't looking to go into business, so at first I didn't take the offer seriously. Not until they threatened to ask someone else – that galvanised me into action!

I got in touch with an old friend and fellow-chemist, Dave Scott. Now he takes care of administrative aspects here, but then he was just finishing his PhD at Manchester. He liked the idea of running the place, and to me it sounded like a great way to keep in with the scene and meet girls ... we decided to go for it! In 1970, the Everyman Bistro duly opened, in just one room, under the old theatre.

I know people credit us with paving the way for Liverpool's restaurant revolution, but nothing could have been further from our minds. All we wanted to do was party on. We soon realised our mistake. Unlike a party, this was something you had to set up every day!

The work was unremitting. I used to go the Liverpool produce market at Edge Lane between six and seven in the morning, come back with our supplies and start cooking. Dave and I would still be here at 1 am. That regime went on for quite a time. You needed to be physically fit and pretty disciplined. I was 25, athletic, a middle-distance runner in fact, and that helped. But, looking back, I wonder how we did it.

The theatre was in a converted Congregational chapel built in 1837, with facilities that were far from ideal. We cooked in a tiny room – now our cellar – and initially, before the theatre was remodelled, we had to close during performances, because the noise from the kitchen would carry through to the stage.

There were a couple of other operational difficulties to contend with. We needed to have as much food as possible ready before the show and it had to be served quickly. But all we had to cook on was a couple of domestic stoves. To make matters worse, being in a completely enclosed basement, we couldn't get rid of the heat from the kitchen.

That's how our well-known selection of salads and desserts developed – as a way of coping with the predicament. They turned out to be a really popular combination. As a lot of people discover every day, you come in, eat a salad and then feel you deserve a dessert. It wasn't planned that way, but some things just work out.

Casseroles were another solution to our problems and we did lots. Spicy lamb and tomato was an old favourite; hazelnut and courgette bake was another. Of course, things like that had to be reheated quickly for customers. But how? The answer was microwave ovens and we're very honest about our use of them – they're out there in full public view.

All our primary cooking, though, we do in a traditional way. Tom Gill is in charge. He's the Everyman's chef and I couldn't do what we do without Tom.

Since many meat recipes are ruled out with microwaves, it has encouraged us to develop our range of vegetarian dishes – probably one of the best in the Northwest. About 40% of our food is vegetarian. It's a reason, I think, why lots of people of different nationalities like to eat here, because they don't feel compromised.

Because of the relatively low percentage of meat dishes and the lack of frying, the food here is perceived as a healthy selection – which it almost certainly is. Our use of saturated fats is fairly low and no substitutes are used. If we do use fat, it would be butter. Very occasionally it would be lard but that would be for a specific, traditional dish. No hydrogenated fats. Plenty of roughage.

We've never thickened anything either: everything is by reduction, not added flour or cornflour. There may be a traditional mushroom soup that's thickened with breadcrumbs, but nothing is unnecessarily thickened and there are no flavour intensifiers.

I was in the city-centre the other day and I heard a couple of young people saying: 'Wish we had a bit more time – we could get up to the Everyman. It's healthy food there, but it's not *bad* healthy food.' Quite a compliment, I couldn't help smiling. Dave and I have been thanked by parents for having healthy food available for their offspring while they were at university – though the offspring probably made more use of the liquid sales!

I suppose you could sum up our approach as sticking to good old-fashioned principles. As neither Dave nor I had any catering training, we just formed our own conclusions, and fortunately they've taken us down the right track.

Our starting point has always been good quality produce, bought locally wherever possible, and freshly cooked every day. In the early years, getting some of the ingredients was a problem. If I asked for herbs down on the market, or anything that was unusual, aubergines perhaps, they'd say: 'Oh, you don't want that, son. No call for it, not worth our while.'

By contrast, basic British vegetables were very easy to obtain and far superior to what we see in supermarkets today. They were locally grown and really fresh. Since then so many of the farmers and market gardeners have gone out of business.

Other producers have prospered though, Mrs Kirkham and her Lancashire cheese, for one. At first we used to have to go up to the farm to get it – or rather, a member of the Liverpool Philharmonic Orchestra used to collect it for us! Nowadays there's a regular delivery.

Despite the difficulties, we found ways and means, because we were determined to create a certain sort of place: one where where you could get good,

honest, nourishing food at affordable prices, where everyone could feel welcome, and where you could relax and meet people.

What I'd seen in London's Soho in the '60s had influenced me – the bohemian, cosmopolitan atmosphere, and relaxed ways of eating in places like the Algerian Coffee Shop and Patisserie Valerie in Old Compton Street, The French House in Dean Street, Schmidt's in Charlotte Street.

But it was my experiences abroad that made the really deep impression. They began when I was about 16. Cycling around Britanny with a friend, I tasted my first oysters and French cheeses. Later, I did a series of long walks throughout Europe and along the North African coast. These exposed me to markets, to the ordinary food and cooking methods of people in different cultures.

If you're walking, you take in all the agriculture, you see what thrives in different environments and how it's respected in the local kitchens. You recognise the separate identity of each and every village, and you notice what they are particularly proud of – like a good restaurant. If it takes local produce and draws in visitors, it can make the difference between a community flourishing or failing.

Paddy Byrne, Everyman Bistro **45**

In France at that time, there were still the genuine routiers restaurants. If you got there just after noon, you could frequently get a splendid three-course meal for a very reasonable price indeed. But that wasn't really the point. The point was that no-one was excluded. Everyone put down their tools, no matter what they did, bank manager or farm labourer. They stopped work and they all shared food.

Right around the Mediterranean, tables were shared. In countries like Austria and Germany too, restaurants had big tables, lots of people coming together – general inclusion. That's the culture I've kept to.

It was very different from what was happening in Britain at the time. Here, restaurants were often such pretentious, self-conscious places and so silent that it was quite painful to eat in them. That's not for me. Food, on its own, without lots of personal interaction is cold, frigid.

The Everyman is a place for social eating. We have several tables that will seat a dozen, most are generous for four. Many people still share, and it's not that unusual for customers to tell you how they met their future wife or husband here. Former staff bring their children; you'll meet people you haven't seen for 20 years. We're even used as a sort of post-box – customers come and ask us if so-and-so's been in. It's that connection between food and lifestyle that interests me.

Good food is much too elitist in Britain. It's been lost from the lives of ordinary people and reintroduced as visual consumerism. Often it's a case of, 'see me, I've got enough money to afford this', rather than any real interest in food. That seems a bit of a shame.

I've always thought of good food as a right, but in Britain we lost our natural good food, and our tradition of regional dishes, in a way that they never did on the continent. It all goes back to our very early, very rapid Industrial Revolution, to the Enclosures Acts, whole families becoming divorced from the land; the population becoming urbanised at an incredibly fast rate.

We were cut off from our roots. They are in the peasant food, and peasant food has been developed over centuries to get the best flavour, the best nutrition out of what is available.

If you go back to the old herbals, in the 17th century we were picking and eating a wide range of greens, rather in the way of the village women that Patience Gray describes in her book, *Honey from a Weed*. She recalls her life among them in Tuscany, Catalonia and Naxos in the 1970s and '80s, how they would go out and pick the early green herbs from the fields, cook them simply and eat them for health – their spring vitamins after the winter.

Our loss of that kind of access to, and knowledge about, natural good food, and the cooking skills that go with it, was compounded by the Second World War. Rationing went on for so long in Britain, from 1940 until 1954. Fourteen years of it – that's a childhood.

More recently, in the 1980s, we saw slot machines and carbonated drinks brought into our schools, playing fields sold off, bad school meals. The teaching of cooking was largely dropped at the same time. I do quite a bit of work with the health authorities on the obesity task force and now the idea is to reintroduce what we've lost. Of course it's not just a case of educating the children, but the parents who missed out too.

Family background played a big part in my interest in food. My mother had her battered copy of the first Penguin paperback of Elizabeth David. There's probably some shared gene, because my brother Tim (who is also a partner here and does the day to day accounting) lectures for the Wine and Spirit Education Trust.

Despite rationing and shortages, family meals were always varied. At school, what amazed me about my friends was they always knew what they were going to get to eat when they went home. This was something I couldn't comprehend. It was only when I left home that I realised people had the same meals every week. I'd imagined my school friends had some sixth sense about what they were getting!

Belly pork, lentils – the small meats and pulse dishes – cheap cuts with vegetables, that was the sort of thing we used to have at home. Beef hearts, lamb flanks, scrag-end of neck in a Lancashire hotpot, where the meat had to be cooked very carefully and bones sucked. The exotic would have been a pot-roast of beef. I can't ever remember having a prime cut of meat when I was growing up. Waste was absolutely taboo and we ate what was in season.

I think seasonality is very important, especially in terms of the ecological cost of eating things out of season, whether they are flown in from half-way around the world, or grown here in energy-intensive ways. However, it's very difficult to apply nowadays when everything is so available and there's so little in the outside environment to remind us of what actually is in season.

Seasonality is talked about in restaurants, but too often it's just an excuse to change the menu, rather than a real knowledge of what's out there. I've got an allotment – in fact, I've worked on one since I was eight – where I grow quite a selection of produce. That lets me know what's in season, and what's coming into season. It gives you a remarkable insight into what you should be buying from the growers and into the intrinsic excellence of fresh produce.

For a number of years I was resigned to the fact that catering had gone the wrong way in Britain, but now I think we might be making headway. All the same, I'd love to be able to go to more restaurants that are easily approached and where you can get a good, honest soup or a decent steak and chips. It's those simple dishes – done really well – that are difficult to get in this country. There often seems to be an unnecessary desire to elaborate, rather than respect the primacy of the material. I think it's partly because so few chefs have good ingredients to work with, and partly because there isn't really the respect for the profession in this country. As a result, chefs are often over-compensating and trying to create dishes before they've understood the basics of cooking leek and potato soup.

The extraordinary can always be good. What I want is for ordinary things to be good. That's the better option."

Paddy Byrne, Everyman Bistro 47

Chef: Tom Gill

"When I was training as a chef, here in Liverpool, the college staff said to me: 'Are you prepared to leave the city when you qualify? You'll need to.' Well, I never had any desire to go and, fortunately, I've never had to.

I started at the Everyman in 1990, left after four years and came back about six years later. Paddy's absolutely the man. It's great working with someone who has so much knowledge and experience. You'll hear other chefs describe him as the godfather of the local restaurant scene. I hate saying 'all that passion' because it's what people always say, but Paddy's still got it.

The diversity of the crowd at the Everyman – professors, students, scousers, artists, actors – is something I've always liked. You're thinking to yourself, 'Now what was she in? Was it Emmerdale … was it Corrie …?'

Most of all, I think it's great cooking the way we do. Everything is prepared on the premises from scratch every day. It's all fresh, honest-to-goodness ingredients. Minimum fuss, minimum interference. Simple, tasty, wholesome food. Dishes differ from day to day but, typically, they'll include soups and salads, pâtés, pizzas, pasta dishes, curries, casseroles, quiches, cakes and desserts.

In the kitchen, we generally start about 7 to 7.30 am, though I always find it's great about an hour before, when there's only me and the cleaner. I'll get on with my first job, and then ideas for the day's menu just start flowing. You think to yourself, I'll do a casserole next – maybe pork with prunes and apple, then … perhaps vegetable tortilla … and it all begins to take shape. The other chefs come along, make suggestions, and in no time, we're away!

Each of us sees our dishes through from start to finish. That's different from an à la carte restaurant where it's about repetition – like a production line. Ask someone to make a goulash and they're quite likely to look at you blankly. They can be good chefs but terrible cooks. At the Everyman it's more cooking than cheffing.

We make our own bread here as well, so early on there's a delicious waft of dough coming up from the bakery. An hour later, you'll walk past, and the dough's proving. Then it comes out of the oven, about quarter-past-eleven, and the smell of fresh bread fills the whole kitchen. I love that. There's something so basic about it.

From noon on, the lunch queues start. Service is buffet-style. The menu is chalked on slates above the counter – we change it twice a day. If you choose a hot dish we'll re-heat it in front of you in a microwave. We are pretty much constantly busy, with no slow-down till about 2 pm.

That's when we'll assess the situation. What have we got left? What do we need for tonight? And the whole process will start again. We cook the food and, as soon as it's cool, it goes in the fridge. The menu is written down, the night-boss comes in, we'll go through it together, then everything is ready for the evening rush.

While I'm doing the orders, I'll form an idea of a few dishes that I might want to do the next day. For instance, we've got a delivery of some really nice outdoor-reared hams coming from Maynard's Farm Bacon – one of Rick Stein's food heroes. We'll cook those, glaze them with honey and mustard, stud them with cloves, and serve with a simple potato salad, a few leaves and some of our bread. Perfect in summertime.

One of the misconceptions about us is that we're a vegetarian restaurant. Obviously, we're not, but it's not such a bad misconception for people to have. It means we're known for having a really good range of veggie meals. And that's something I'm very pleased about, because, even now, there are so few places around offering that.

Another misconception is that we're a healthfood restaurant. Again, we're not, but the food is healthy – because it's all fresh and good quality. Yes, we use a little bit of butter, yes, we use a little bit of cream occasionally, but you're not having that every day.

I was talking to a guy in a pub recently who turned out to be a chef. So I started telling him about our buffet system, how dishes get reheated in a microwave –and he gave a sharp intake of breath. But then I explained how all the food is prepared from scratch, from produce that comes in fresh every day; how we make all our own dough – bread, pizza, pastry; everything except filo. He told me how all his stuff was out of tins – and then it was my turn for a sharp intake of breath!

It's a similar story with our desserts. Not long ago we had a food salesman in, trying to sell us some. When we told him that we made them all ourselves, he looked quite taken aback!

If we could get to a situation where more people just cooked simple, home-style food like the kind we have at the Everyman, it could raise nutritional standards significantly.

It's so important that we help our children to learn about food. At home, I always make sure that my daughter gets involved – even if it's only, 'rip this lettuce up, while I do this', or 'throw a little olive oil on that.' She's eleven so as far as I'm concerned she should be in and around the kitchen, getting the feel for food, just knowing what different things are, like a squash or an aubergine.

When I was a young boy, I used to make scones with my nan, and I think that my interest in cooking may have stemmed from that. Every Sunday it used to be: 'Nan, can we make scones?' I used to make weird triangular things, but these experiences make a big impression on you when you're little.

I think the problem is there aren't enough parents with the time, or knowledge to cook with their kids. Fortunately, when I was at school, they still taught Home Economics. I don't believe they do any more. In Joanna Blythman's book, *Bad Food Britain*, there's a chapter about how lessons now are almost based in a food factory. Instead of being taught how to cook, it's all about designing a crisp packet or some industrially manufactured convenience food or an airline meal. Food Technology they call it. I found that shocking.

Some of the food we made at school was, frankly, quite bad – scone-based pizzas and that kind of thing. But at least we were in a kitchen, getting our hands dirty, learning a little bit about how to cook. We were taught about nutrition too, in a lesson called Life Skills. There is absolutely no question that kids should know what it's like to be in a kitchen, getting their hands messy, making food.

I always think of that scene in one of Jamie Oliver's television programmes, when he went to a school in Italy to look at the food they were doing for lunch – organic parmesan cheese, organic aubergines, organic tomatoes in sauce. And one of the funniest things I've ever seen – he gathered all these Italian dinner ladies round and showed them some British turkey twizzlers. They literally recoiled. 'Ugh', they said, 'you let your children eat that?'

Now a good wholesome dish, uniquely traditional to Liverpool, is scouse. I've chosen it for this book. I didn't actually do it at the Everyman until a couple of years ago. I put it on the menu as a reaction against the negative attitude some people have towards it. 'Oh, not scouse!' they say dismissively.

You wouldn't hear a French person saying: 'Oh, not cassoulet!' They'll argue about it, fight about what should go into it, but they won't dismiss it. It matters too much for that.

Well, I wouldn't dream of not having scouse on the menu now. We've become a little bit famous for it, and if you can make black pudding trendy and sexy, why not scouse? Let's be proud of this dish.

The recipe varies greatly. In fact, there are only three ingredients everyone can agree on: potatoes, carrots and onions – the holy trinity of scouse! After that the arguments start.

When I did the food for my cousin's 30th birthday party, I included scouse. As I was serving it, one guy's saying: 'That's proper scouse that, proper scouse.' Another fella, in his 80s, he's going: 'That's not scouse that. What have you got in there, lamb? Should be mutton. It's definitely got to be mutton.'

I thought: brilliant, it matters enough for people to argue, to get passionate about it! That's what I loved about my mum's reaction when I told her I was doing scouse – and putting beer and black treacle in it. She was horrified. 'You can't make scouse!' she said to me.

Then she tasted it. She loved it.

The black treacle gives it a great colour and works so well with the maltiness of the beer and the sweetness of the lamb. People are usually very complimentary and it's become one of our most important dishes. I've no problem with anyone slagging my scouse off – if they can back up their opinion and say why!

If our experience is anything to go by, people are getting more and more interested in local specialities. Every month we hold a pre-booked Supper Club when we serve a regionally-based set menu, cooked to order. Themes have included Lancashire, local British seafood, strawberries and asparagus. They've all been sold out.

But whatever the geographical origins of dishes at the Everyman, they all have one thing in common: good, fresh ingredients. That, basically, is what it boils down to. Cook with good, fresh ingredients and you can't go far wrong."

Chinese Spiced Crab Cakes with Carrot, Lemon and Sesame Salad

SERVES 4

For the Crab Cakes
480g white crab meat
30g fresh ginger, finely chopped
4 spring onions
1 red chilli, de-seeded and finely chopped (optional)
Zest of 1 lemon
1 small bunch coriander
4 tsp mayonnaise
4 tsp oyster sauce
2 tsp Chinese five spice powder
3 eggs
75g white breadcrumbs
75g plain flour
Groundnut oil for frying

For the Carrot, Lemon and Sesame Salad
4 large carrots
1 lemon, juice and zest
Dash of sesame oil
Small handful of sesame seeds, toasted

Crab Cakes **1** Place the crab meat, ginger, spring onions, coriander, chilli (if using), lemon zest, mayonnaise, oyster sauce and five spice in a large bowl and mix well. **2** Beat the eggs and add a small amount to the mixture to bind it together. Add some breadcrumbs if it seems too wet, and check for seasoning. **3** Shape the mixture into four, evenly sized cakes and place on a tray, lined with grease proof paper. Place in the freezer for 30 minutes. **4** Arrange 3 shallow dishes in a line, one containing the flour, one containing the beaten eggs, and another containing the breadcrumbs. Remove the crab cakes from the freezer and, one by one, coat them first in flour, then egg and finally breadcrumbs. **5** Heat a large frying pan over a medium heat and add the oil. As soon as the oil begins to smoke, carefully place the cakes in the pan. They should take about four minutes each side. Make sure they are hot in the middle! **6** Serve with carrot, lemon and sesame salad.

Salad **1** Peel the carrots, then using a vegetable peeler, peel long ribbons of carrot and place in a bowl. **2** Add all other ingredients.

Chef's Alternative For a more 'English' crab cake, omit the ginger and chilli; replace the coriander with tarragon; replace the five spice with Worcestershire sauce. Omit the oyster sauce and use 4 dessert spoons of mayonnaise instead of 4 tea spoons. Serve with a mixed leaf salad.

Tom Gill's Lamb Scouse with Red Cabbage and Brown Bread

SERVES 4 GENEROUS PORTIONS

For the Lamb Scouse
225g minced lamb
225g diced shoulder of lamb
4 medium potatoes, peeled and quartered
2 large carrots, peeled and cut into fairly large chunks
1 onion, diced
1 small piece celery, tied together with some rosemary and thyme
2 medium leeks, washed and sliced into rounds
225ml Brewer's Revenge beer from George Wright Brewery
1-2 ladles of hot lamb stock

For the Paste
1 heaped tbsp tomato paste
1 heaped tsp wholegrain mustard
2 tsps black treacle
A generous splash of Worcestershire sauce

For the Bread
225g strong white bread flour
225g wholemeal flour
50g melted butter
15g dried yeast
Pinch salt
Pinch of sugar
Just over 200ml lukewarm water

For the Red Cabbage
$1/2$ head red cabbage, finely sliced
Knob of butter
Generous splash of cider vinegar
Small handful of brown sugar
1 tbsp redcurrant jelly
Splash of red wine
Salt to taste

Paste [1] Mix all the ingredients into a paste.

Lamb Scouse [1] Heat a heavy based pan with no oil and, when hot, add the meat and stir quickly and constantly until browned. [2] Add the paste and stir into the meat. [3] Add the potatoes, carrots and onion and stir. [4] Add the hot lamb stock and beer. The liquid should just cover the other ingredients. Drop in the bundle of celery and herbs, cover and simmer very gently for approximately 1 hour 15 minutes, stirring occasionally. [5] Add the leeks and simmer until the lamb is tender. Season with salt and black pepper.

Red Cabbage [1] Place all the ingredients in a heavy based pan, cover with a lid and cook very gently until the cabbage is tender, approximately 35-45 minutes.

Bread [1] Mix together the flour, salt and sugar in a bowl and add the melted butter. In another bowl add the water to the yeast. [2] Make a well in the centre of the flour and pour in the yeast liquid and mix together to form a dough. [3] Turn the dough on to a lightly floured surface and knead for a good 10 minutes. [4] Place in a bowl, cover with cling film and set aside to rise, in a warm place, until it has doubled in size. [5] Knock back the dough, flattening it firmly with the knuckles to expel the air bubbles. [6] Form into one or two ball shapes, as preferred, and leave to rise again in a warm place for 30 minutes. [7] Preheat oven to 220-230°C / gas mark 7. Place dough on a lightly floured baking tray and bake in the centre of the oven for 25-35 minutes or until the base of each loaf gives a hollow sound when tapped.

Alternatively, simply serve a good, purchased, rustic bread of your choice.

Pam Wellings' Curd Tartlets with Caramelised Berries

MAKES 12 INDIVIDUAL TARTLETS OR 1 LARGE TART

For the Pastry
250g butter, diced
175g caster sugar
2 medium eggs, beaten
550g plain flour
Pinch of salt

For the Curd Filling
300g cream cheese
200g caster sugar
1$^1/_2$ tsps cornflour
3 medium eggs
3 egg yolks
1 tsp brandy
1 orange, finely grated rind only
300ml double cream

Pastry 1 Grease 12 deep, round, fluted tartlet tins about 7cm diameter. 2 Beat together the butter and sugar until creamy (but not fluffy). Scrape down the sides of the mixing bowl, add the beaten egg and mix well. 3 Add sieved flour and salt; bring the mixture together to form a firm dough. Refrigerate, covered, for about 1 hour. 4 Gently knead the dough and roll out on a cool, highly floured surface. Cut into rounds and line the prepared tartlet tins. Leave to rest for a further 30 minutes in the refrigerator. 5 Bake the pastry cases, blind, in a preheated oven at 180°C / gas mark 4 for approximately 7-10 minutes until lightly golden. Remove and leave to cool.

Curd Filling 1 Beat together the cream cheese, sugar and cornflour. Add eggs, egg yolks, brandy, orange zest and cream and mix together thoroughly. 2 Spoon the mixture into the pastry cases. Bake in a pre-heated oven at 180°C / gas mark 4 for 35-40 minutes until the pastry is lightly browned and the filling set. 3 Top tarts with sprig of fresh redcurrants, dusted with icing sugar.

For the Caramelised Berries
A mixture of strawberries, raspberries, loganberries, redcurrants, whitecurrants and blackcurrants (a punnet of each)
175g granulated sugar
125ml water
125ml cranberry or orange juice

For Serving
Vanilla Cheshire Farm Ice Cream (optional)

Caramelised Berries 1 In a heavy based pan, heat the sugar and water until the sugar has dissolved. 2 Bring the mixture to the boil and boil rapidly until the mixture turns a golden brown. Do NOT stir. 3 Add the cranberry or orange juice to the boiled mixture. Be VERY careful at this point as the mixture will spit. 4 When the mixture has settled, using a heatproof spatula, stir the syrup until you have a smooth, lump free consistency. 5 While the syrup is still hot, pour over the prepared berries and leave to cool.

To Serve Serve the caramelised berries with the tartlets and some vanilla flavoured Cheshire Farm Ice Cream.

Mick Evans
Personal Shopper
to the Trade
Liverpool

It's 6 AM ON A SODDEN JUNE MORNING and the rain is lashing down relentlessly on Liverpool's Wholesale Fruit and Vegetable Market. It's an extensive site, about three miles from the city centre. Trucks, vans and private cars are parked haphazardly about a large tarmac square, hemmed in by rows of big industrial-sized lock-ups. They call these 'stands' or 'stalls' and that's where you'll find the wholesalers and their produce. Some are open, but more have their grey, roll-down shutters, rolled down, shut. The market isn't what it was. There's a modicum of traffic on the move, at the crawl; and nippy forklifts, zipping in and out, taking you by surprise in the half-light. It's cold and bleak. Conditions don't look promising for a photoshoot and, to make matters worse, we can't find our subject.

Then, just as our sprits are beginning to flag, we spot him. All around, dripping men are rubbing their eyes, but Mick Evans is bright as a button and lively as a cricket. He's with Paddy and Tom from the Everyman Bistro and the wisecracks seem to be flying thick and fast.

Mick is Paddy's man in the Market. Every night he gets up about ten-thirty, has a good breakfast, checks his orders, and makes his way here for about half-one in the morning. Because he has his own stand, he's allowed in early, along with the farmers and market-gardeners. It means he can get a headstart on the all-important job of the night – trawling the market to see what's what, seeking out the right produce for his many and varied customers. Shops and sandwich bars are numbered among them, as well as cafés, restaurants, pubs and private caterers, and they all have distinct requirements.

'There's varying degrees of everything', says Mick. 'Take bananas for instance. Shops want them slightly backward; sandwich bars want them coloured, because they go straight on the counter; restaurants want them ripe. So it's having that varying degree, not of quality but of condition. You have to have that in 99% of the products. 'I walk about four or five miles a night, backwards and forwards round these stalls, until I'm happy with what I've got.' No wonder he's so slim.

Behind the stands like Mick's, which open onto the square, is a second circuit, served by a wide covered way. Here you can cheat the weather and the darkness to wander in comparative comfort, searching out all the natural wonders gathered here.

Exquisite little jewels of shiny redcurrants nestle next to soft, matt-velvet raspberries. Light green gooseberries lie gorgeously with succulent crimson strawberries.

Stands full of flowers strike an unexpectedly feminine note in the masculine world of the market. There are both homely and grand to choose from: chrysanths and carnation sprays; tall white trumpet lilies, stiffly elegant; impossibly perfect gerberas in orange, carmine, yellow and pink. Sky-blue delphiniums, pink paeonies; waxy purple orchids, graceful golden rod and long-stemmed red roses ... stock enough to fill the florist-shops of Merseyside is sold here.

Among the produce too, the colour is dazzling. Enormous sacks of orange net enclose giant white onions; swedes are in red nets, drumhead cabbages in green. Carrots and tomatoes blaze side by side. Bright blue plastic crates hold a perfection of portobello mushrooms; next to them enormous fans of the oyster variety have been arranged in flamboyant display. Under the prosaic label 'Mushroom Mix' is a medley of wrinkled brown shitakes, yellow oysters, smoothly rounded chestnuts and clusters of tiny little hatpin jobs, still growing, like a dense Lilliputian forest.

Cold stores and wooden pallets punctuate the place. The ubiquitous forklifts veer about, traditional handcarts trundle past, and occasionally a man goes by carrying a box of veg on his head.

As produce comes over to Mick from the different wholesalers, it's sorted out, customers' orders are made up and loaded on the firm's two vans. He explains: 'I'm responsible for the invoicing and the lads (there are three of them) are responsible for knocking the orders together. If there's something they think isn't right for somebody, they'll tell me, and it has to be changed. Every morning, on a continual basis, you have to watch what comes over from the stalls for quality. Never forget you're dealing with nature. These products aren't made in a factory. They're not guaranteed. Fruit can come in pitted because of damage by bees, or veg may be wilting because it's been in hot sun.'

By six to half-past each morning, the loading is complete but, before deliveries begin, the crew may have to pick up other items for customers – from the wholesale meat and fish market on the far side of the 19 acre site, or from the cash-and-carry. 'We do a full service. Customers ask us to pick up the likes of frozen chips and peas. Cheeses, such as the camembert I came back with this morning, have to be ordered. We'll supply milk and creams too, but I make sure people understand I'm secondhand with the likes of all that – I'm not a dairyman.'

The day doesn't end with the deliveries: 'If customers have left something off an order, they'll ring or text and we'll drop it in a bit later. Some days you've got the phone going every two minutes and you've got to plod on, whatever the time. Other days, you don't get bothered at all.'

A lot of Mick's chefs like to deal with a single supplier – one invoice, one transaction, one person. He sums up succinctly: 'I'm a commodity. I save these people time and money. You could describe me as a personal shopper for them. I do all the running round, getting them what they want and how they want it – and if they want something different, I'll find that for them too.

'They'll see a celebrity chef like Gordon Ramsay on the telly and he's using baby gourds, so it'll be: "Mick, we want baby gourds!". If it's something in season, it's not a problem; if not, it has to be ordered in specially. But that's not how Paddy works, He wouldn't use something that wasn't in season.'

For the most part, Mick never sees the chefs he supplies. They leave orders on his 24-hour answering machine. It's different with Paddy. Their relationship is a personal one, stretching back some twenty years, to when Mick first started on the Market.

It was December 1987, he'd been working in a garage but the job finished. 'Les Rice owned this business then and he knew me mum. He knocked on the door and said: "Do you fancy a start? It's early but you get the rest of the day to yourself." So he was an out-an-out liar!' Mick laughs.

He took the job, on the clear understanding it was just to make a bit of money for Christmas and he'd be looking for something else in January. 'I'm still waiting for January!', he jokes. 'I don't know what happened but I came along and just

fitted in.' Les had a weak heart and retired three years later, leaving Mick to take over the business. He still trades as 'L. Rice'.

The Market may have been the saving of him. At fourteen, he parted company with his school, the prestigious Bluecoat, in Liverpool, and was packed off to Wales where he worked for a while on a livestock farm. 'I was a pain in the arse as a kid. Rebellious. School didn't interest me, and whatever you do in life has to hold your interest.'

This business hits the spot for him. In his stand, still surrounded (for our benefit, at this late hour) with mouth-wateringly good-looking produce, Mick is indisputably in his element. He tells tales from the delivery round. 'One young commis chef was robotically putting spinach on a plate so I asked him if he'd tasted it. No. So I told him you've got to taste it to know what you're doing. So he took some and spat it out: "Ugh – that tastes as if it's just come out of a field!" (general laughter). Another one said to me, "These vegetables have got dirt on. Shouldn't they be in plastic bags?" And you just think to yourself, why do I bother?'

Before long a curious, good-natured, all-male audience has collected to watch Mick being put through his paces for the camera. 'Just keeping the wheels of industry turning eh Mick?' suggests someone. 'As you do', comes the cheeky reply. 'Look at that insolent saunter!' laughs Paddy, admiringly. A group of guys spill out of the Market Diner next door and treat Mick to a burst of the Hokey Cokey: 'You put your left leg in, your left leg out …' As if on cue, two forklift drivers approach from opposite directions, gaze, pass and execute a synchronised balletic reverse to take a proper look. 'You're a bit late', shouts one, 'we start here at 4 am.'

The night's work is drawing to a close. That's why the traders who've furnished Mick's photogenic produce have time to come over for a look-see. Some are growers as well as suppliers. Howard Langley has been bringing in produce from his Wirral farm for nearly as long as Paddy's been running his bistro. New potatoes, rhubarb and purple kohlrabi have come from him today. Then there's a quartet of growers with time-honoured family names from the Lancashire side of the River Mersey: Lennie Rimmer grew the cauliflowers; John Baybutt the iceberg lettuces; Jimmy Molyneux, the cabbages; Ronnie Prescott, the asparagus and the caulis too.

Paddy remembers when the Market used to be chocabloc with farmers, not just the few there are now, and scurrying barrows would be everywhere. He laments the decline: 'The Market occupies about a third of its old space. Some of the wounds were self-inflicted: people didn't respond to the changing demands in the '70s and then the supermarkets ate up their trade.'

'There's far fewer traders than when I started', agrees Mick. 'It used to be the four blocks, every single stall open, every morning but', he points out, 'the variety of produce is greater than it's ever been. The likes of Paddy and a few others here and there may have been instrumental in changing that. And you'd be amazed at the amount of stuff that leaves here before four o'clock every morning.'

And does Mick actually eat the fruit and veg that surrounds him day in, day out? You betcha. 'I pick at it a lot through the night and during the morning – strawberries, raspberries, cherries, apples, peaches, nectarines. Cherry tomatoes are a favourite.' And how sweet, succulent and utterly delicious are the little plum tomatoes he's handing out now. They are from Flavourfresh Salads at Banks, Southport in Merseyside – no wonder they're a big favourite with several top chefs and leading food-stores.

Is this diet contributing to Mick's healthy outdoor glow? 'Yes', he says with a smile and a chuckle, 'and I think it's certainly contributed to my lad's! He starts school at eight, finishes at half-two, comes here with me of an afternoon and never stops eating fruit and veg. He's taller than me, a good build and he's only 14!'

The photoshoot is finished, our well wishers have dispersed, the car-park has cleared and only the dumpsters, empty crates and boxes are left. 'Michael, always a pleasure, never a chore!' says Tom in a farewell-flourish. The sky is still leaden. Time to adjourn to the diner for a cuppa. There's a lot still to do this afternoon and Mick needs to be in bed by five.

George Wright Brewing Company

Rainford, Merseyside

THERE IS A GREAT TRADITION OF ARTISAN BREWING all along the backbone of the Pennines, from Cheshire in the south to Cumbria in the north. In the 1960s it nearly died, as the giants of the industry began to swallow up the smaller fry and produce beer according to new imperatives. Predictability, ease of handling and increased shelf-life, took precedence over flavour, variety, and the skill required to master the vagaries of a living product.

The bland and gaseous brews which followed soon fermented seeds of revolt. The Campaign for Real Ale (CAMRA) was formed in 1971 and began a national fight-back. That gave birth to the micro-brewery, a plant with limited output, focussed on producing tasty, traditional draught beer from the cask, served without the aid of extraneous carbon dioxide.

As a result, Britain now has about 600 of these real-ale breweries. Upwards of seventy of them are in England's Northwest, a few large, most small, all characterful. One such is the George Wright Brewing Company. It's the choice of Paddy Byrne, patron of Liverpool's Everyman Bistro. 'Beer is our national drink', he proclaims, 'and it's a shame it's invariably excluded from our better restaurants. We stock products from a number of local breweries but I've chosen George Wright beers because they are very popular and amazingly consistent.'

The brewery is on Merseyside, but in a location worlds away from city-centre Liverpool. Rainford is a village on the West Lancashire Plain, surrounded by farmland and a scattering of woods; sequestered in the lee of the A570. Turn off the bypass, down a winding country lane and you'll come across a completely incongruous 'business park' marooned amidst the fields. At its far boundary stands an anonymous industrial unit. Nothing outside even hints at the activity within. Step inside and the alchemy begins.

The cave-like interior is aglow with gleaming metal. Light bounces off the diamond-dazzling surfaces of machine-tooled stainless steel vats; off the silver and coppery glint of pipework connecting them; off the high-level walkways that service them. The only brighter prospect in the place is the brewer himself – Keith Wright. His face radiates the kind of pure delight that comes only from doing something you love, and doing it well: 'Beer is the number one drink in the world. I love the taste, I love the flavours, I love the diversity, and I want to make the tastiest beer humanly possible!' Could there be a more authentic mission-statement?

To pursue his passion, Keith has designed and built a very remarkable micro-brewery, probably the most technologically advanced in the entire country. Brewing is done with great finesse and efficiency here, with virtually every stage of the process automated and computer-controlled. In the jargon, it's a recipe-driven, programmable logic control (PLC) brewery. 'That means – and this is where my head is swelling', he laughs, '– from anywhere in the world, via the internet, we can choose what we need to brew, load a recipe menu, and the plant will make only that beer.' And the beer will be unfailingly consistent.

This level of sophistication and precision does not come cheap – in time or money. What on earth made a man, who began brewing simply as a hobby, go to such lengths?

It all started when he couldn't get the beer he wanted near his home in St Helens, where all the pubs were owned by the same brewery. In 2002, Keith decided to supply the deficiency. He was running his own engineering company, designing hygienically sensitive plants all over the world, and power stations too. But that left weekends free, so together with business-partner and fellow CAMRA activist, George Dove (since retired), he bought a small, second-hand, 5-barrel micro-brewery on the other side of the Rainford bypass. Each man contributed half his name to create that stalwart of the trade, George Wright, and in no time at all they were producing award-winning, high-quality ales. But inconsistency, a common occurrence in micros, was a problem. 'We won the Southport Beer Festival with a spectacular brew, but it wasn't quite the same next time we made it.'

What to do? Obvious. First, acquire a 7,000 square foot building; design and build a fully-computer-controlled 25-barrel brewery that will allow you to produce a perfect brew every time; then shut down your engineering company, so you can concentrate on your brewing. Keith is not a man for half measures: 'Well, I had the ability to build a PLC brewery, so that became a challenge in itself. Running both businesses was difficult, so a decision had to be made as to what I wanted to do with the rest of my life. I decided to be a brewer.'

And a very good one too. Since 2005 he has been producing his traditional bitters, milds and stouts on this site; a range of six regular beers, all with evocative names, each with its own distinctive flavour, each as worthy of lyrical description as any wine. Take Pipe Dream best bitter: straw in colour, 'a light and fruity ale with a hint of grapefruit which leaves a lingering malty dryness in the mouth'. Mmm … lip-licking stuff. It won the highly covetable Silver Award in its category at the Great Britain Beer Festival in 2007, no mean feat.

How does Keith devise new beers? Every month he makes a 'special' (like Brewer's Revenge, the choice of chef Tom Gill for his scouse recipe). These give him the chance to try something a little bit different. He can put the plant into manual operation, gradually alter elements, and produce a new taste.

He takes his inspiration wherever he finds it. He'll explore fashionable flavours in other foods, in restaurants, to see if they would match any of his beers. Even at

breakfast, crazy as it might seem, he'll find himself thinking: 'What would bacon-and-egg flavour beer taste like?'

He samples other brewers' offerings too: 'You can generally tell what they've used and how they've brewed it. I've tasted wonderful beers, beers in distant parts of the country, beers so good that you'd want to move house, just for the taste!

'At the moment I've got a passion for getting passion-fruit flavours out of my hops. I'm always looking for a newer, tastier drink. ...'

Keith works his multifarious alcoholic magic out of just four basic ingredients: malt, hops, yeast and water. The technology is just an aid: it's the ingredients that matter and he sources them with the greatest care – even the water. 'In a brewery we call water 'liquor', the reason being that before we produce the beer, we have to produce the water – by removing from it the minerals and salts we don't want, and adding back the ones we do. So, if I want to make a Burton-upon-Trent style beer, I first have to replicate the water from that location.'

George Wright Brewing Company, Tom Gill's supplier 67

As for malt ('grist' to a brewer), it's made from barley and there's a whole industry before a brewer gets his malt. Two weeks before we met, Keith was in Suffolk, walking the barley fields, testing the grain. That's sold to Muntons, the maltsters in nearby Stowmarket who he also visits. They soak the barley to start germination, then kiln it, to dry it and impart colour and flavour. 'They are trying to get as much starch as possible in each grain for the brewer to convert into sugar. We're a 100% malt brewer. We don't use added sugar; all our alcohol and sweetness come from the grain.' So to ensure the quality and traceability of his malt, Keith buys it through the Assured UK Malt scheme, from this single supplier.

It's a similar story with the hops, some of which are added for bittering, others for aroma and, above all, flavour. There are scores of varieties to choose from, each with their special attributes – spicy, citrus, floral, earthy, grassy and so on. As with all food recipes, the magic is in the mix. George Wright is a whole-hop brewery: they use the actual flower, no pellets, no chemically produced hop-liquid. They buy from a single UK hop-merchant, the highly-regarded firm of Charles Faram, and Keith makes sure he visits the hop-growers too.

Then there's the yeast. To truly appreciate that, you must follow Keith up on to the walkways and wait while he removes the lid from the appropriate vessel (everything is completely enclosed in this brewery). It is then the rich, sweet, wall of aroma hits you, rising from the thick, creamy froth below.

Next to the ingredients, the most important thing is cleanliness, and Keith approaches the issue with characteristic thoroughness: automated washing throughout – every vessel, every pipe – supplemented by manual attention. To ensure his casks are sterile, he has even designed and built an automatic cask washer.

All the time he is improving; refining his methods and products, innovating and developing. Expansion is planned. Bottling is the next step, giving him the opportunity to reach new markets; after that, another fermenting vessel. But he will have to watch his outlay. 'My wife, Elaine, who does the hardest job – accounts and sales – has been taking a closer look at my expenditure here, with the result she's put me on spends!' He laughs uproariously. 'I haven't had that since I was at home with my mum! It's a bit of a joke between us. But it has eaten up a lot of money, this process.'

It's just a small business, with three other staff apart from Keith and Elaine. However, it is a fascinating one. No wonder tours of this brewery are popular. With all his accomplishments, Keith Wright is a remarkably modest man, genial, humorous and welcoming. He'll fire you with his enthusiasm for one of the oldest foods on earth, even if – heaven forfend – you're not actually a beer drinker. 'Some argue civilization came about because of beer', he says. 'Men liked the taste so much, they stopped being hunter-gatherers and grew barley for beer. True or not it's a story I like.'

Wards Fish

Birkenhead Market, Wirral

FISHMONGERS ARE HARD TO FIND THESE DAYS. Over the last twenty years there has been a decline of more than 75% in their ranks. Since 2000 alone, the numbers have fallen from just under two-and-a-half thousand to little more than one-and-a-half thousand. The loss is a desperate one, especially when you see what a truly superb fishmonger has to offer.

One that really has the wow factor can be found in the Market Hall, in Birkenhead. Ward's Fish, which has just celebrated its eightieth anniversary, is legendary for miles around. You can see why the minute you arrive at the counter. These fish look so fresh, you wouldn't be surprised to see them move of their own accord – even the fillets!

It's a delight to stumble across Wards by accident, to see this quality for the first time. You cannot help but revel in the gorgeous display and variety of fish, eyes still bright, scales still crisply gleaming. The contrast between this and the average supermarket offering is enough to bowl anybody over. Come to Wards and see how fresh fish should look!

Shining silver sea bass; firm-bodied mackeral; Cornish brill and wild turbot; langoustines; lobsters; oysters and scallops; huge gape-mouthed halibut and fresh anchovies all on ice-strewn slabs. Then come the kippers, tiny marinated sardines, potted shrimps and natural smoked haddock …

Emily Ward, wife to a ship's cook, set up the business in 1927, on a busy thoroughfare in Birkenhead. It quickly prospered, but neither Emily nor her husband were destined to benefit from the fruits of their labours. Both died in their forties, and it was left to their son, Norman, to take matters in hand. He inherited his mother's business acumen, and built the company up. At one time it supplied all of the fish and chip shops from North Wales to the southern limits of Liverpool.

In 1976, Wards moved into the new Birkenhead Market, and today the business has passed to the fourth generation of the family. Simon and Nigel Buckmaster run the business alongside their father, Ron. Since 1987 they have held the Seafish Quality Award, in recognition of their commitment to the highest standards in fish marketing.

Working as a team, they have expanded the range to the point where they now describe themselves as food suppliers rather than simply fishmongers. In addition to the traditional fishmonger sales of game and poultry, they also sell pork from Edge & Son Butchers of New Ferry, wild mushrooms, fresh truffles, caviar and foie gras. One of the specialities on offer is Gressingham duck – a cross between Peking duck and wild Mallard. In their opinion, and that of many top chefs, its rich meaty flavour makes it the finest tasting duck available. Game is sold fresh in season – hand-dressed or in the feather – and a range of frozen game is available all year round, including all cuts of wild venison.

At weekends there is an influx of people planning dinner parties, hoping to impress friends with their culinary skills. They seek out more unusual fare and Wards is more than up to the challenge of providing it. One couple come from Wolverhampton every month to replenish their freezer. Wards' dedication to quality and service pays dividends: not only does it draw new customers in, it keeps them coming back, again and again.

Although firmly committed to the traditional aspects of their work, the team at Wards is not afraid to embrace new ideas. Free vacuum packing was introduced some time ago, not only to preserve freshness, but also for customers' convenience and to ensure that the products retain all their original taste and nutritional value. There is a free local delivery service and customers can also shop online. Fish is dispatched in insulated boxes and maintained at the correct temperature during transit with reusable ice packs.

Christmas, a particularly busy time for the stall, sees Simon, Nigel and their staff, selling free-range geese, farm-raised 'wild' boar and, of course turkeys. They supply both Kelly Bronze and Golden Promise turkeys, which are free-range and grown slowly on a drug-free, seventy per cent cereal diet. Both breeds are hung for a minimum of seven days to develop flavour and tenderness.

However, fish and seafood remain the first passion of these men and they pride themselves on offering an experienced, specialist service. Wherever possible they source locally, to reduce the travelling time for the fresh fish. So, for example, their stall stocks Anglesey mussels and sea trout. But since they insist on sourcing the best, they'll source supplies from fishing ports as far afield as Cornwall, Yorkshire and Scotland.

Good food doesn't just happen, it takes care and knowledge and dedication. And behind all really good food retailers there is passion. At Ward's it is apparent in every aspect of the work which Simon and Nigel undertake. The just-caught freshness of their fish, the pristine uniforms of their dedicated staff, the artistry of their displays and the rapport they have with their customers, all confirm this passion. Contrast the typically sterile encounter between customers and supermarket staff with the friendly and informative exchange which is an integral part of shopping at Wards. A laugh, a joke, as well as expert advice on food preparation and recipes, are standard. This is food retailing at its very best and Simon, Nigel and their dad enjoy every minute of it.

Want to be a bit more adventurous in your cooking but short of ideas? They can offer you plenty. Not sure how to cook a particular type of fish, or game? They will give you step by step instructions. If you live in the Northwest and you love food, and have not yet discovered this little jewel, take a trip to Wards in Birkenhead and sample some of the finest food in the region – or anywhere else in the country.

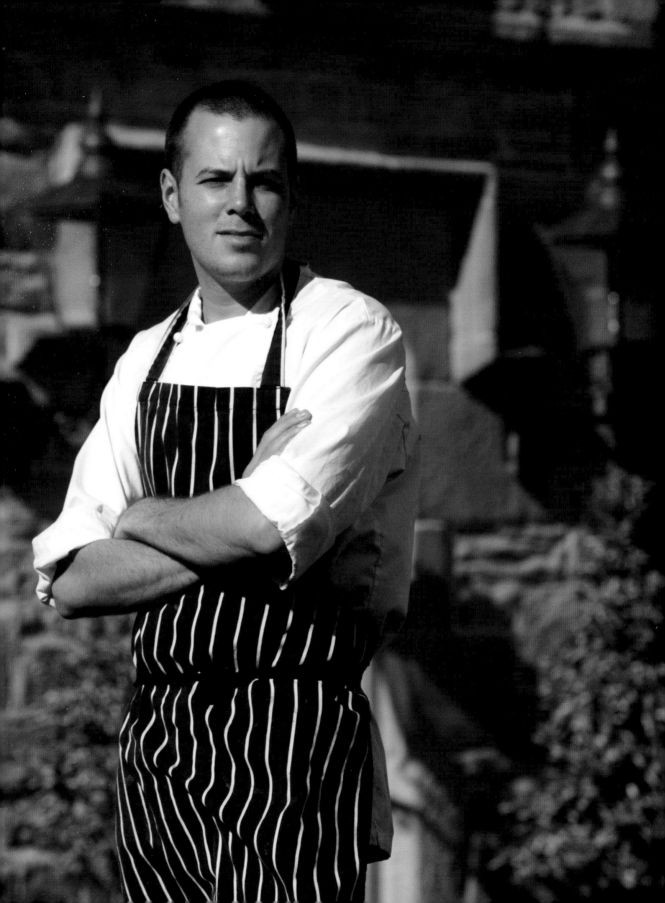

Warrick Dodds

Cassis Restaurant

Stanley House Hotel, Lancashire

ON A HILLTOP, COMMANDING THE ROLLING PASTURES and wooded slopes of the magnificent Ribble Valley, is a mullioned manor house, its honey-coloured sandstone so crisp and clean, its box parterres so new-made, you might imagine yourself in the 17th century – or else on a film-set. This is the award-winning Stanley House, meticulously restored from near-dereliction and opened as a luxury hotel in 2004. Step inside to a series of individually designed rooms, bewitchingly opulent, superbly appointed. Step outside, and discover Cassis, the fine dining restaurant, housed in an accomplished conversion of the manor's spacious farm buildings. The exterior is all restraint; the interior, all exuberance. Baroque rules. Silver thrones, clad in velvet, adorn the foyer. A cascade of crystal leads to the restaurant which forms a tour de force in purple, reflecting the blackcurrant of its name. By day, you can survey half the county through its ample picture windows and, on summer nights, watch wine-dark sunsets sink before you. The denizens of this realm seem intent on perfecting every detail for the pleasure of their guests. None more so than Head Chef, Warrick Dodds, and Restaurant Manager, Laurent Duval. Each regards the other as an indispensable partner in taking fine-dining to the pinnacle of performance.

"I JOINED CASSIS AS HEAD CHEF IN THE AUTUMN OF 2004, when we opened. I was 28 and, for the first time in my career, I had the wonderful opportunity to develop my own style of food. I think I've established that now. It's been described as 'French-inspired' fine dining but it goes a lot wider. There are influences from around the Mediterranean to North Africa and further afield, while some of the strongest are much closer to home.

Nigel Haworth, who I was with for seven years at Northcote Manor, and Paul

Heathcote, who I was with at Longridge for two-and-a-half, have both been really strong influences on my whole approach to cooking.

Like them, I believe you have to start with first-class produce. Next, it's about preparing it to absolute perfection, through every single stage, from start to finish. Then it must be served to perfection.

This is why it's so important for me to work closely with Laurent, our Restaurant Manager. Whether it's the choice of crockery or the weekly menus, we'll discuss everything necessary to make sure that both our operations gel. I've been in too many places where I felt front-of-house was lacking, but here I feel very comfortable with it. Both of us share the same goal: to take Cassis to the highest level we can.

I think my ambition goes back a long way. As a child, I always wanted to be a chef. I don't know why. Perhaps because my older brother, Lawrence, wanted to be one. Right from the age of about ten or twelve, all I wanted to do was cook. I was probably only the second boy in the whole school ever to do Food Studies and it was the only subject I ever concentrated on!

Once, I brought in a pigeon to cookery class. Everyone else was doing chicken or lamb, but my brother was training to be a chef so he'd got me a pigeon and shown me how to cook it. I did it with blackcurrant sauce! I was about 14. The teacher couldn't believe it – she didn't know how to do it herself! It created quite a sensation.

I learnt a lot at a very early age, because of my brother, and because I was really interested. Catering college was the next step: three years at Blackpool, but if I could have gone straight from school to a well recognised establishment, I'd probably have far greater experience now.

College was good, especially for some of the basics, but when you go into an establishment it's a real wake-up call to see the way things are done in the here and now!

I was lucky enough to have six months in Franco Taruschio's famous Walnut Tree restaurant in Abergavenny and saw a lot of really good produce come in. I remember the fish, the seafood – lobster, langoustine, spiny crab, winkles. I learnt about truffles, Italian cheeses and hams, and went mushroom picking for ceps there, too. The food was very rustic and, much as I liked it, I wanted to do more fine-detail cooking.

At the time, my brother was working at Paul Heathcote's, in Longridge. They'd just achieved their second Michelin star, and I managed to find a way in, as a commis chef. It was a very, very hard kitchen when I started.

There I was, barely eighteen, and I found myself working alongside people from Le Gavroche – the seminal three-star restaurant! So I had to learn very quickly!

You had to get things right at Longridge. It was a 14-mile journey back into work for me otherwise, so I had no option. I'd stay till all hours if necessary, come in on my days off if I had to.

Without a doubt, discipline is a key part in character-building for chefs and it

needs to be taught at an early age. If you have to correct your mistake straightaway, you don't repeat it. If I hadn't taken the bollockings when I was a young lad, then I wouldn't be where I am today! It was the only way that I learnt.

Once I found my stride, it just got better and better. I became chef de partie and did the pastry section, larder, bread and canapés. I loved my time with Paul. But, from a two-Michelin star establishment, I wanted to go to a three-star and test my own capabilities at a higher level.

I knew someone who worked at Nico's in Park Lane. So off I went to London, did a stage and got a job there. I learnt a helluva lot, in every aspect. The food was a lot more precise – mind you, there were a lot more chefs to prepare it! I noticed how perfect everything was. Little things, like petit fours, would be just so right. The quality of the produce coming into the kitchen was excellent too – truffles, meat, fish, everything that came through that back door.

In terms of quality it wasn't a that big a leap from one restaurant to the other – some things at Heathcote's were a lot better – but overall, Nico's was attaining a consistently higher level. I knew that, one day, I wanted to be able to achieve something like that.

I enjoyed it there, got promoted and after two-and-a-half years, the opportunity came up to go to Nigel Haworth's kitchen at Northcote Manor. So it was back to Lancashire, just a few miles from here.

Nigel is one of the best chefs I've ever worked with. He taught me so much about flavours and precision. I won Young Chef of the Year while I was there and got promoted to Head Chef at 24. Four years later, Cassis came along and, with it, the chance to make a mark in my own right.

When I cook, my aim is to capture the essence of the product and bring out its flavour to the maximum. I like to use simple ingredients, of the finest quality, prepare them to absolute perfection, and let them speak for themselves as genuine items.

In the past, I think I've over-complicated dishes. What I'm trying to do now is simplify them. You don't need to put five, six, seven other ingredients on the plate – maybe just one or two. When it's such a perfect product, why spoil it by putting other things alongside?

For instance, I do a dish using white asparagus. When I get the asparagus in, first I check that they're all perfect. Then I get them peeled down, cut to the right length, and all cooked for exactly the same time in seasoned water. From the trimmings, I'll make a creamed asparagus mousse. I'll serve it with a salad of baby white asparagus shoots. The only accompaniment is truffle and hollandaise sauce. That way I have a dish made from what is basically a single ingredient, used to its full potential – and the flavours are so identifiable!

You've got to be able to identify what you're eating. There's no doubt about that in my mind. When I order fish, I want to see fish. Why mess around with food when it's perfect already?

I think a lot of people fail on the basics of preparation. Take sauce-making. It's no good getting the flavour right but not quite getting the texture. It has to be spot on from start to finish.

The guys here know, if they do something wrong, they have to get rid of it and do it again. I try to get them to understand the fine detail of their work, to be very focussed on what they're doing. The standards have to be there. My approach is to be disciplined but fair – and to make sure they enjoy their jobs as much as I enjoy mine. That way we get the best results.

I believe it's important for the guys in the kitchen to be able to put forward ideas of their own, and to learn different dishes which we work on together. Experience I had in the USA convinced me of that. Part of my prize, as Young Chef of the Year, was a two-week stage at the famous Chicago restaurant, Charlie Trotter's. Every guy had one job and one job only in the kitchen. It was like a production line – the Ford of food! The benefit was consistency, but it was a bit boring, and difficult to improve your knowledge, just doing one thing all day.

We have excellent kitchen facilities here, with equipment that allows us to use the latest techniques. For instance, a lot of our meats are now slow-cooked at a lower temperature, using a water-bath. That way the muscles don't contract and meat is unbelievably tender – like butter! After it's cooked, you let it rest, then pan-fry it for flavour. Even with foie gras, I don't pan fry it any more because so much fat is lost. I poach it in a pouch at 54 degrees, then finish it with a blow-torch for the fried flavour. That way it's a lot more succulent.

However, at the end of the day, it's all about the quality of the ingredients. Here, we check everything as it comes through the back door. If it's not good enough, it goes back to the supplier. I always try and incorporate seasonal produce into my menus, because to get the best from a product you have to harvest it at its best and that's when it's in season.

My ingredients are sourced for quality, of course, and will come from all over the country and some from abroad, but an awful lot is produced right here, on our own doorstep. I get local ham and pork, lamb from Bowland Forest, ducks and chicken from Goosnargh, local potatoes, peas and tomatoes, fish from Fleetwood. All our milk and cream come from Eddie Cowpe's dairy, close by in Samlesbury.

My game supplier, Ian Banks is just outside Goosnargh. He brings me whole deer, partridges, pheasants, wild duck – teal, mallard – rabbits if I want them. You can even go out with him on a shoot. He supplied me at Northcote Manor, too, and I've always found that the quality he delivers is just brilliant. His ducks are fantastic – cracking flavour to them!

We're really lucky in the Northwest having so much top-quality local produce. Michelin talk a lot about terroir and using local produce. I believe we have the best in the whole of the country, but we've yet to be recognised for it.

There's excellent cheese being made all round the area, you can see prime cattle right across the region – or just go down the road six miles to Goosnargh and find Reg Johnson's ducks. All the top chefs are using Reg's ducks now – Gordon Ramsay's using them – because they're the best.

We have so many amazing local producers and they care, they really care about what they do. The way I am with cooking, they are with producing. They take a proper pride in it.'

Laurent Duval

"WARRICK AND I BOTH BELIEVE that it's essential that the chef and the front-of-house work together. Ours is a symbiotic relationship. What begins in the kitchen we like to carry forward in front-of-house: to complement fine food with fine wine, a beautiful table, comfort and the best of service.

My starting point, as a restaurant manager, is simple: what are my guests' expectations? They want to be served very good food, fast, and with a smile.

You cannot have an enjoyable experience in any restaurant without feeling relaxed. Your state of mind while having a meal will affect the way you perceive it. So, it is the job of the restaurant staff to put guests at their ease. Be friendly and be helpful, is what I tell my guys. For example, there is a lot of French and Italian terminology in the menu – out of necessity – because many dishes spring from those traditions. Not everyone knows these terms, so we will explain them. Guests can relax on sofas, enjoy a drink, and choose from the menu at their leisure.

I design the service to be as simple and as non-intrusive as possible. Naturally,

everything that goes on the table, cutlery, plates, glassware, has to be polished and spotless. This is compulsory. The linen has to be white and pristine. This too is compulsory. For extra comfort, our dining chairs have a special little swivel, so that guests can be seated nice and smoothly at their tables, and leave them in the same way. Attention to detail is important in the restaurant, just as in the kitchen. The final touches to a dish are made by the chef, but once the dish is served, the final touches are made by the front-of-house.

For example, the choice of wine to accompany the food, is very important. For fifteen years I was a sommelier and, in matching wine to food, there is a science that is really, really interesting. Basically, you analyse the chef's dish and you try to find flavours that will match every aspect of it. If you do that successfully, then the dish served to the guest will be that much enhanced. This makes the difference between a good experience, and a very good experience!

Nowadays all English youth wants to be a chef! They see it as a career with cachet and the promise of stardom. But being a commis chef is painful work, and it is a misconception that it's easier to be successful in the kitchen than in front-of-house. What's more, the rewards for a top restaurant manager can be considerable.

To be a good maitre d' you need a range of skills – as a business strategist, an organiser, a manager of staff and finance and of course, you must have wide breadth of knowledge about cuisine. You must be able to answer all your guests' questions about the menu, and in some depth.

Waiters must be knowledgeable too. Traditionally, haute cuisine restaurants, like the legendary Tour d'Argent in Paris, for example, have always had a wealth of highly specialised people in front-of-house – canardier, crémier, and so on. Now these positions are becoming obsolete, so the average waiter will need to have a wider knowledge in the future, in order to take over those specialities.

A waiter is anything but a servant. It is necessary to know about cuisine, cheese, carving, cocktails, beverages of all kinds – and be a psychologist into the bargain! In fact, a waiter has to be someone exceptional. The job is physically as well as mentally demanding and you work many hours, so people need to be committed to what they do and have a passion for it, especially in fine dining.

Front-of-house has a lot of career potential, but you must start early. In France, it is possible to take a first diploma as early as 13, two by 16, because if you are not academically inclined, you get the option, throughout your education, to do technical, practical courses with a lot of work experience. Although I did the Baccalauréat and a master's in management, in a sense, it's a waste of time, because there's no substitute for practice.

I place a lot of importance on staff training. Probably the most enjoyable thing, apart from the guests' satisfaction, is to see the evolution of young staff. They come through the door, scared to say two words, partly due to the language barrier –because my brigade is mostly French – partly due to lack of confidence. You work on that and you build them up. You give them a code of behaviour, you teach them how to relate to customers, how to relate to management, how to achieve success. It is like witnessing a coming-of-age. There is a bit of the fatherly attitude in that, which is great.

Nothing is more edifying for me than to see some of the guys who I have trained reach the top of their profession in this country, and in France as well. For instance, one of my head-waiters is now restaurant manager at the three-star Arpège in Paris, while another is restaurant manager at John Burton-Race's Michelin-starred New Angel in Devonshire.

All the great restaurants in England have a great front-of-house manager – Le Gavroche has Silvano Giraldin, Gordon Ramsay has Jean-Claude Breton, and Alain Desenclos has been at Le Manoir since day one.

It's like performing live on stage every night – and that goes for all levels of the restaurant, whether it's in the kitchen or the front-of-house. Hiccups happen, but you're trying to prevent them and overcome them. If something does go wrong there's no point hiding from it. Explain to your customer, because there is nothing worse than waiting and not knowing what's going on. If a problem is handled well, most people will cut you a little slack!

* Warrick Dodds is now Head Chef at The Sparling, Barton, Lancashire.

Ballotine of Foie Gras and Ham Hock with Spring Pea Purée and Mustard Mayonnaise, Honey and Mint Dressing

SERVES 4

1 lobe best quality foie gras
2 ham hocks
2 onions, chopped
3 whole, peeled carrots
4 sticks celery
2 large potatoes for dicing
2 bay leaves
2 sprigs mint
2 sprigs thyme
1 parsley stalk
500g chopped parsley

For the Pea Purée
500g fresh peas
200ml cream
1 leaf gelatine

For the Garnish
1 punnet pea shoots
4 soft boiled quail eggs
8 cubes pickled beetroot, cut into 2cm cubes
8 batons chives
For serving, toasted brioche

For the Mustard Mayonnaise
2 egg yolks
150ml very light olive oil
1 tbsp prepared English mustard
Salt and pepper
1 tbsp white wine vinegar

For the Honey and Mint Dressing
12 mint leaves, finely chopped
2 shallots, chopped
300ml very light olive oil
2 tbsp honey
100ml vinegar
Salt and pepper

1 Put the ham hocks into a large pan, cover with water. Add chopped onions, 2 of the carrots, celery and chopped parsley stalks together with salt and bay leaves. Cook for five hours on a low heat until the ham comes away from the bone. Remove the ham hocks from the pan and strain. Reduce the remaining liquid by half. **2** Fry the foie gras in a non-stick frying pan, keeping the lobe whole. Season, add thyme and cook for about 6 minutes until the lobe is cooked. Cool and reserve. **3** Dice the potato and remaining carrot into 1cm squares and cook in boiling water until just beginning to soften. **4** When the hocks have cooled sufficiently, take the ham off the bone and dice. **5** Combine with the chopped parsley, salt, pepper, diced potato and carrot. **6** Chop the mint finely, season with salt and pepper and add to rest of mixture. Add some of the foie gras fat and some of the reduced liquid to keep the ham mixture moist. **7** Cut the foie gras down the centre. Place 3 sheets of cling film on worktop and place the ham mixture on to it. Pat it down slightly, place the foie gras on top and roll into a perfect cylinder, approximately 8cm in diameter. **8** Tie both ends and refrigerate for 5 hours.

Pea Purée **1** Soak the gelatine leaf in a little water until soft. **2** Bring the cream to the boil and reduce by half, add the peas and season with salt and pepper, then purée in a food processor until smooth. **3** Pass through a fine sieve, add the softened gelatine and stir. **4** Take a large plate and place a ladleful onto it, make a perfect circle, approximately 10cm in diameter. Refrigerate.

Mustard Mayonnaise **1** Put the egg yolks in a food processor and mix until very pale in colour. **2** Slowly add the vinegar and oil until the tone of the motor changes. **3** Add the mustard and season, place in a squeezy bottle.

Honey and Mint Dressing [1] Place the honey, vinegar and chopped shallot into a bowl. [2] Slowly add the oil and whisk. [3] Season with salt and pepper then add the finely chopped mint.

To Serve [1] Cut a slice of the chilled foie gras roll (the ballotine), 1cm thick, and place on a plate in the centre of the pea purée. Arrange 3 pea shoots around the rim. [2] Place 2 cubes of beetroot opposite one another on the slice. Cut the soft boiled quails eggs in half, season with salt and pepper, and place opposite one another on the slice, forming a cross with the beetroot cubes. [3] Squeeze a little of the mayonnaise on top of each half egg, then place a chive baton on top of each. [4] Drizzle some of the honey and mint dressing around the dish. [5] Serve with slices of toasted brioche.

Pan Roasted Roe Deer with Parsnip and Vanilla Purée, Pickled Red Cabbage, Bitter Chocolate Sauce and Sweet Quince

SERVES 4

4 small loins of roe deer

For the Venison Marinade
Freshly picked thyme
Crushed juniper berries
Olive oil
Salt

For the Parsnip and Vanilla Purée
400ml cream
2 vanilla pods
100g unsalted butter
4 parsnips

For the Quince Purée
500g quince
100g sugar
100ml water
Squeeze of lemon juice

For the Cabbage
1 red cabbage
300ml water
300ml white wine vinegar
200ml balsamic vinegar
350g sugar
40g salt
1 star anise
10 cloves
5 pink peppercorns
5 black peppercorns
2 cinnamon sticks
5 bay leaves
3 juniper berries
1 tbsp mustard seeds
4 dried red chillies

For the Garnish
12 spring onions
12 red radishes
570ml water
250g unsalted butter
Salt to taste

For the Sauce
50g bitter chocolate
2.4lt veal stock
600ml chicken stock
500g chopped vegetables:
2 carrots, 1 onion, 2 celery sticks,
1/2 bulb garlic
1 bunch thyme
600ml port
200ml sherry vinegar
1 clove garlic
600g venison bones, lightly roasted

Pickled Cabbage [1] Cut the cabbage into very fine ribbons. [2] Place all other ingredients in a pan, bring to the boil and reduce by two thirds. [3] Meanwhile, salt the cabbage, place in a colander and leave for 4 hours. [4] Then wash off, place in a suitable sized bowl, and once the liquid has cooled down, pour over the cabbage and leave for about 2 hours.

Sauce [1] Fry the chopped vegetables for a couple of minutes on a high heat. [2] Cut the garlic clove in half and lightly crush with a knife blade and add, along with the port, thyme, and vinegar, then reduce by two thirds. [3] Add the chopped, roasted bones and chicken stock then cook for 40 minutes. [4] Remove the bones and vegetables and pass the liquid through a cloth. [5] Return to the stove and reduce until it reaches a sauce consistency. [6] Chop the chocolate finely and whisk it into the sauce. Season with salt.

Parsnip and Vanilla Purée [1] Peel and finely chop the parsnips. [2] Melt the butter and add the parsnips, add vanilla from the pods. [3] Add the cream, stir and simmer slowly for approximately 10-15 minutes until the parsnips are soft cooked. [4] season with salt and purée in the food processor until smooth.

Quince Purée [1] Peel and chop the quince, add the water and sugar. [2] Bring to the boil and simmer for 10-15 minutes until the quince is cooked. [3] Add the lemon juice. Purée and pass through a fine sieve.

Garnish [1] Heat the water whisked with the butter to form an emulsion. [2] Cook the radishes in this for 2-3 minutes until a knife will go through, cook the spring onions for about 1 minute.

The Meat [1] Overnight, marinate the venison in fresh thyme, crushed juniper berries, olive oil and salt. [2] Cook the loins in an oven preheated to 180°C / gas mark 4 for approximately 12 minutes.
     OR
[1] If you have the facility place each loin in a vacuum pack bag and cook in a water bath for about 30 minutes at 55°C. [2] Remove the loins, and to obtain a roasted flavour, roll in icing sugar and pan fry until nicely caramelised. [3] Rest for 20 minutes then reheat in a pan with a sprig of thyme, basting with melted butter.

To Serve [1] Drain some cabbage and gently heat both purées. [2] On the plate, place a blob of parsnip purée and drag a spoon through it to form an elongated leaf shape. [3] Next to it place a circle of quince purée. [4] Cut 2 slices of the meat, on an angle, with a really sharp knife and place to one side of the plate, opposite the purées. [5] Place a neat domed portion of cabbage between the purées and the meat. [6] Garnish with radish and spring onion, spoon a little sauce over the meat.

Chef's Tip As an accompaniment, I like to serve garlic and thyme dauphinoise potatoes, presented in a copper pan.

Iced Strawberry Parfait, with Strawberry Crisps, Strawberry and Basil Sorbet

SERVES 4

For the Parfait
2 egg yolks
100g caster sugar
25ml water
100g strawberry puree
250g whipped cream

For the Nougatine Disc
50g glucose syrup
75g fondant icing
60g nibbed almonds
10g butter

Parfait [1] Whisk the egg yolks until fluffy. [2] Place the sugar and water in a pan and boil until it reaches a temperature of 118°C. Pour over the egg yolks, add the purée and whisk until cold. Whip the cream into soft peaks and fold into the egg mixture. [3] Fill four 8cm rings and freeze.

Nougatine Disc [1] Boil the glucose syrup and the fondant icing until the mixture turns golden in colour. [2] Add the almonds and the butter then stir. [3] Turn the mixture out onto greaseproof paper or non-stick mat to cool. [4] When cold, crack the praline into pieces, put in a food processor and blitz into a powder. [5] Line a baking tray with greaseproof paper and, using a sieve, lightly dust with the powder until completely covered. Place in an oven 140°C / gas mark 1 for 8 minutes or until the caramel melts and forms a thin sheet. [6] Remove from the oven, allow to cool and cut into rounds the same size as the frozen parfait.

For the Strawberry Crisps
100g Fresh strawberries

For the Sorbet
200g strawberry puree
100g sugar
2tsp lemon juice
100g chopped basil

Strawberry Crisps [1] Thinly slice the fresh strawberries and place on greaseproof paper or non-stick sheet. [2] Leave overnight in a conventional oven at 90°C / gas mark as low as possible to dry out.

Sorbet [1] Put all the ingredients in a saucepan. Bring to the boil. [2] Pass through a fine sieve then churn in an ice cream maker until set, or freeze in a container stirring well every 30 minutes until set.

To Serve [1] Place the parfait in the centre of a plate. [2] Put the Nougatine disc on top. [3] Place 8 dried strawberry slices around, and a quenelle (or well formed oval scoop) of the basil sorbet on the top. [4] Garnish with 2 strands of pulled sugar if required.

Ian Banks

The Deer Hunter

Eaves Green Game Farm
Lancashire

NOTHING STIRS BUT THE WIND IN THE HEATHER, high on a stone-studded moor in the Forest of Bowland. No trees grow here to check its onward sweep: through heathland grasses, over rocky outcrops and blanket bog, down steeply incised cloughs. Skimming the green velvet pastures of river valleys below, it rolls on, to buffet the heights of blue misted fells beyond.

This July day opened with unremitting rain. Now, on the cusp of evening, it has relented. And under a cloud-strewn sky four men, clad to merge with their surroundings, move quietly, haltingly, through the natural grandeur of this isolated wilderness. They are stalking deer.

Ian Banks leads the party. He's a Lancashire game farmer, who has shooting rights on about four hundred acres hereabouts, near the ancient village of Caton on the south bank of the River Lune. It's just a tiny patch in the three hundred square miles that make up the Forest. The deer, wild and elusive creatures that they are, could be anywhere. Red deer and roe deer, the native species that have roamed Britain for millennia, roam here. Hunting them, however, is strictly seasonal, as it is for all six of the UK's resident species of deer. Since it is July, the male roe – the buck – will be the only permissable quarry.

Deer stalking is a new venture for Ian. He rears game birds on his farm and, in the past, has always bought in venison for customers like chef Warrick Dodds, who is with him today. But now he has decided to do everything himself: hunt, kill, dress, deliver. Perhaps it was always just a matter of time before Ian would engage in this age-old branch of venery. He is, after all, a former gamekeeper on the Duke of Westminster's great estate of Abbeystead nearby. What's more, the whole vast tract of Bowland has been managed mainly for game ever since the Norman kings designated it a hunting demesne in the eleventh century. It is a 'forest' in the medieval meaning of the word – a royal deer park – not in our modern sense of woodland. There have been few trees on these uplands since our forbears cut them down in the Bronze Age.

Despite the lack of cover, and despite high numbers of their kind, the deer are not easy to locate. Dawn or dusk is the best time for roe deer, when they are moving into feeding areas. But it's not guaranteed even then. Just now, Ian's busy getting the lie of the land. He hasn't been up here for a few weeks and growth has changed the terrain dramatically, as he knew it would. The hinds have had their calves too, so they will be even more secretive than usual.

He watches and waits. Still, silent, patient. If roe are there, the slightest untoward movement, a scent on the wind will alert them, but if you stay completely immobile they will carry on grazing. Once, a score of hinds walked within twenty-five yards of him: 'You've not to move a millimetre. They might be eyeballing you for four or five minutes and it's all a question of whether you can stop still that long.'

Ian shares his knowledge freely and modestly. But not here. Stalking must be wordless for the most part, so we talked beforehand, against a background of constant chirping, at Eaves Green Game Farm, some twenty miles to the south. It's set in a small area of Lancashire that might well be called the golden triangle of Goosnargh – so remarkable is it for exceptional food producers.

The landscape is in complete contrast to Bowland: pastoral, settled, tamed. Ian lives outside the village. There's a long complex, of farmhouse and converted outbuildings in local stone, much extended into a smart and spacious family home, complete with decked and parasolled patio. Around it, are six acres of land where Ian rears partridge, pheasants and wild ducks for shoots, together with a processing plant where he prepares game for the table.

If the scene sounds a bit mixed between commuter and countryman, the answer may lie in Ian's family background. As a third-generation scion of famous Preston jewellers, George Banks, young Ian was fully expected to join his older brothers in the business. Even at school, the careers teacher had him pigeonholed: 'No need to see you Banksie, you'll be going in with your dad.'

'No I'm not', came the instant rejoinder. 'I'm going to be a gamekeeper.'

Even so, he was still following in the parental footsteps. His father reared a few ducks and pheasants behind the house, taught his youngest son to shoot and the two would go out together after rabbits and game birds. 'He was very careful with guns. As a kid I had a toy one and I wasn't allowed to point it at anybody! That's how safety conscious he was and I'm exactly the same. Up on the fells, you must know the safety of where you can shoot and where you can't shoot. For instance, you must never shoot a deer if it's stood on the horizon because, if you did miss, the bullet would be over the top and could go anywhere. So you must always make sure there's a backdrop to the beast you're shooting.'

Ian thinks he probably saw the best of his dad, 'Because when he was with me he was always relaxed. My brothers worked with him and, as a child, it seemed to me they were always arguing – before they left the house in the morning and when they came home in the evening! I decided I didn't want to join them. I wanted an outdoor life.'

At sixteen he joined a youth training scheme on a small shooting estate at Garstang. That came to an end, but it won him an introduction to the head keeper at Abbeystead and every Saturday, even as he trained to be an electrician, he'd go

up to the estate, just to help the keepers. Six months later, as he lay in hospital after an appendectomy, his dedication was rewarded with the offer of a job. 'It was just brilliant. My dad used to come up and go beating. The Queen would visit and she would be working the dogs and Prince Philip would be shooting. My dad met the Queen and it was all just amazing really!'

By the time Ian had been gamekeeping for about six years, his father had become so keen that he was planning to go into business with his son. Then, suddenly, a freak street accident cut short his life and left Ian to go it alone. That was twenty years ago. 'He was 64, about to retire and really looking forward to all this', says Ian, indicating the game farm. 'He would have been very much involved.'

And, no doubt, very interested in the way it has developed. Today Ian hatches, rears and sells many thousands of birds for shoots, as well as being partner in one himself. The work is seasonal, ending when shooting begins in the autumn. That's when Ian turns his attention to preparing the carcasses for food. He buys back most of his birds from the shoots. They are plucked, dressed, packed and refrigerated or frozen – up to 600 a day – then sold to restaurants, butchers and private buyers.

Ensuring quality is very important to him, though not always easy when your product is a free-range creature shot out of the sky. 'Consistency is what chefs

want from me and that's what I give them. I'm not afraid of going into the kitchen and asking them to look and see whether what I'm delivering is good enough for them. After all, it's no use a Michelin guy walking in and finding things fine one night and not the next.' Ian eats his own produce and is particularly appreciative of the 'wonderful things' chefs do with them.

He is similarly attentive with his venison. The beast must be neither too young, nor too old. 'Then Warrick would want it hanging for two or three weeks.' He doesn't sell venison all year round, just in season. 'I could sell it frozen or defrosted, but I don't do that.'

The husbandry of the birds appeals greatly to this gentle, good-natured man: collecting the eggs each day, incubating them, hatching them, then rearing them up, indoors and outdoors, through their various stages until they are sent to the shooting estates. That's at six weeks for duck; seven for pheasant; twelve for partridge. Then the gamekeepers take over responsibility for the next few months. 'We've really got to look after them. The better they're bred here, the more we'll have and the better birds they'll be. Pheasants, especially, don't rear in the wild very well and if they were left to their own devices there would be a lot less of them.'

He likes the idea that the birds he rears, unlike farmed chickens, have a chance to get away and live on in the wild – as many do.

> "Consistency is what chefs want from me and that's what I give them."

Ian Banks is a natural countryman, connected to the land and the life it supports. He knows our food must be either grown or reared. Unlike so many of us who eat meat, Ian remains in touch with the age-old practices of rearing, hunting, killing; the cycle of life, death and renewal, which puts the meat on the table. In his quiet way, he regrets the town and country divide, the notion that the vacuum pack is meat's natural environment; that so many children don't know where their food comes from, and so many adults don't want to.

He's probably never happier than when he's close to nature, out in the covers with his working dogs or, in particular, out on the fells, deer-stalking. It thrills him just to see these noble beasts and so far, every time he's come up, he's had a sighting. Seeing other wildlife thrills him too: a badger, just twelve feet away, the image captured perfectly on his mobile phone. Then there are Bowland's rare, protected, upland birds such as the hen harrier, peregrine and ring ouzel. But even if he sees or hears no wildlife, he is content to experience the thrill of this sublime country at what seems like the top of the world. And that is fortunate for, on this day, no deer were seen at all.

Ian Banks, the Deer Hunter. Warrick Dodds' supplier 93

Eddie Cowpe
Huntley's, Lancashire

THERE ARE NOT MANY FARM SHOPS where you would arrive to find the owner manoeuvring a digger around huge piles of earth. But this is Eddie Cowpe, a man on the move, with the bit well and truly between his teeth. Eddie is one of those people who never stop, and just now he is absorbed with a massive expansion of his already very successful business at Huntley Gate Farm, close to the village of Samlesbury, near Clitheroe. The new complex includes a food hall, bakery, wine shop, clothing store, antique shop, forge, butchery – and more to come.

The first member of the Cowpe family settled in Samlesbury as long ago as 1208 and, as well as setting up the farm, operated a ferry across the River Ribble. The family has continued farming in the area ever since. So, it seems particularly fitting that these new enterprises should be realised in 2008, right on time to mark the farm's eight hundredth birthday.

Back in 2001, when Foot and Mouth Disease hit the farming industry like a sledgehammer, Huntley's suffered, like all the other farms in the region. In fact, many farmers were so devastated by the outbreak that they had to be treated for post- traumatic stress disorder. After it was all over, Eddie Cowpe looked at his own business and knew he must transform it if he was going to survive. He took stock of the situation and decided to build an ice-cream factory and 750 square feet of farm shop, selling his meat, milk and home-made ice cream direct to the public.

The geographical location of Huntley Gate Farm helped a lot. It is close to the M6 and just off the A59, the main road between Preston and Blackburn. The shop was an immediate success and Eddie has been expanding ever since.

As well as the dairy herd, the farm breeds its own beef cattle, sheep, wild boar and rare breed pigs. Eddie points out: 'We don't force our cows into producing milk intensively, which is one of the reasons that we get a really good product. What you feed your cows affects what you get from them. Milk is one of the easiest things to taint. You can even tell which field the cows have been grazing in, from the taste of the milk they give. We are not organic but we do have a closed herd. We have never had a case of either TB or BSE. We use a minimum number of antibiotics and no artificial fertilisers on the land.' Huntley's grow their own crops of maize and wheat to supplement the cows' diet, so they know exactly what the herd has been eating.

This solid, old-fashioned good husbandry, reaps its own rewards. Both members of the public, and chefs like Warrick Dodds, flock to the farm for Huntley's famous milk and cream. Eddie respects his customers' powers of discernment and believes that they can tell the difference in the taste and the freshness of his dairy products.

His award-winning ice cream, Moo 2 You, has been a roaring success since it was originally launched. If the words 'ice cream factory' conjures up an image of industrialised production – think again. Whilst Eddie only uses top quality equipment, he is not a great fan of the high-tech approach and prefers to trust in the skills of his highly trained workforce, who make the ice cream largely by hand.

But why produce ice cream? The venture began when Eddie discovered some old recipes and contacted a friend in Yorkshire, who already made the stuff. His friend thought the recipes looked very exciting, and after tweaking them slightly, he spent three to four days a week, for about a year, teaching Eddie how to become an ice cream maker. Now Huntley's are producing between five and six thousand litres a week at the farm.

The range of flavours has kept on growing. There are eighty different varieties to date, including some very tempting creations such as Custard Cream and Melon and Ginger. And the all-time favourite? It's still Vanilla of course! One of the strong selling points of Moo 2 You, which is widely available through independent retailers, is that much of the fruit, and all of the cream, come straight from the farm, so customers can have a very clear insight into the provenance and content of what they are eating.

The farm shop sells fresh fruit and vegetables grown on the farm, while the butchery stocks top quality home-reared beef, Ribble Valley lamb, traditionally reared poultry and game in season. Master butchers, John Simpson and Ken Westall, always happy to advise customers, pride themselves on the proper preparation of all their products. As well as the farm's own products, the shop's shelves are filled with those of specialist local suppliers, making the enterprise a real asset to the local community.

> What you feed your cows affects what you get from them. Milk is one of the easiest things to taint. You can even tell which field the cows have been grazing in, from the taste of the milk they give.

A particularly intriguing feature of this rural business complex must surely be the two highly successful restaurants on site. Huntley's By Day is open from breakfast time to early evening. Then Huntley's At Night takes over! They both offer home-cooked food made with a lot of produce that is local. With all this enterprise, no wonder 2007 saw Huntley's win a Best Rural Retailer Award, as well as Lancashire's Tourism Team of the Year.

Never one to rest on his laurels, Eddie has also been busy creating a maze of tall grasses as an all-year-round attraction for families. During the summer there is PYO too, which is especially popular with parents who want to show their children where food comes from. But the crowning glory for Eddie is his new food hall, with its cheese and fish counters, and a place for making jams and preserves which is open to the public. 'All you need to fill your shopping basket,' says Eddie proudly.

In the course of the coming year, he expects to see the staff complement at Huntley's rise to more than one hundred, a development which will have a significant impact on the local economy. 'Our vision has always been to create a family destination, but also to promote the idea that local families and rural businesses can be successful. Since I was fourteen, I have always had ambition. I enjoy what I'm doing, so why not keep on doing it?' He shrugs and as he heads back towards the cabin of his digger. Time to get stuck into the real work again.

Steven Doherty
First Floor Café
Lakeland, Cumbria

RENOWNED CHEF, Steven Doherty, has a reputation as a pioneer. Mentored by Albert Roux, he became Head Chef at Le Gavroche in the '80s and the first Briton to lead an establishment in receipt of that ultimate accolade – three Michelin stars. After more metropolitan glitter at executive level in London and Amsterdam, and becoming only the fifth chef in this country to attain the exclusive Master of Culinary Arts Award, a yen for country pleasures, hands-on cooking and his native north drew him to the inspirational landscape of England's Lake District. This is where he trailblazed the gastro-pub in the '90s, with Marjorie, his wife and business partner. Acclaim was virtually instant. But after a decade of success democratizing good dining, another innovative prospect of even greater potential beckoned: the high-quality, in-store café.

It's located in picturesque Windermere at the spectacular, award-winning headquarters and flagship-store of Lakeland, the creative kitchenware company. Bounded by a sleek curve of glass and steel, the First Floor Café seems to float above the store. For a modest outlay, customers can enjoy stylish surroundings and exceptionally good food, expertly prepared from the best, local, seasonal produce that Steven can buy. Needless to say, it's hugely popular.

"THERE'S A WONDERFUL FEELING OF SPACE HERE. Our panoramic window lets diners feel as if they are part of the landscape. In winter, when the trees have lost their leaves, you can almost see Lake Windermere – almost, but not quite!

We wanted to create a very wide-open, light environment in natural colours. So we've used wood and local slate, glass and steel – modern and traditional materials. It's a timeless design. You could come back in twenty years and it would still look good.

We opened in April 2004. The Rayner family, who own and run Lakeland, had asked me if we would be interested in submitting a tender. We were successful and had the opportunity to help with the development and design of the café. We aimed for a very simple style, nothing pretentious. We chose the name on the

same basis. I just wanted the place to be called what it is: the First Floor Café. I took my inspiration from the Fifth Floor Café at Harvey Nichols.

Lakeland are very specific about how they do things, and they wanted to build a relationship with somebody who understood and was sympathetic to their requirements. Customer care and customer service are key priorities and this is fully reflected in the café. To begin with, we've made sure people have plenty of room at the tables. And, because our visitors like their food to arrive within minutes, my menus are constructed using ingredients and dishes which I know we can fire out quickly.

That is the remit. It's just a question of how you use your skill to interpret that and make it work. For example, a special dish-of-the-day which is very popular with our customers, is seared salmon with oven-roasted courgettes and cherry tomatoes, on pesto mashed potato with a tomato salsa.

What we do is blanch some sliced courgettes, sear the salmon in a frying pan and add the cherry tomatoes to blister them. Then, when an order comes in, we'll have a very hot oven, put in a dish with some olive oil, and put in the pre-seared salmon with the tomatoes and courgettes for three or four minutes. The mashed potato is already hot. We add the pesto. That goes in the dish. The salmon, courgettes and tomatoes come out of the oven and then, on top, a little salsa, and juices from the dish. Bingo! That's how we construct a dish. It's going to take us five or six minutes. No problem at all!

Of course our menu offers plenty of choice besides 'specials', from soups and savouries and sandwiches to a whole host of sweet things. As for cakes, we just can't keep up with the amount we sell here. I'd have to take on another two people to do it, so I've out-sourced it. A lot of our cakes are made by Lisa Smith

who runs a business called Ginger Bakers in Kendal. She's had her kitchen adapted at home and makes fantastic hand-made cakes.

Whatever we do, we use quality ingredients and suppliers with integrity. For instance, my first-course recipe for this book, cheese on toast, uses five. The cheese is Birdoswald Organic, a lovely, crumbly cheese, similar to Caerphilly. It's made here in Cumbria by Eric and Dianne Horn up at Gilsland on Hadrian's Wall, using milk from their herd of pedigree Ayrshires.

The bread is baked by Aidan Monks at Munx Lakeland Bakery, just down the road from us in Staveley – his bread is fantastic. Cream of Cumbria Butter, by Sue Forrester, will go on the toast.

I've combined that with Michelle Partington's delicious Savin Hill bacon which she produces from her own Middle White pigs, reared locally in the Lyth Valley. Then it's served with Lizzie Smith's wonderful sweet mustard relish, Cumbrian Mostarda, which not only won best chutney and preserve, but new product of the year in 2007 at the Northwest Fine Food Awards.

I've chosen natural, un-dyed, smoked haddock for the second course. That comes from Neve's in Fleetwood who supply my fish. The quality is first class. I'm serving it on 'dug today' potatoes – just fantastic – from Booths. They're a family-owned supermarket chain, here in the Northwest, who have a real commitment to selling high-quality local produce. We're lucky enough to have a branch within sight of the café.

Those are just a few of our suppliers. We list a lot more on our menu. What they all have in common is the high quality of their products.

Let's look round the kitchen and you can see how we do things. It's designed to deal with big numbers smoothly and efficiently, so we're very organised. The orders come in, get done, hot and cold each have their own area, and they're back out again.

The big pan on the stove is our stock-pot. It holds about 25 litres. We make all our own soups, for which the starting point is good stock. This is made just the way I've always been shown by the Roux brothers, though we use beef, not veal bones. Pigs' trotters give it the gelatinous content and we cook it, as you'd expect, for twenty-four to thirty-six hours, strain it, reduce it down. We add water to get a second stock which we use for braising. The process takes about five days from start to finish.

Normally, we do one stock pot a week. Sometimes we'll have a second – it depends what's on the menu. Cooking next to the stock-pot are ham knuckles. That's for our pea and ham soup which we make from ham-stock every day. We take the ham off the bone and flake it and that's what goes into the soup.

We can't cook to order here. Sometimes, perhaps, chargrilled vegetables, bruschettas or things like that. Otherwise, it's impossible because we are so busy. The café seats 100. We have 8 staff in the kitchen and 24 front-of-house. We are open seven days a week during the daytime, closed in the evenings. On an average day we'll serve around 600 customers – 800 to 850 when we're busy. Sometimes more.

Because of the café's popularity, we can't take bookings by phone, only from personal visitors. We tell them how long they will need to wait for a table (the time is displayed electronically in our entrance area, too). Then we give them a pager, so they can look around the store, and we can call them when a table is ready.

We've found the paging system works really well. But we also provide seating that is never reserved. There's a dais that runs round the rear of the room where people can sit and order whenever they want.

The First Floor Café is the best move I've ever made in my career! Although, having said that, in retrospect, everything is right at the time.

When I left catering college in Southport in 1976, London was the place to be. There weren't many independent restaurants then. Most were in five-star hotels that weren't catering for ordinary people in any way.

I started as an apprentice at the Savoy. It was an incredibly structured environment, with military-style discipline. There was a brigade of nearly a hundred. The Executive Chef was Silvano Trompetto and he was like a colonel in the army. When he'd come through you'd say: 'Good morning, sir'. It wasn't 'chef' but 'sir'.

We had two restaurants, various private dining rooms – all named after the D'Oyly Carte operas – and two main banqueting rooms, the River Room and the Lancaster Room. The food was okay, but it wasn't what I'd expected, so I started sniffing around to find the best places. That's what took me to Albert Roux at Le Gavroche.

I started as a dogsbody in September '78 – and from then until December I just worked like a dog! I have never worked as hard anywhere in my life!

We weren't doing lunches, just dinners. We used to go in about 1 pm, have a break at 3 pm for lunch – and that was it! I used to walk home every night about 1 am. I'd moved to a flat in South Kensington so I'd be able to do it, because there were no buses at that time of night. Actually, it was nice to walk back.

I lost-one-and-a-half stone in three months – and I'd only weighed ten and a half to start with!

Albert Roux was there every day, every service. He taught me. He really did teach me how to cook. Without a shadow of a doubt.

Albert and I – this is absolutely true – we actually made what became the iconic lemon tart recipe, together. He'd got a recipe from his brother at the Waterside Inn, made it, and said: 'This is no good, we'll have to change it! We'll do this and this …' and we did – and it worked!

Interestingly, we never really used it much – only ever as a special. It never, ever went on the à la carte menu, because we wanted it to be fresh. We used to do it in summertime, serve it with fresh raspberries, perhaps some raspberry sorbet. And that was it. Nothing else.

When I first saw the tarte au citron I didn't realise it was going to become such a classic. It's everywhere now!

I spent fifteen years working with Roux Restaurants, including a spell as Group Executive Chef, which gave me experience catering for large numbers that has proved very useful here. Later, I was part of Albert's consultancy team that opened the Grand Hotel in Amsterdam, and after spending two years there as Executive Chef, I wanted a real change.

Albert said: 'If you want to do something different, go into pubs because the market is about to open up.' So, in 1993 Marj and I left London for the Lake District. We'd spent our honeymoon up here, at the Sharrow Bay Hotel, we'd been back several times for anniversary dinners, and we just loved this part of the country.

Our first pub, the Brown Horse at Winster in the Lyth Valley, was an absolutely phenomenal success. Both Jonathan Meades in *The Times* and Emily Green in *The Independent* named us pub of the year. We weren't doing anything formidable – steak and kidney pudding, roast pork with stuffing, that kind of thing – but people just loved it.

In '95, we moved two miles down the road, to the Punch Bowl Inn, at Crosthwaite, and that just took off. Jonathan Meades gave us an incredible review in *The Times* and the 'phone didn't stop ringing for two weeks! We were full for a year on the back of that.

The Punch Bowl was one of the very first gastropubs. But we didn't go into it because we wanted to have a gastropub. We did it because it felt right. We could serve simple food, of very high quality, that people could afford to eat on a regular basis, whether it was a ham sandwich at lunchtime or something like lamb shank with braised beans for dinner in the evening.

The Punch Bowl won all manner of awards over the years, but more and more people started following our example and diluting what was already a pretty static market. By 2005 we were faced with a choice: re-invest, add more bedrooms and stay another ten years, or sell. We were already running the First Floor Café and we decided to concentrate our efforts here and sell the Punch Bowl.

I believe the next five years is going to see a massive fall-out in the pub market, but I think places like the First Floor Café are going to become the restaurants of tomorrow.

The shorter working day here brings personal benefits too. Apart from the chance for a social life, it has given me more time to spend on the Academy of Culinary Arts, on issues like the slow food movement, and on judging food industry awards and training initiatives, such as the Roux Scholarship and the Gordon Ramsay Scholarship.

Food education in general, across the age-range, is a big interest of mine. Not long ago, I had a very encouraging experience at a school just outside Shap in Kendal. We were doing a tasting day with some 6–10 year-olds, under the Academy's Adopt a School Scheme. We did a few foods, including lettuces, and the children could identify all the different flavours: radicchio – bitter, rocket – peppery, and so on. They were very young children, I was impressed.

Then we looked at eggs and I asked: 'Who knows about eggs?' All these hands went up, and I said: 'Why's that?' It turned out they were all farmers' kids, helping their mothers and fathers round the farm, and they were really clued up! They knew the difference between eggs – free-range, organic, standard supermarket – and they could tell if they were fresh or not. They said to me: 'Oh look at the white, it's all over the plate – well that's not fresh!'

It was a revelation! But then you go to another school and the poor things have never seen celeriac or a turnip. It's pretty sad.

Not everyone cares about food. It's just fodder, fuel, for some. It's the same with supermarkets and other retail outlets when it comes to their restaurants and cafés. For the most part, there just isn't that commitment to serving really good food made with high quality ingredients.

Early influences are very important. My grandmother ran a grocery shop in Manchester, made her own brawn and potted beef and cooked her own hams to sell there. I remember seeing her do it when I was about four or five.

This is where I developed the taste for all these flavours and foods. She used to cook tripe all the time – I still love it. When I was seven, my father changed jobs and we moved away to live in Formby, near Liverpool. But my mother had inherited this style of cooking from my grandmother. She used to cook offal quite a lot – kidneys, braised hearts – and rabbit stew, pig's trotters, soups and broths, which I just loved.

While Le Gavroche was being relocated in the early '80s, I spent two years in France, outside Lyon, and, of course they're really into that kind of rustic stuff down there. I was working for the great Alain Chapel, in the village of Mionnay, where he took over his father's auberge and elevated it into this great culinary exemplar. They called him the three-Michelin star chef's chef! I had some memorable dishes down there.

One of my all-time favourites is what the French call tête de veau. I'd probably choose that for my last dish on earth! But I love good Chinese food as well … so it would have to be stir-fried lobster, which is one of the best dishes you could ever eat, followed by tête de veau and a bottle of Beaujolais – I'd be in heaven!'

Marjorie Doherty

"I thought I was a good cook till I met Steven! It was 1982, he'd just come back from France and had the whole of January off. He was meant to go down to London to see Albert Roux but he was stuck in Formby because of a rail strike. So you could say British Rail brought us together!

Friends introduced us, but we'd met before, and it was: 'I know you!' from both of us, simultaneously. We were engaged three months later.

I'll never forget our first meal, on our first date. It was at a bistro in Liverpool and he ordered a salad – not as a main meal, but as an accompaniment – and then ate it after his main course. I thought: 'What bizarre eating habits!'

Of course, I knew nothing of his world then. Going out for dinner was not something my family did. I certainly never thought I would find myself sitting down to eat in Alain Chapel's, later that year. What an eye-opener – brilliant!

We're so lucky now, living here in the Lake District. Steven didn't want to go on working in London or being an executive chef with all that administrative work. He wanted to get back to his pots and pans.

We had a great following at the Punch Bowl but I wouldn't go back now. We enjoy what we're doing here too much, despite the hard work. It's a wonderful venue, a spectacular building in a really good location, and we have the culinary freedom to do things differently.

Eating with people is about sharing food – that's the joy of it. If Steven came to your house and was presented with beans on toast, he'd be perfectly happy. It's the effort that's gone into it that counts."

Birdoswald Organic Cheese on Munx Bakery Rye Toast with Savin Hill Bacon, Lizzie Smith's Cumbrian Mostarda & Sue Forrester's Cream of Cumbria Butter

SERVES 4

300g Birdoswald cheese
8 Savin Hill bacon rashers
1 jar Cumbrian Mostarda
1 roll Cream of Cumbrian butter
8 slices Five-grain rye bread from Munx Bakery in Stavely, toasted

1 Cook the bacon until crisp and keep warm. **2** Roughly grate the cheese. **3** Lightly butter the toast then sprinkle with the cheese and grill until melted. **4** Top with bacon and serve with the Mostarda.

Poached Fillet of Locally Smoked Haddock on Dug Today Potato Mash with a Creamy Grain Mustard Sauce Topped with a Local Free-Range Poached Egg

SERVES 4

1 kg potatoes, 'dug today' from Booths, peeled
225g unsalted butter, softened
Ground white pepper
Freshly grated nutmeg
2 large naturally smoked un-dyed haddock fillets, halved
Full fat milk

For the Sauce
225ml Double cream
2 tsp grain mustard
1 tsp Dijon mustard
Sea salt

For the Eggs
1 tbsp white wine vinegar
4 medium eggs, very fresh

1 Cut the potatoes into large dice and cook in boiling water until soft. **2** Drain well and put through a sieve, mouli-legume or mash with a fork. **3** Beat in the softened butter, season with white pepper and a grating of nutmeg to taste. Keep warm. **4** In a shallow pan, poach the fish in water with a splash of milk to cover (no salt) and simmer for 8 minutes.

Sauce While the fish is poaching, bring the cream to the boil in a heavy bottomed pan. Whisk in both mustards and add a pinch of salt. Keep warm.

Eggs **1** Fill a deep saucepan with water, bring to the boil and add vinegar. **2** Break an egg into a tea cup and tip, very gently, into the water at the point when it is bubbling. **3** Quickly add the other eggs, one at a time, and poach for 3-4 minutes with the water at a rolling boil. **4** Using a slotted spoon, remove the first egg and press with your fingertip to check it is properly cooked – the white should be set but soft to the touch.

To Serve **1** Remove the fish from the poaching liquid and peel off the skin. **2** Neatly spoon some mashed potatoes onto 4 warmed plates. **3** Place the haddock on top of the mash, coat with the sauce and gently place a soft poached egg on top of the fish.

Rum and Currant Baba with Whitehaven Rum & Low Sizergh Barn's Organic Cream

MAKES APPROXIMATELY 12 BABAS USING AMERICAN NON-STICK MUFFIN MOULDS

For the Dough
15g fresh yeast
200ml warm milk
1 tsp salt
500g plain flour, sifted
6 eggs
150g butter, softened
1 tbsp caster sugar
75g currants, soaked in boiling water for 1 hour

For the Syrup
85g sugar
2 cloves
1 cinnamon stick
Juice of 1 orange
Juice of 1/4 lemon

For Serving
Sizergh Barn's organic cream, whipped
Whitehaven rum

Babas [1] Place the yeast and half of the warm milk in a bowl and beat lightly with a wire whisk. Add the salt. [2] Add the flour and eggs, knead dough until smooth and elastic – about 10 minutes in an electric mixer with a dough hook or 20 minutes by hand. [3] Beat the softened butter and sugar together and slowly add this mixture to the dough a little at a time, making sure it is fully mixed each time. Add the currants. [4] Continue to mix until the dough is perfectly smooth, glossy and fairly elastic. Add the remaining milk, a little at a time, until the dough is supple – it should not break when stretched. [5] Cover the dough with a baking sheet or damp cloth and leave to rise for 1 hour in a warm place. The dough should double in volume. [6] Knock back the dough by flipping it over once or twice with your hand to remove some of the air. [7] Pre-heat oven 220°C / gas mark 7. [8] Divide the dough between the moulds (about 2/3 full) and leave to rise in a warm, draught free place for about 40 minutes. [9] Place the moulds on a baking sheet and bake in the preheated oven for 30 minutes. [10] Reduce the temperature to 200°C / gas mark 6 and bake for a further 15 minutes. [11] Remove the babas from the oven, remove from moulds and place them upside down on the same baking sheet. Immediately return them to the oven and bake for a further 5 minutes to ensure they are evenly cooked. [12] Place on a wire rack and leave to cool for at least 1 hour.

Syrup [1] Meanwhile, make the syrup by putting all the ingredients into a pan and bringing gently to the boil. [2] Stir until the sugar has just dissolved and reduce the heat to a simmer for 3 minutes without further stirring. Leave to cool slightly. [3] Place the babas on their 'heads' in the syrup for 10 minutes then turn them over to stand in the syrup for another 10 minutes.

To Serve [1] Remove the babas from the syrup with a slotted spoon and put into individual serving dishes. [2] Pour a good measure of rum over each baba and serve with whipped cream.

Chef's Tip The syrup can be stored in the fridge and used again. Babas are best made 1 day ahead or frozen before soaking in syrup.

Chris Neve
Cream of the Catch
Lancashire

IF EVER A MAN EMBODIED THE HEALTH-GIVING PROPERTIES of the product he sells, it is Fleetwood fish merchant, Chris Neve. Lean and lithe, he moves with an easy energy that belies his years, more than thirty of them spent at the helm of leading seafood supplier, C & G Neve.

What Chris doesn't know about the business of fish is probably not worth knowing – that is if you're looking to catch, buy, sell and, ultimately, eat them at their best. And he does love to eat good fish. To cook it, too. He really does.

As you tour the processing plant, and Chris directs your attention to one box of glistening fish after another, he'll not only tell you where it was caught and give you a thumbnail sketch of the species but, like as not, reel off a recipe in passing. Above all, he'll assess the quality: 'Beautiful, them', he says, looking into a box of lemon sole. 'They're from Peterhead – North Sea. If you get them from the Faroes, they just don't keep. A Cornish lemon is even better. Or Devon – they're wonderful round there. I love to make goujons of lemon sole.'

He wears his knowledge lightly, delivers choice morsels of it laconically, then, like a true raconteur, finishes with a dramatic punchline or an unforgettable fishy tale. There's an undercurrent of humour propelling things along, sometimes dry, sometimes uproarious, seasoned with just the right amount of salty language for effect.

More boxes are unveiled and a refreshing ozone rises from each one. The variety is glorious: haddock from Shetland, hake from the North Sea, mussels from Menai; silvery wild sea bass out of Morecambe Bay; oysters from Loch Fyne.

The familiar and the unfamiliar are stacked, side by side. Langoustines and scallops from Scotland; brill, turbot, plaice, Dover sole – prime fish from the Irish Sea. There's locally caught grey mullet; wild sea trout from the mouth of the Lune; mackerel and monkfish. Razor clams (named for their uncanny resemblance to the cut-throat instrument) lurk in their dark, shiny cylindrical shells. Beside them, the soft, opaline bodies of calamari, or squid, which can be found all round the coast. On these last Chris confides: 'I'll cook them whole. I just pick out the small ones and fry them in a bit of butter and oil.'

We're in what they call the Fish House, 17,000 square feet of big, bright, arctic-white interior, where the fish come to be prepared. Underfoot there is water and ice; overhead, unrelenting fluorescent light, reflected in it. Ceiling and walls shine. Stainless steel equipment gleams. Brawny-looking men in baseball caps,

wellington boots, white suits and long white waterproof aprons, work steadily at various stations. For the uninitiated, the sheer whiteness of it all is painful on the eyes. It's numbingly cold too, what with water for washing everything – fillets, floor, hands, equipment – and whole areas devoted to refrigeration. But the entire crew works with forearms bared.

This is a hardy, physical, emphatically male world. 'Some of these lads have been with me 25 years', says Chris. Perhaps that's why the atmosphere feels relaxed. There's a bit of chat, some banter with the boss, all in the rich north Lancashire tones of Fleetwood. Mainly though, there's quiet concentration, because this is engrossing work that requires attention. Here, fish are gutted, skinned, boned, filleted, trimmed, and cut to the specific requirements of customers, all over the country and abroad, be they restaurants (he supplies 350), supermarkets or other wholesale suppliers.

We stop to watch a filleter perform his mesmeric sleight-of-hand on plaice, slicing into the slippery flat fish with a narrow blade and deftly parting flesh from bone to produce a perfect fillet every 30 seconds. 'Very skilful', comments Chris admiringly. He did the job himself in his youth. Now, the training isn't there for young people and the result is a skills shortage in the industry. Machines are taking over. They are widely used today by big mass-market processors. They lack the finesse of the skilled human hand and Chris laments the loss of quality, but mechanisation deals with the volume. At Neve's, it's used for salmon. Vast quantities of this – the nation's favourite fish – go out every day. On the far side of the room, tended by watchful eyes, a conveyer belt carries the coral pink fillets into a pin-boning machine.

It's early lunchtime and most of today's fish has been finished. The rigid plastic crates it arrived in are stacked empty and upside down. The waste boxes are filled with heads and fins, skin and bones and offal: there's about 50% discarded in the processing of fish.

By two, the day shift – who started work at 6 am – will be off home. The results of their labours are all around, neatly arranged in more boxes, some with handwritten labels, listing the destination and contents in abbreviated trade lingo. Here are red mullet fillets for a pub; perfectly matched cod loins for a restaurant; herring fillets for a hotel; pearly-pink skate, off the inshore boats, and Cornish sardines for a supermarket.

Some red-gold gurnard, for a customer in Colchester, catch Chris's eye. He looks joyfully at their plump little bodies covered in glinting papery scales: 'There was hardly any on the market this morning', he says, 'and then, one of the boats came in early for weather. He had eight boxes and they were absolutely living! I love it when they're like that!' He lingers on the words, infusing them with feeling.

We leave the cold of the Fish House for the dry warmth of a room where fish is being packed exclusively for Booth's supermarkets: individual portions, with parsley garnish, weighed, priced and labelled. 'Lovely fish, all picked out for them. Those cod steaks – you don't see many of them – they're for the Kendal shop.'

Neve's supply a couple of supermarkets direct and Booth's is one of them. Others are supplied indirectly, through third-party wholesalers. 'We used to do – (he names a supermarket chain), but I kicked them into touch. They employed these young people – probably university graduates, but they knew nothing about fish. They were programmed to buy as cheap as possible.' His voice rises in disgust, cracks in disbelief. 'Their attitude was terrible. I sent them an e-mail: "From today I'm not supplying you any more." They sent one back: "You can't do that".' He laughs, as much as to say – can you believe it? He's a good-humoured, equable man, but he won't be messed around.

He hates to compromise on quality. As they'll tell you down at Fleetwood's daily fish auction, Chris wants the best and he's prepared to pay for it. Auction manager, Terry Houghton, is unequivocal: 'He pays for the quality of his fish. He runs an outstanding quality operation.'

And Chris likes to be recognised for that: 'There's a French supermarket supplier who buys our fish and he says we come top or second in their quality league all the time. They appreciate the quality – and they'll tell you that. They'll say, "I can buy it cheaper, but I still need the best for some of my top customers." That's terrific. You'll put yourself out for that.'

We emerge from the packing room and into the sunshine. We're heading for the Smokehouse now, at the end of the road. C & G Neve is all along this stretch, filling a block between two parallel streets just off the main road into Fleetwood, just where the factory belt peters out and dock and town begin.

It's a perfect location, for road transport, and for allowing Chris Neve to shuttle between his daily sites of business: the dock, the fish auction and the factory. The firm runs its own fishing trawler, The Artemis, and acts as agent to another 25 independent fishing vessels. The dockside is also home to the auction hall where Chris can be found any time from about five in the morning, inspecting the catch, reaching 'understandings', conversing with some of the 33 other registered buyers, before selling starts at 7.30.

As we walk, he recalls the early days of C & G Neve: 'We started up in a shed in 1976. Me and our kid, Gerard. Dad used to help us like.' Now it's a multi-million pound operation, split into three companies, employing 90 people and occupying 26,000 square feet of plant.

'At crucial stages like, I've always been lucky.' And he tells how he bought the main factory. The former owners had spent millions refurbishing it, then closed it. 'It'd been empty for three years and we were running out of space, so I rang up the agent and he said, "Make us an offer." Well, I didn't know how much and he said he couldn't tell me, so I thought I'd try £70,000 and see what happened. I was driving somewhere when I had a call to say it was ours. Afterwards, the bank manager came and looked and said: "You got a good buy there." The agent told me: "You know, we hadn't had an offer on that place in three years and, after we'd done the deal with you, the phone never stopped ringing!"'

We turn into the warm and aromatic Smokehouse and the welcoming presence of Elsie Riches who runs it. We see trays of golden mackeral topped with coarse ground black pepper: 'Go on, taste it.' It is meltingly delicious, firm textured but tenderly yielding.

They smoke salmon here too, but it's a cut-throat game according to Chris, so, mainly, they limit supplies to their own customers. Then there's cod. They started supplying this to a wholesale company and now the customers won't take anyone else's. 'That's purely quality again', says Chris. 'A lot of people think, if you've got crappy fish, smoke it. Well, if you smoke crappy fish, you get crappy smoked fish!'

The natural smoked haddock looks beautiful but it can be very awkward. 'Early on in the year when haddocks are spawning, you can't get a good haddock', Chris explains. 'Then, shortly after they finish spawning, they start to fatten up, but they're very soft because they haven't got the muscle tone yet. Steven (Doherty) will ring me up and complain: "These haddocks aren't good enough." And I quite agree. They ain't. And I do try to pick him the best out all the time. But I know if Steven rings up there's genuinely something wrong. He's a top man, without a doubt.'

We turn into the warm and aromatic Smokehouse and the welcoming presence of Elsie Riches who runs it. We see trays of golden mackeral topped with coarse ground black pepper: 'Go on, taste it.' It is meltingly delicious, firm textured but tenderly yielding.

Aidan Monks
Munx Lakeland Bakery, Cumbria

THERE IS SOMETHING ABOUT THE SMELL OF FRESHLY BAKED BREAD, which is deeply satisfying. It resonates with some deep and atavistic need within us. After all, bread, in its myriad forms, is a staple of the diet worldwide. Yet, here in Britain, we have allowed almost all our independent artisan bakers to disappear. We have paid the price for this folly. The once common experience of popping round the corner to buy freshly baked bread, so warm, so crusty, so tasty that you just had to tear a corner off and eat it plain and unadorned on the way home, has gone. In its place are industrialized offerings, sadly inferior products on the whole.

Fortunately, the beginnings of a reversal in this trend can be discerned. The last few years have seen the resurgence of the artisan bread maker. A front runner in this new movement is Aidan Monks, who set up his first bakery in Kendal over twenty years ago and now runs Munx Lakeland Bakery in the Cumbrian village of Staveley, just east of Windermere.

Bread making is in Aidan's blood. His grandfather was a baker, and Aidan can vividly remember, as a boy, smelling the wonderful aroma which enveloped the old Lakeland bakery. Yet he did not go straight into baking. He first trained as a chef and studied hotel management at college. At the end of his course, he was offered the chance to go on a scholarship to the Institute of Culinary Arts in Boston. Whilst there, the big emphasis on artisan breads caught his eye and the American entrepreneurial spirit made him feel confident that he could set up his own business on his return home.

However, his real eureka moment came one cold day on top of the Eiffel Tower in Paris. He was eating a freshly-baked baguette so delicious that he decided there and then that this was exactly the sort of bread he wanted to make. He holds in high regard the training bakers receive in France. 'The French', he says, 'train in college for five years and then have to work in the five different regions of France before they get a job.' Determined to emulate his continental counterparts when he set up his business, Aidan employed a French baker, who initially came over for several days each month, to teach him the necessary skills.

When he opened that first bakery in the centre of Kendal, there was nobody else producing baguettes of any kind, let alone French artisan breads. He made pastries too, and sold them in his adjoining café. But, like many small entrepreneurs, it wasn't long before he was feeling the strain: 'The business began to run us, rather than us running the business.' It was clear the café was a distraction, so he sold up, moved to Staveley and concentrated on the bakery: 'I knew artisan bread was on the up. I think it's still right at the start of a revolution.'

Not surprisingly, Aidan is scathing about much of the bread available at present, stripped as it is of all the nutrients that make it worth eating and that give it taste. 'There is a revival in artisan bread and people are beginning to realise, that it is worth paying for.'

He would like to see more artisan bakeries opening up. 'It will help people become aware of what really good bread tastes like', he says. He certainly doesn't want it to remain a niche product, something sold only in farmers' markets and specialist shops. 'To me, it is about bringing real bread to ordinary people, not just dedicated food lovers. Bread', he explains, 'is about time and fermentation. A modern processed loaf takes around two hours to be made from start to finish, whereas naturally leavened bread takes up to twelve hours simply to prove. And it is time which gives properly made bread such fantastic flavour.' Modern loaves also have more gluten added to speed up the process and this, Aidan firmly believes, is why so many people find bread indigestible nowadays.

'People have begun to think that bread is not good for you. Whereas we believe that what we make is the staff of life and is very good for you indeed,' he insists. He is also keen for people to pop into his bakery and see how the bread is made. It is the way to understand the process and to realise that, by taking care and time, and using the best ingredients, you can create light and beautiful bread that is a joy to eat.

You can't help but fall in love with Aidan's passion for real bread. It shines through in everything he does. Even when he has found himself up against it in the business world, his unswerving belief in his craft has helped him through. The venue for his activities must surely be an inspiration too. Staveley is a lovely village. It is set at the junction of two rivers, in the Kentmere Valley, cradled

between three hills, Reston Scar, Piked Howe and Lily Fell. Munx Lakeland Bakery is on the site of an old bobbin mill, now converted and home to twenty small businesses.

Aidan has just moved from his original premises in the Mill Yard to a spanking new building, glass-faced and full of light. Here he is now able to produce bread all day, every day. Just upstairs is Lucy's Cookery School, where he can share his love of baking and his skills with other enthusiasts. As you watch him demonstrate the technique for kneading dough, the rhythm becomes hypnotic. He makes it look effortless but, when you try it yourself, you quickly realise the level of skill required to create a perfect loaf. Aidan's dough is wetter and more gelatinous than might usually be imagined but this, he explains to his students, is what makes great bread. 'The more water in the dough, the greater the spring in the bread.' The result is that his loaves are much lighter and fluffier than their traditional English counterparts.

These new premises of Munx Lakeland Bakery have been planned with sustainability and energy-saving in mind. Aidan has installed wood-burning ovens which not only produce great tasting bread, but also save two-thirds of the power of a conventional oven. And the owners of the Mill Yard have planted 15,000 trees on their land, which will be used to fire them up. The Mill Yard also has its own water turbine on the River Kent, which provides another twenty per cent of the bakery's energy needs. Munx can also use the fresh, natural spring water in the making of their bread.

But in the end, everything comes back to Aidan's all-consuming passion for the bread-making craft. 'I love baking best of all,' he says. 'I would be happy baking all day.'

Munx Lakeland Bakery. Steven Doherty's supplier 121

Nigel Haworth
Northcote Manor
Langho, Lancashire

The setting for this Michelin-starred restaurant is the very picture of an English country-house hotel. Victorian, mellow in brick, stone, high gables and half-timbering, it is framed by manicured lawns and scenic views. A productive kitchen garden reflects the changing bounty of the seasons. An air of serenity and impeccably managed comfort pervades the interior: oak panelled lounges with leather wingbacks before open fires; attentive staff; luxurious bedrooms with high-tech facilities. It melds the best of the traditional and the contemporary.

A similar theme infuses the food of chef-patron, Nigel Haworth, a proud member of the Academy of Culinary Arts. His menu is a paean to local produce and traditional regional dishes, subtly combined with skilful innovation and hints of other lands. He lauds his native Lancashire as the premier county for artisan food producers and has become their ambassador, par excellence. Their photographs line the walls of his new Ribble Valley Inns, where he also celebrates the fruits of their labours, and brings them before a larger and increasingly appreciative public. It is a role he embraces with missionary zeal. Chance, conviction and irrepressible curiosity have led him to this point, through a life he describes as an intriguing journey.

"I HAD A WEIRD KIND OF COMING TO THIS CAREER. It's the very truth, and a bit scary, but I woke up one morning and decided: I'm going to cook. It was as simple as that. I had no persuading from parents, no dissuading either; no influences from in or out of school. I never took home economics, I never had anything to do with cookery. I was going on sixteen and I just decided I wanted to be a chef.

My mum thought I was absolutely crackers. It wasn't a fashionable choice then. In fact, in those days, you'd be termed 'girly' if you went to cookery classes. I trained at Accrington and Rossendale Catering College with a wonderful old pastry cook, called Mrs Smithies. She didn't so much teach you as adopt you, and she loved me to bits. I'll never forget coming home on the bus with my first lemon meringue pie. I knew I'd made the best one in the class (or at least I thought so) and I knew cooking was for me. It came relatively easily – and I just loved it.

The reward element appealed. It was the fact that you could do a job and immediately have something tangible, a product – and judge your own performance too. Instantly, food was me. When I went fishing with my dad at our caravan, people on the site would come round to eat my mackeral. I'd put what they called jus de Paris with it, a mixture of lemon juice and Lea and Perrins sauce. It just seemed very natural to cook for everybody.

After I finished college, I went south. The way it happened was quite tragic. My best mate, Chris Andrew, and I had jobs in Germany but the Christmas before we were due to go, Chris got killed in a car crash. My world fell apart. I ended up going to the Royal Berkshire Hotel in Ascot, then to the Grosvenor Victoria in London. I stayed a year, tried to get into the Café Royal and couldn't, probably because I wasn't tenacious enough. I am quite shy by nature and that may have played a part.

But I was desperate to work under somebody really good. I was getting promoted too quickly. I was sous-chef at 19 and it was just a farce. It's the old story: if you're quite good, people spot you, you get fast-tracked, but you're hollow.

One chef in the brigade had been working in Switzerland and he kept saying how good it was. I decided I'd go there and re-train. That was 1978. I spent four-and-a-half years there, at several hotels, including the Schweizerhof in Lucerne with Natalie Viscardie, one of Switzerland's finest chefs. I took a sugar course, too, with Willy Pfund, then 70-odd, and known as the best sugar man in the world. I was made up doing that! I used to do a lot of butter carvings as well. When I first came to Northcote Manor, I'd stay up all night doing them. I specialised in Capodimonte figures and I would carve them quite finely. It's years since I've done any, so I don't know what I'd be like now!

After Switzerland, my plan was to go to Hong Kong – a place I love – but I'd met a girl back here in Lancashire. I was nearly 25, which seems so young nowadays, but then it seemed like time to get married and settle down. We parted later, but the decision to come home changed my whole life and brought me to Northcote Manor. I have her to thank for that.

I began by lecturing at my old college and cooking at Foxfields, then the best restaurant in the area. But it wasn't the kind of food I wanted to do. As for the college, I loved to teach cooking but there weren't enough people wanting to love to cook. Too many were there just to pass the time of day, and that wasn't good enough for me. I was so fed up, I decided to get out of the business altogether.

One Sunday afternoon, my Auntie Edith found me filling in a form to join the Lancashire Constabulary. 'What on earth are you doing?' she said. 'You must be crackers after Switzerland and all that hard work!'

'I know, but there's nothing here. It's a desert. I feel like I'm just completely wasting my time.'

Then she said: 'Northcote Manor is under new ownership and Craig Bancroft's

just come back to take over as manager. Why don't you give him a call and tell him you know me.'

Who, I wondered was this Craig Bancroft?

It turned out my Auntie Edith had looked after him when he was a little lad, after his parents split up. He'd gone on to train with Trusthouse Forte, in a series of five-star establishments and now he'd been brought back to Lancashire to turn around Northcote Manor. So I rang him and went down. He was 22, a sort of blue-blooded, public school-educated chappie – and he was fine about me starting as chef. But the new owner thought I was too highly qualified and asking too much money – I'd just got a mortgage and I wanted a hundred and forty quid a week.

A bit later they rang and asked if I was sorted out. Well, I wasn't. In fact I was desperate. On the other hand, the Manor had a poor reputation in those days and, although the new owner intended to transform it into a first class hotel and restaurant, it seemed like a huge risk to me. But, I was so bored and unhappy, I decided to take it. That was 1984. The rest is history I suppose! Every time I wanted to leave, Craig would windle something out of me. One of the main factors was, I'd promised my wife I'd stay in the area while we brought up the children, so she'd have family around her while I was working such unsociable hours.

The Manor prospered. Before long, Craig and I acquired shares and, in 1989, we took over as joint proprietors. I concentrated on the kitchen, Craig on the

Nigel Haworth, Northcote Manor 125

rooms and front-of-house, particularly the wine cellar, for which he's built quite a reputation. It was a tough journey: long hours; months without days off. You had to give blood really. We both did. You forget what it was like. It was such a culinary desert round here. There weren't people with the vision, or the knowledge, to back you in those days.

Before long, though, we started to win awards and, eventually, in 1996, a Michelin star. I always remember Paul Heathcote ringing me up and saying: 'I think you're going to get a call today …', and lo and behold, about an hour later, I did! Nevertheless, I was really surprised. We'd strived and strived for it. I think it's done us a lot of good, too. Some chefs will argue that the Michelin star is not an emblem of desire but, ultimately, there's nothing else that chefs in the world of fine dining look to as a gauge. It's the star system that really counts.

Fortunately, we've retained ours, enjoyed some success and got some great staff around us. Our goal now is to develop Northcote Manor still further, as a country house hotel which will be recognised throughout Britain – and to have a bit of fun, as well as stretching our abilities in the process.

In 2004, we embarked on a new venture, Ribble Valley Inns. These are pubs that celebrate the food of the area. We use the best local, seasonal produce available and we have traditionally inspired menus. The Three Fishes at Mitton opened in the September and we followed it up with The Highwayman, near Kirkby Lonsdale, in 2007. They're places where everyone can feel welcome and enjoy themselves, including children.

As soon as I decided on the concept I knew there was something right about it. For years, Craig and I – and everybody else – had talked about the middle market in Britain being so barren and the need for real food there. In other european countries there's much more quality at that point.

Also, when I'd go over to various places in Europe, I'd always find traditional restaurants. That's something so completely missing in the UK. Probably, after thirty or forty years, Indian and Chinese restaurants are traditional here now. But there still is very little traditional English food. That gives us huge scope. I am adamant I'm going to try and do something really interesting. And if I get the bit between my teeth, who knows where that journey will end?

The pubs are about trying to do quality in volume, which I suppose we're not famous for as a nation. That's the challenge – doing four of five hundred covers on a Sunday, doing it well, and doing it with real food, like Reg Johnson's Goosnargh chicken breasts, Andrew Sharp's Herdwick lamb cutlets or Michael Price's beech smoked salmon from the Port of Lancaster Smokehouse. Or a really good fish and chips. That was one of the things made me do the pubs – because there was only the Inn at Whitewell where I could get good fish and chips! That can't be right, can it?

The temptation is, once you've found a producer, to use them lock, stock and barrel. But if I don't think a particular product is good enough, I'll say to the people – are you up to the challenge of getting it there? Interestingly, a lot of them are. It's a two-way partnership.

Nigel Haworth, Northcote Manor 127

I get very inspired, just meeting the producers and working with them. It's a privilege – they're tremendous characters and so dedicated to what they do. Take Peter Ascroft, one of our best friends. He grows cauliflowers over at Hesketh Bank, beetroots and potatoes too.

Cauliflower is the forgotten vegetable, but a great product so we've worked hard with Peter, and we've got lots of things we do with them. We started by asking when's the high season for cauliflowers round here? It's summer, whereas I always used to think of caulis as a winter vegetable. We're harvesting them golf-ball size and treating them almost artichoke-like. We're keeping some of the leaves on, leaving a longer stem and cooking them with a lot of care, so that we get a beautiful cauliflower. We might serve it with a little caper butter, or just cut in half. Or we might tempura that and serve it with a sarsaparilla dip.

We're doing cauliflower panna cottas, or you might call them blancmanges. What you have to do is shred the cauliflower up and cook it very quickly: sweat it off in a little bit of butter, put the cream into it, bring it up to the boil, take it off and cool it, food process it, pass it and set it with vegetarian gelatine. You get incredible flavour. It's wonderful with oysters or Dublin Bay prawns. We can do all sorts of dishes, but I tend to have ones that evolve into something different every year.

We hang pictures of our producers in the pubs, list them on the back of our menus and on the websites, so we're opening up our suppliers to everyone else. For recipes to go with the produce, I'm writing The Three Fishes cookery book. If we're going to get cooking food better in the Northwest and throughout the UK, then we've got to share our information. I think most chefs, now, are aware of that.

I'm probably a bit of a man on a mission. Certainly, with the style of food we do. It's an evolving menu. The direction is given purely by who and what you discover; the area; the seasons; what's out there in the kitchen garden. I've altered all my menus to change weekly, so that we can link in with the seasons. That's not easy!

Tuning into the seasons is very inspiring though. It's the waiting and waiting and waiting for something – like strawberries. Or when a crop is over – like asparagus – and I can say to the staff: 'Right, after next week, that's it – no more asparagus!'

I had a supplier ring me up yesterday: 'Why aren't you buying these girolles off me?'

'Because they're out of season.'

'What do you mean?'

'Well, I'll buy girolles when the Scottish ones start in August. I don't want your South African ones. They don't inspire me.'

I can't get through the amount of produce I've got in my own kitchen garden here at the Manor, so I don't need to buy things coming in landslides from the big suppliers! That's a bit like going to a supermarket. It's the easy way to shop.

I try to make sure that I'm cooking, as much as I believe, English food, sourced regionally, here. But, I don't ban anything. If I want to use Perigord truffles, I will.

My real passion is food. I love all kinds, from all over the world, although here it feels right to cook regionally. The most important thing about food is that you care. If I see chefs not caring, I'll get annoyed. I like to see food respected, handled carefully. There are a lot of chefs who aren't cooks, just imposters who wear white. And there are a lot of people out there in kitchens who don't care about what they do. I think that is one of the hardest things to take.

The next generation of cooks is so important, and education about food in schools, and more widely, is vitally important. Here we train our own apprentices. We have seven at the moment and another three coming on board. We teach them to care about produce, right down to the humblest vegetable and salad leaf that comes out of our organic kitchen garden. They've got to want to know about them. What's the point of Andrew Mellin, our head gardener, growing them otherwise? So I send the chefs out there sometimes for a bit of digging. They don't particularly like it, but that way they can understand the roots of what they're doing – literally!

Bringing staff on is a real motivational factor for me. Our head chef at Northcote Manor is Lisa Allen, and we first met when I was presenting student prizes at Lancaster and Morecambe College. I suggested she got in touch if ever she was looking for something in the area. So when she left David Everitt-Matthias, at Le Champignon Sauvage, we took her on as a demi-chef de partie. That was about six years ago. She worked her way through the ranks to become head chef three years later.

Her leadership qualities were apparent right from the start. Now she heads a brigade of 14 and, in the very masculine world of chefs, she can match up to the lads and frighten them to death if she wants to! She's a fearsome competitor, incredibly hardworking, with a very inquiring mind. She embraces what I think and like about food, and brings something to the party herself. She's our specialist on the jellies and caviars, and extremely good on the finesse side of things.

I enjoy the relationship I've got with the chefs. Is it mutual? I think so. They'll hate me and love me at times. I'll drive them mad, because, in some ways, I am a perfectionist. I don't suffer fools in the kitchen, and that can be horrible. If there's anything I have a short fuse with, it's when I'm working with people and I tell them three or four times about something and then, they go and do it again! Well, bloomin' 'eck!

When I was starting, I wondered what it would be like to be a head chef – which was one of the reasons I had to take on Northcote Manor. Then I used to watch Craig signing the cheques and I wondered – and this may sound bizarre – what would it be like to do that? Then: 'What it would be like to be a director?' So, I suppose, I'm always wanting to know – what's the next level? I find life a really intriguing journey.

Similarly, with food, I think I'll never be satisfied – but that doesn't mean to say that I'm not happy. It means that I'm always progressing. There will always be something round the corner that intrigues me, that drives me on. As we become a bit more successful, we'll probably be able to throw the dice a little bit further and say: 'Go on!' And if it doesn't work it isn't going to kill us. That excites me.'

Morecambe Bay Shrimp Organic Porridge with Tomato Relish

SERVES 1

For the Tomato Relish

¹/₂ onion, finely sliced	3 pinches salt
500g chopped plum tomatoes	4 pinches sugar
²/₃ chopped red chilli	1 dsp tomato purée
3 dsp olive oil	200ml tomato juice
1 clove garlic, chopped and puréed	¹/₂ lime, juiced

Tomato Relish **1** Moderately heat a thick bottomed pan, add the olive oil. **2** Cook the onions until just turned brown. **3** Add the chilli, garlic, salt and sugar. **4** Add the tomatoes, tomato purée, tomato juice and the lime juice. **5** Cover with a lid and gently simmer for 20 minutes. **6** Pass through a fine sieve and keep until required.

For the Tarragon Paste

90g tarragon, cut with scissors
90g parsley, washed thoroughly and finely chopped
60g toasted pine nuts
6 cloves roasted garlic
250ml olive oil
5g salt
145g grated Lancashire cheese

For the Tarragon Butter

100g unsalted butter, softened
10g shallots, finely diced
20g tarragon, chopped
Pinch cayenne pepper
1 tbsp lemon juice
Maldon sea salt to taste

Tarragon Paste Place all ingredients into a liquidiser, blend to a smooth paste.

Tarragon Butter Place all the ingredients into a bowl and mix until light and fluffy.

For the Vegetable Nage

¹/₄ head celery	0.25lt white wine
1¹/₄ whole leeks or trimmings	¹/₂ bunch tarragon
¹/₂ bulb garlic	¹/₂ bunch thyme
1¹/₄ heads fennel	1 bay leaf
250g celeriac trimmings	¹/₄ bunch parsley
3 carrots, peeled	5 pink peppercorns
1 onion, roughly chopped	5 coriander seeds
1.5lts water	1 star anise

Vegetable Nage **1** Peel, wash and chop all the vegetables. **2** Place in a large pan then add the cold water and white wine. Add all the herbs and spices plus the garlic then slowly bring to the boil. Simmer for 20 minutes. **3** Remove from heat and allow to cool. Leave to rest for a day then pass through a sieve and store.

For the Shrimp Porridge

50g Morecambe Bay shrimps
10g organic oatmeal
2 knobs tarragon butter
3-4 dsp tomato relish
75ml vegetable nage
1/4 tsp tarragon paste

1/2 spring onion, finely sliced
1/2 plum tomato (chopped into fine dice)
1 dsp chopped chives
Pinch salt
Few drops lemon juice

Shrimp Organic Porridge **1** Melt the butter in a heavy bottomed pan, add the spring onion and then add the organic oatmeal. **2** Add the vegetable nage, tomato relish, and tarragon paste to the mixture. Bring to the boil and stir gently for 2 minutes. **3** Add the shrimps, chopped tomato, chives and lemon juice. Check the seasoning. **4** To garnish, put the tomato relish, tarragon, pesto and the olive oil on a warm dessert spoon, place on top of the porridge.

Milk Fed Bowland Lamb, Madeira Sauce, Lamb Sweetbreads, Cauliflower, Barley and Summer Savory

SERVES 4

For the Lamb
2 boneless best ends of lamb
25ml clarified butter
Salt and pepper

For the Lamb Sweetbreads
200g lamb sweetbreads (soaked in the fridge for at least 12 hours in cold water, changing the water every 4 hours)
200g onions, sliced
25ml clarified butter
1 clove
1 bay leaf
4g sea salt
Pinch icing sugar for glaze
Water to cover

For the Pearl Barley
125g pearl barley
700ml chicken stock
½ bulb fennel, roughly chopped
3 sprigs summer savoury
Pinch salt

For the Baby Leeks
12 baby leeks, remove the outer leaf, trim the base and wash carefully
250ml water
10g salt
10g sugar
25g butter

For the Cauliflower
4 golf ball cauliflowers
50g butter
25g melted butter
10g chopped chives
Salt to season

For the Madeira Sauce
150g chopped onion
40g butter
150ml Madeira
500ml lamb stock
500ml chicken stock

Pearl Barley [1] Take the summer savory and carefully pick the leaves from the stem (cut the leaves carefully with scissors) and reserve. [2] Place the pearl barley, chicken stock, fennel, and summer savory stalks into a medium sized saucepan, season and cover with a lid and allow to simmer until tender (do not allow to boil). When the pearl barley is ready remove the fennel pieces and summer savoury stalks. [3] Add the cut summer savory leaves, correct the seasoning. [4] Reserve and keep warm.

Baby Leeks [1] In a medium sized pan, bring the water, salt, sugar and butter to the boil. [2] Cut the leeks across into 3 equal pieces, add the leeks, cook until just tender. [3] Remove and place into a bowl of iced water. [4] When cold, take the leeks out and place on kitchen paper to drain. [5] Reduce the cooking liquor by half and reserve.

Lamb Sweetbreads [1] Place all of the ingredients in a pan, except the butter and icing sugar, and just cover the sweetbreads with the cold water, bring to the boil, simmer for 1 minute then remove from the heat and allow then to cool in the liquid. [2] Once cooled, peel off the outer membrane, place the sweetbread back into the cooking liquor until ready for use. [3] In a hot non-stick pan add the clarified butter. Drain the sweetbreads well then put them into the hot pan and gently colour before sprinkling them with a little icing sugar to glaze. [4] Remove from the pan and put on a small tray and keep warm.

NB. The sweetbread stock can be used for making soups or as an alternative for chicken stock in the Madeira sauce.

Cauliflower [1] Remove two thirds of the outer leaves of the cauliflower. Trim the stalks then cut the cauliflower in half. [2] Put 1 litre water into a medium pan and bring to the boil, add the butter and seasoning. [3] Place the cauliflower into the boiling water, seasoned with chives and salt, and cook carefully for 3 minutes until tender. [4] Remove from the pan when ready and reserve.

Madeira Sauce [1] Gently cook the onions in the butter until they turn a golden brown Add Madeira and reduce by two thirds. [2] Add stocks and reduce to approximately 300ml, and season to taste.

Lamb [1] In a hot frying pan add the clarified butter and seal the lamb quickly, place in the oven and cook for 8 minutes at 180°C / gas mark 4. [2] Remove from the oven and allow to rest.

To Serve [1] Prepare pearl barley, cauliflower, leeks, sweetbreads and Madeira sauce. [2] Take the lamb and gently baste with the butter on the top of the stove for 2-3 minutes. Pop the sweetbreads under the grill to keep warm. [3] Take the warm plates and on the left hand side place two to three dessert spoons of pearl barley. [4] Put the leeks into the reduced cooking liquor. Reheat for 30 seconds, remove from liquor and drain well. [5] Place a few baby leeks on top of the barley. Put the cauliflowers at the side of the pearl barley. [6] Place the sweetbreads at the front of the plate, take the lamb and cut in half across the loin. Carve the pieces four times lengthways. Place the lamb on top of the pearl barley and garnish with the remaing leeks. Pour sauce around and serve.

Blackcurrant Compote with Hunters Moon Ice Cream

SERVE 4

For the Ice Cream
250ml milk
250ml cream
5 egg yolks
100g sugar
300ml Bowland Brewery's Hunters Moon beer

Ice Cream **1** In a heavy bottomed pan bring the milk and cream to the boil. **2** Whisk together sugar and egg yolks until light. **3** Pour the milk and cream onto the yolks, whisking constantly, place back into the pan, cook out until it thickens (the mixture should just coat the back of a spoon), then pass through a fine sieve. **4** Leave to cool. **5** In another heavy bottomed pan reduce the beer by half then add to the other mix. **6** Pass through a fine sieve and then churn in an ice cream maker, or freeze in a shallow tray, stirring every 30 minutes until the ice cream is frozen.

For the Blackcurrant Compote
500g fresh garden blackcurrants
300g caster sugar
$^1/_2$ Lemon

Blackcurrant Compote **1** Wash the blackcurrants and mix with the sugar. **2** Place on a low heat and gently simmer for 2-3 minutes. **3** Remove from heat and cover with cling film and allow to rest for 30 minutes. **4** Gently drain the fruit through a large sieve. **5** Add a squeeze of lemon to the liquor and allow to cool. **6** Chill the fruit in a bowl in the fridge. **7** The compote should be served well chilled. **8** Garnish with garden herbs and flowers.

For Serving
Sprig mint
Sprig basil

To Serve **1** Divide the blackcurrant compote into 4 chilled bowls. **2** Place a scoop of ice cream in each bowl on top the blackcurrant compote. **3** Tear the basil and mint and place around the berries.

Peter Ascroft
Cauliflower King
Tarleton, Lancashire

RAISING CAULIFLOWERS MUST RUN IN PETER ASCROFT'S BLOOD. His father, and both his grandfathers, did it before him, farming this flat, fertile Lancashire land, that stretches along the coast between Southport and Preston. It's good black earth inland, a gift for growing root vegetables and salad crops; while the silt out on the marsh is ideal for brassicas.

Traditionally, these were the fields that fed the cities of Liverpool and Manchester and all the mill towns of Lancashire. They are still a powerhouse of fresh produce, pumping out potatoes, carrots, tomatoes, lettuces and all the rest – in their millions – filling our supermarket shelves. You can see glasshouses and field-crops to either side of the Southport New Road. What you can't see from there is the hidden world of the marsh, where lone and level fields stretch far away: acre upon acre of tilled soil; mile, upon mile; row upon parallel row of plantings, that seem to meet on the distant horizon. It is an awesome prospect.

This is the world of Peter Ascroft. He's a big man: strong, calm, reflective, good-humoured, with a nice dry wit. A man at ease with himself. He farms about 250 scattered acres, many of them around the tiny hamlet of Holmes where he lives; some between the villages of Tarleton and Hesketh Bank; then a great expanse, out on the marshes beyond. We meet on a fine day in mid June, slip into his daughter's car (the only vehicle not in use on the farm), and take a tour.

Cauliflowers are Peter's main, but not his sole, crop. He doesn't favour the modern monocultural trend. Together with his wife and business partner, Rosalind, he prefers to grow a variety of arable crops in rotation, so that the goodness stays in the soil and pests and diseases are kept to a minimum. Close to home, on low-lying black peat, he grows beetroots, traditionally planted to counter the dreaded clubroot that attacks caulis.

His beetroots are renowned. There are familiar red ones; raspberry-ripple style 'Candy' pink ones; and the Golden variety. Imagine the patterns those three could make on a plate – Nigel Haworth already has.

Golden beetroot was the first crop Peter Ascroft ever grew for Nigel, the only chef he supplies directly. 'A middleman introduced us about 5 years ago. Nigel wanted to promote local produce. He wanted to connect with local farmers and have some input into their products, and he were looking for people who would work with him. He saw beetroot as a good vegetable but, if you put it with a fish dish or a chicken dish, it stains everything. So we did Golden. You get the beetrooty flavours, but it doesn't stain. We've got a chutney manufacturer in the Brecon Beacons that's taken it up now – and it is nice as a relish – but we're still waiting for it to take off in a big way!'

Perhaps it would if only us shoppers could buy it more easily. It's the same story with purple carrots – so good and so hard to find. Peter grows them for Booths. He got out of orange carrots, partly because competition is fierce, the profit-margin slim and he hasn't enough land to grow them on a viable scale; partly because he'd have to spend about £50,000 on a machine to polish them. Yes, polish them. Polishers came in a few years ago. They're designed to remove the surface membrane from carrots and polish them to a 'deep glow'. When carrots are displayed on the supermarket shelf, days – and even weeks after washing – they still look 'fresh'. It seems we don't only like our veg washed these days, we like it shined up too: shiny carrots, shiny parsnips, shiny swedes – 'And shiny potatoes that taste crap', adds Peter.

He's an aficionado of potatoes. He grows various varieties. For the chip trade there's Maris Piper; an up-and-coming variety called Markies; and one he's trialling, Cabaret (dubbed 'a new chip on the block' by Potato Review). But right now he's remembering the misfortune that befell Wilja (which he also grows), the best all-round potato for home use in Peter's judgement. It lost popularity when washing came in, all because 'the skin set like crazy-paving. It won't polish up bright and shiny either. But Booths have always stuck with Wilja, selling them dirty.'

'Since time began, people have known that vegetables last longer with the dirt on. The more you do to a vegetable, the more you shorten its shelf-life.'

He stops to point out a plot of land he's turning organic. 'It's a good little field', he says, with a note of affection, 'and we keep saying we should be going organic. It's no good knocking it', his voice rises on a note of determined optimism, 'we must give it a try.'

Then we're on the move again, driving past the farmhouse where he was born and where he still rents the fields. It's black mineral soil here – good for potatoes – but as we ride out towards the marsh we're on peat again, planted up by lettuce and celery growers who'll pay good money for this choice land.

A few miles on, we're nearing Hesketh Bank, home village to Peter's wife and where there's more family land. Now we turn off Shore Road, once lapped by the waters of the Ribble estuary, and head out across the Old Marsh. This was the first area to be reclaimed for cultivation. Beyond is the New Marsh and, beyond that, the Out Marsh – extending about a mile and a half in all. As England's east coast erodes, here in the west it grows.

We bump along the punishing field tracks, the little car protesting. 'Come on girl', coaxes Peter. 'Are we going to make it or are we going to have to go and get the tractor?' We make it. And what a sight. Sky, space: infinity. A vast, wide-open expanse of dark earth, pin-striped with plants. In the distance, trundling back and forth across the horizon, is the planter, an amazing machine that seems to have greenery growing out of it.

It's six miles from here to the farm. A long way to travel with your tractor and your wagons. What makes it worthwhile? On the marsh, the natural PH of the silt is between eight and nine, so brassicas don't get clubroot, because the high alkalinity kills it off. That means you can grow superb cauliflowers and cabbages every year, if you've got the skill.

46,000 brassicas will go in this week, mainly white cauliflowers, a few thousand of the spiky green Romanesco; a few thousand Savoy and green cabbages. 'That's what I planted last week; that's what I'll plant next week. In a couple of weeks time we'll plant four times as much. And I'm not a big grower in the scheme of things – I'm just small fry.' His voice is deep. His accent is the gentled Lancashire of these parts, with its rich, rounded 'r', the occasional dialect word, and a rhythm and a phrasing to the speech that's poetic at times.

Peter Ascroft, the Cauliflower King. Nigel Haworth's supplier 139

'What we tend to do is cut wor cauliflowers in the morning and do wor planting in the afternoon.' Peter's been cutting caulis since he was eleven years old, nigh on forty years. The day he left school, it was off his bike and straight out into the fields. 'That's what lads want – they want work – and then they wouldn't be doing so much rappocking about, making mischief. Me cousins' lads help me here.' Peter's cousins and half-cousins are legion round about; the Ascroft name figures prominently too (and that is how you spell it, by the way – no 'h').

Caulis are still cut by hand these days and it's demanding work. Planting them, however, has got a lot less labour intensive. The seedling plugs are brought up in trays from the glasshouses at the farm; loaded onto a neat bit of kit at the back of a tractor where three guys sit, putting them into planting cups which then drop them into the soil, correctly spaced. His father used to grow about twelve acres of cauliflowers: Peter grows one hundred and twelve acres, with the same number of staff.

The cauliflower is an exacting vegetable to grow. They say it responds to the moon: always growing more strongly on a waxing moon when the curd is ripening. It is certainly highly sensitive to soil and climate. If a cauli catches a little too much sun, the curd will turn yellow and, although the delicate taste may be the same, the shopper will spurn it for a white one. In Lancashire, it is a summer crop. 'We can't grow them in winter – the weather freezes them', Peter explains. 'They look just like a sorbet when they're frozen, then they go to mush when they thaw out.'

But in season, they're a real treat to eat, cooked or uncooked: 'When I'm cutting in the morning, the first one that's not good enough to pack I eat raw. Then, I usually have one for my tea, cooked. A cauliflower, this time of the year with some new potatoes and a bit of bacon is a meal fit for a king! The trouble is, people think all you can do with a cauliflower is boil it.'

"Since time began, people have known that vegetables last longer with the dirt on. The more you do to a vegetable, the more you shorten its shelf-life."

Far from it, as a visit to any recipe website will confirm – or a trip up to Nigel Haworth's Three Fishes for his ever-popular cauliflower fritters. 'Mmm, they're very good', says Peter, 'and he does a good cauliflower soufflé, does Nigel.' You bet.

He sighs: 'If cauliflowers were a Tuscan speciality it'd be – oooh we must have some of these! Instead, people take them for granted and stop thinking about all the different ways you can enjoy them. The vegetables we grow in Lancashire are as good as any in the world if you eat them seasonally.' And what a harvest of them there is to be had around Tarleton, grown here by generations of hardy farmers, knowledgeable about their crops, in harmony with the land.

Back on the village road, a pause to breathe it all in. A westerly breeze ripples through the low-lying fields on this sunlit, and otherwise still, summer's afternoon. The roads are unfrequented; scarcely a vehicle passes in ten minutes. Tall, feathered grasses wave along the verge. This is truly a place apart. And a hard one to leave.

PORT OF LANCASTER
Smokehous
w. polsco.co.uk
E-MAIL sal
Port of Lancast
Smokehous

Michael Price
Port of Lancaster Smokehouse
Lancashire

IT WAS ALMOST FORTY YEARS AGO when Michael Price's father, John, decided that it was time for a change of career. At first, this erstwhile art teacher searched for a small farm to take over but, along the way, he discovered a smoking kiln and started to experiment, curing fish in his back garden. He never looked back. Since then, the Port of Lancaster Smokehouse has grown into a thriving business. The products it makes and sells have won numerous awards and are highly sought after by people from all over the UK.

John and his wife Pat were joined in the business around sixteen years ago by their son, Michael. He has a passion for the sea, and loves nothing better than fishing off the dock, in Morecambe Bay or local rivers, and bringing back his catches, ready for the smoking to begin. The smokehouse itself is situated on the eighteenth century Glasson Dock, at the estuary of the River Lune. The views are stunning: Sunderland Point to Morecambe Bay and onwards to the Lakeland fells, drawing you to cross the water towards them.

Following winding coast roads, past boats, two estuaries and grassy banks, suddenly you turn a corner and come upon a small group of unprepossessing industrial units. In among them is where the transforming magic occurs; where fine fresh foods are preserved, and their flavours and textures captured and enhanced by this age-old curing process.

The range of foods which pass through the smokehouse is too extensive to list in full. It includes various types of sea and river fish; almond and cashew nuts; back bacon; eels; unshelled prawns; cheese, and locally made black puddings and sausages. Each type of food is treated in a slightly different way. For example, the almonds and cashews are first mildly flavoured with sesame and pumpkin seeds which have been blended with fine olive oil, before being smoked for two days over a hickory fire. Freshly caught haddock, on the other hand, is first gently soaked in brine and then subtly smoked over oak wood for up to four days. The Prices are fastidious in trying to use local fish wherever possible. 'The fish comes in from Fleetwood docks, or from the rivers, and can be here within an hour of being caught, says Michael. 'You can't get fresher than that.'

Smoking is an ancient and very efficient way of preserving food which removes the need for artificial additives or preservatives. The woods used in the process – mainly oak and beech – impart a distinctive flavour to the food. Oak alone can sometimes be too harsh, but blended with beech it creates a more rounded taste. For chef Nigel Haworth, at Northcote Manor, Michael has developed a special blend of juniper and beech, to produce a unique-tasting smoked salmon. Whatever the food, smoking should always complement its flavour, never mask it.

The demand for organic smoked food is also continually increasing and the Port of Lancaster Smokehouse is one of only a tiny number of smokehouses in the country, which are licensed to produce organic smoked foods. Seasonal produce, such as salmon and sea trout from the River Lune, as well as pheasant, partridge and other game from local estates, are smoked at certain times of the year. The Prices also offer a service to those who want to smoke their own produce. Catch your fish, or shoot your own game, and they will smoke it for you.

Alongside the Port of Lancaster Smokehouse, is the Price's own specialist shop, which offers a wide selection of fine foods. In addition to all the glorious smoked meats, fish and fowl, are Morecambe Bay shrimps, cheeses, chutneys and preserves; mustards, olive oils, coffees and fine wines. The shop does a roaring trade, not only serving the local community but also a large clientele who travel from much further afield. For those who cannot shop in person there is an internet mail order service which has also helped to spread the word about this little gem of a business. The Prices attend farmers' markets and food festivals throughout the country, bringing their products to a wide and appreciative audience. Keen to play their part in the Slow Food movement, keen to ensure sustainability in their work, the Prices are proud of their products and their contribution to the local economy.

"The fish comes in from Fleetwood docks, or from the rivers, and can be here within an hour of getting caught, you can't get fresher than that."

Port of Lancaster Smokehouse. Nigel Haworth's supplier 145

Paul Heathcote
The Longridge Restaurant
Lancashire

LONGRIDGE WAS THE FIRST of Paul Heathcote's many restaurants. This is where he famously raised traditional British dishes to the realms of haute cuisine, gained two Michelin stars, and ushered the produce of Northwest England into the national limelight. The restaurant is named after the Lancashire town in which it stands, a place prominent in the 19th century for its gritstone, much of which went to build the city of Preston and the docks of Liverpool. What was once the Quarryman's Arms is now the Longridge Restaurant. A blue heritage plaque provides a potted history. Carved above the entrance are the date, 1808, and tools of the quarryman's trade.

"CHAMPION OF BRITISH COOKING? I don't know about that. Certainly, I was probably one of the first chefs to come back to the Northwest and really attempt to do something different.

It was 1987, a turning point in my career. I'd left the Manoir aux Quat' Saisons to take up a position as Head Chef at Broughton Park Hotel, just outside Preston, At that time, the Northwest had a very poor reputation as an eating ground. There were certainly no Michelin starred restaurants and the produce available was poor.

I recall a conversation in my first week with Chris Neve, one of the best fish merchants in the region. It was about fresh fish. He told me he didn't really have any call for it! Cod, a few kippers, yes, but as for selling fresh scollops or lobsters or crab, or something like monkfish or skate – there just wasn't the demand. He had a lot of frozen fish, but all his fresh stuff, his premium stuff, went down south.

That was the state of Fleetwood Fish Market. At Preston Market, when I asked for things like peppers or artichokes, they called it 'queer gear'. In Manchester it wasn't much better. I remember my first few weeks, going round, looking at the produce and thinking: 'This is a pretty big disaster.'

Since my background had been working for London's Connaught Hotel and for people as passionate about food as Francis Coulson at Sharrow Bay and Raymond Blanc at the Manoir, it came as a bit of a shock!

So I knew there was a lot of work to do. The suppliers had to be better. Finding them wasn't going to be easy; they'd have to be educated and, for it to be economical, they'd need other buyers to support them besides Paul Heathcote. So I got together a group of half-a-dozen like-minded chefs across the region – people who wanted to put the Northwest back on the culinary map.

We started finding new producers – cheesemakers, like Ruth Kirkham, for example – and we managed to inspire existing ones to develop, people like Reg Johnson, with his Goosnargh chickens and ducks.

At the time Reg was a local farmer who supplied chickens and turkeys to the hotel. When he arrived at my back door, I asked him, what for me, coming from the Manoir, was a very natural question:

'Do you do corn-fed chickens?'

He looked at me as if I'd got two heads!

'No', he said, 'I just do these.'

Well, after a couple of weeks, Reg came back: 'I've been reading up about these corn-fed chickens and I wouldn't mind having a go. Will you give me your opinion of them?' Well, of course, I was delighted.

So my relationship with Reg's corn-fed chickens was literally from birth! Unfortunately his first batch popped their clogs at 7 or 8 weeks because he'd given them too rich a feed. It took him a couple of years or so to perfect them and then I made the switch.

Up until then I'd been buying Poulets de Landes and Poulets de Bresse from France, but I didn't believe that was the solution. Buying a British chicken was the solution. Getting someone to breed it in the Northwest was the perfect answer.

So Reg and I ended up with Goosnargh corn-fed chickens and, later corn-fed ducks, which have now become synonymous with nearly every good restaurant in the Northwest and farther afield. The Ivy buys from him, Gordon Ramsay buys from him – Reg Johnson supplies a lot of great restaurants and great chefs.

I think, perhaps, I educated Reg, and another guy, called Eddie Holmes, who was my veg supplier until he retired recently. In the early days, Eddie'd bring in a box of artichokes and say: 'Is this what you want?'

So I'd pick one up, put it over the side of the table and knock the stalk off to see how stringy it was and say:

'No. Get another box.'

'What's wrong with them?'

'Look – they're as stringy as anything!'

'Oh! I didn't know that.'

'Well go back and educate your guys on the market.'

And so he'd go back and say: 'These bloody artichokes are crap!'

'What's wrong Eddie? Got out of bed the wrong side this morning?'

And he'd show them what I'd shown him.

I think Eddie used to enjoy the banter, the fact that somebody had shown him why an artichoke was not as good as it should be and the fact that he could educate somebody down at the market. So there was this to-ing and fro-ing and the message got fed down the line.

It was almost about having a point to prove: that our produce here in the Northwest wasn't as bad as everyone made it out to be – even if it was in those days!

The fact of moving back to my home region, my beloved north, and finding it in such a poor state after seeing the city lights was something that I felt needed changing. And it's a trait of my personality that I don't like being beaten. I don't give up very easily.

Those first three years back home, before I opened Longridge in 1990, were important in developing relationships with suppliers and getting them to change. Relationships grew into friendships and into an appreciation of good produce. There was a number of big success stories: Chris Neve expanded his business enormously, Ruth Kirkham became quite famous and it certainly changed Reg's life!

Slowly but surely other producers started to develop and grow. And it encouraged chefs to attempt to cook to a higher level. My reward was getting a Michelin star in 1992, the only one, I think, in Lancashire at the time. Then, in '94, when I received two stars from Michelin and the Egon Ronay Chef of the Year, there was a lot of notice outside the Northwest that maybe there might be something happening here. Nigel Haworth had got a Michelin star at Northcote Manor, Paul Kitching was making a name for himself at Juniper, and The Chester Grosvenor already had a

Michelin star. A resurgence of cooking had started in the Northwest!

It certainly set some excitement going that you could cook good food, that customers would patronise the places that served it, that you could use British produce, that you could make a living out of it, and that there was something creditable about it.

Those were the early days of the region starting to make a name for itself. Now there's a very strong stable platform here of good producers, good produce, a good supply network and a lot of up-and-coming talented chefs. There will certainly be a far greater and more accoladed chef than Paul Heathcote some time, that's for sure.

There will eventually be far more *great* restaurants in the Northwest, too – there's a lack of them at the moment. Most cities of a certain size in European countries have a great restaurant. We've got a lot of good places in the region, but considering how some of our cities have changed – Manchester and Liverpool have changed enormously for example – we still lack the numbers of top quality establishments. There'll be far more of them in another 10 years time, far more great restaurants and far more very good ones.

People have credited me with reinventing British cooking, but the fact is, I've never been a believer in cooking from farther afield when you can find something great on your own doorstep. So the use of foie gras or truffles – which, by the way, I enjoy enormously – would not come naturally to me.

I got far more excited when I finally found a great suckling pig – and because it was just a few miles up the road in Garstang! That's Pugh's Piglets. When I first visited him he was producing about 20 pigs a week. I think he does about 200 now.

Anyone can use truffles, anyone can use foie gras and, understandably, it's a bit difficult to cook badly with them. But finding a great suckling pig, or mixing some blood up and turning it into a black pudding, that used to give me a far bigger kick!

It's great that black pudding can go on a restaurant menu in London now and be perceived as fashionable or sexy. Equally, I think that when you look at things like pig's cheeks and oxtail, it's quite nice that we do now use them in abundance. I wouldn't take credit for them all by any means, but it is nice that we now look at British produce in a different way.

People ask me where my ideas for dishes came from. It wasn't from researching people like Mrs Beeton or Eliza Acton. Occasionally, I got an old cookery book out and read it – and I was probably more likely to pick up a French one – and think: 'Well, they've used pig cheeks ... we have pigs, they have cheeks ... I know they've put truffles with it ... but why can't we put parsnips, or swedes?

'Now what do we need to do to marry these ingredients together? What else do we need to add to make it balance?'

It's instinctive, I just look at it as food and think what I can do to make it better. Pig's trotters, for instance. They were made famous by Pierre Koffman at La Tante Claire and later emulated by Marco Pierre White. I ate it at both restaurants. Then I thought: 'What can I do to make this dish better?' That's a bit arrogant perhaps, because Koffman and White are both brilliant technicians and brilliant chefs. They might think my version was pretty awful, I don't know.

They used morrel, truffles and chicken mousse in theirs, but for me, this is an old-fashioned British dish, so I stuffed mine with ham hock and served it with onion sauce and a pea purée. Then, to stop it being a bit of a fight on the plate, I sliced it nice and thinly.

My wife, Gabbi, was brought up on pig's trotters. Her father was Italian, but he used to cook pig's trotters every other week – I think she was the only person in her school ever to have eaten them!

A lot of my taste is in my head, to be honest. Occasionally you're surprised, occasionally you get it wrong, occasionally things go together you'd never believe would. But unless you experiment you're never going to get there.

Raymond Blanc gave me one great lesson which changed the way I viewed food. One day, when I was cooking in the kitchen at the Manoir, he put his hands up at the side of my head so that all I could see was straight ahead: 'Paul', he said, 'you're like a racehorse with blinkers on. All you see is the winning post. Look to the sides.'

After those great French influences at the Manoir and the Connaught, my cooking could have easily gone down a different route. But if I were to credit any one person with changing my viewpoint on food it would have to be Francis

Coulson, first and foremost. He and Brian Sack created Sharrow Bay, the legendary English country house hotel in the Lake District. Their influence was the first great learning curve of my career and will stay with me all my life.

Francis and Brian saw customers and staff as no different, except that staff serve and need to understand the customer – we used to eat the same food the customers ate. I've tried to take elements of their hospitality and the way they thought about the customer. One of my first edicts here was go out and greet the customer and, when they leave, see them to the door, if possible. We need great hellos and goodbyes because a customer should be treated the way you'd treat a guest in your own home.

We work very hard to train staff, to retain staff, to build a team culture throughout the company. You need to learn from people, keep your eyes open and the blinkers off. For instance, I took 22 of our people down to Berkshire to spend the day with John Campbell, Executive Chef at the Michelin 2-star Vineyard, Stockcross. They embrace sous vide cooking and the techniques that are used for cooking at lower temperatures for a longer time. John's an immensely detailed technical chef and it was great to have an insight into his mind – which works totally differently from mine!

By complete contrast, it was poor cooking – my father's – that got me into this career. He really couldn't cook and as my mother worked two nights a week and my sister showed no inclination whatsoever to cook, it was left to me on those occasions. I found I liked it and I was good at it. When I was about 13 or 14 years of age, I got quite excited about it. So, at 16, I left school to do a 3-year catering course at Bolton Technical College.

Actually my father's achievements had a lot to do with it too. His career was in health and fitness and he was an extraordinary man in his sporting prowess. For example, on his 40th birthday, on the same day, he ran 40 miles in less than 4 hours, lifted 40,000 pounds in weights above his head in less than 40 minutes, did 400 sit-ups and then played 4 games of squash, finishing off with the world champion. He did the same on his 50th, but in multiples of 5!

So although sport was one of the two things I excelled at in school – the other was art – it leaves you with a bit of an achievement bar if you want to follow your father into his chosen profession!

Sport has always been a bit of a passion in our family. I get up about six in the morning and run for up to three-quarters of an hour, sometimes with Nigel Haworth. We talk about food, if we have any breath left. It's very sad! On a Saturday morning I play squash and in the season, if I'm picked, cricket for Chipping, which is just up the road. If I start putting on weight my father mentions it, so I realise I've got to do something about it. Eating less is not the solution!

Longridge restaurant was my only ambition when I opened it. At one point, in the first 12 months, we were virtually bust. Then, thanks to a review in *The Guardian* by Matthew Fort, suddenly, we were filled out for eleven weeks solid. Later I met him and he became a good friend.

Since then I've changed direction – I've become a serial restaurant opener! I've got 15 now, offering a variety of different eating experiences. I don't cook in the kitchen but I do have a lot of chefs who I try and influence – and it's nice to see chefs develop from your own stable.

I don't think my passion has diminished – if anything it's increased in terms of using produce from within the area. Most of our restaurants have suppliers that all come from the Northwest. I still have a lot of my old ones who have grown businesses alongside us.

Longridge restaurant is my baby. It's the place I visit more frequently than anywhere else. It's still the one that gives me an enormous amount of pride.

It's smart but informal, intimate. I'd never want it to be stuffy – that's never been my style. But the service should be professional and the food should be stunning, and I think it is at the moment."

Hash Brown of Black Pudding and Lancashire Cheese

MAKES 8

450g Maris Piper potatoes
1 egg white
2 large slices good black pudding cut into 8 pieces
120g Mrs Kirkham's Lancashire Cheese
1 tsp chopped parsley
1 tsp chopped chives
Salt and pepper

1 Leave the potatoes in their skins and cook in boiling water until only just firm. Drain and peel. **2** Grate the potato into a bowl and mix with the herbs. **3** Add a pinch of salt to the egg white, beat with a whisk and mix with the grated potato. Season with salt and pepper. **4** Pat out an eighth of the mix in a circle larger than the black pudding. Place the pudding and 15g cheese in the middle, fold over the potato and pat into a circle. **5** Deep fry at 160°C until golden brown or shallow fry for approximately 3 minutes on each side.

Goosnargh Duck with Spiced Apples and Braised Beetroot

SERVES 4

For the Duck and Braised Beetroot

4 duck breasts

6 medium sized beetroots, topped and tailed and peeled with a knife (or 12 baby beets)

25g butter

½ glass red wine

½ onion, chopped

2 cloves garlic, finely sliced

1 dsp Balsamic vinegar

1 tsp Demerara sugar

Sprig of thyme

4 black peppercorns, slightly crushed

50g cold diced unsalted butter

Handful of spinach

Aluminium foil

For the Spiced Apples

1 Bramley apple, cut into 8 pieces

20g icing sugar

Few drops olive oil

Good pinch mixed spice

The Duck and Beetroot **1** Cook the duck breasts, skin side down, in a frying pan for about 8 minutes and allow to rest. **2** Place the peeled beetroot in a large pocket of aluminium foil along with all the other ingredients except the butter. **3** Seal tightly and place in an ovenproof dish with a generous amount of water in it to prevent burning the foil. **4** Bake at 160°-170°C / gas mark 3 for approximately one and a quarter to one and half hours. **5** Open the foil with caution as the steam could burn. Test with a sharp knife to see if the beetroot is cooked and soft (otherwise return to the oven for a further few minutes). **6** When cooked drain the juices through a sieve into a pan, bring to the boil and whisk in the butter to make the sauce.

Spiced Apples **1** Sieve the icing sugar into a hot pan and allow to caramelise to golden brown (take care not to burn either sugar or fingers!). **2** Add the apples, sprinkled with mixed spice and toss until richly covered. **3** Serve with a little wilted spinach.

Rhubarb and Elderflower Custard Trifle

MAKES 8 INDIVIDUAL PORTIONS IN GLASSES OR 1 LARGE BOWL

For the Base
2 sticks of rhubarb, chopped into 3cm lengths
Water
1 packet of ladies finger trifle sponges (about 20)
200ml sherry

For the Custard
500ml double cream
100ml milk
1 vanilla pod, split and seeds scraped
6 egg yolks
30g caster sugar
2 heaped dsp cornflour
4 dsp elderflower cordial
250ml double cream for topping the trifle

Grated chocolate for decoration

Base [1] Place the chopped rhubarb into a large flat pan and just cover with water, bring to the boil. Allow to boil for 30 seconds and remove from heat. [2] Leave until the fruit is soft but still firm enough to hold together. [3] Put the sponges with the rhubarb and sherry, mash well together. Divide between the glasses and chill well.

Custard [1] Place the cream, milk, vanilla in a pan and bring to the boil. [2] Whisk the yolks and sugar together and dissolve the cornflour in the cordial before adding to the yolks. [3] Pour a little of the hot cream onto the yolks and whisk well before returning everything to the pan and cooking until thick and creamy. [4] Remove from the heat and allow to cool before dividing between dishes and chilling for a couple of hours.

To Serve Whisk the double cream until it leaves a trail and top the trifles, decorate with chocolate.

Reg Johnson

Just moving things along …

Goosnargh, Lancashire

THE VILLAGE OF GOOSNARGH (pronounced 'Goosnar') is just a hop, skip and a jump from Longridge. It's a pretty little place with a medieval church, next door to an elegant Georgian mansion, and two venerable inns contending for custom on opposite sides of the road. Prosperous modern housing enfolds the ancient centre, then gradually peters out into farms and fields on the edge of the majestic Ribble Valley.

This is where you'll find Reg Johnson and his Goosnargh ducks. Behind the quiet family farmhouse, the yard is alive with purposeful activity. There's the sound of a mill at work and of grain cascading from hopper to trailer. The trailer is hitched to a tractor, and minutes later it's on the move. Men in white hats, overalls and aprons pass between outbuildings. Delivery vans come and go. But of ducks, there's not one to be seen.

The reason is simple. They live indoors. So do the corn-fed chickens. In open barns, with natural ventilation and fresh straw underfoot, they lead warm, dry, well fed and unstressed, if relatively short, lives. Reg is very particular about this rearing method. It goes hand-in-hand with his trenchant views on the importance of disease prevention, proper welfare standards and high quality feed.

His birds grow at their own natural rate. No growth promoters, antibiotics or other medications are added to their feeds, which are specially formulated and mixed on site to produce birds of exceptional quality and flavour. The same approach, with the same notable results, is applied to the firm's turkeys and geese – except the geese, being immune to most diseases, are free-range, out grazing in the fields by day, indoors and secure from predators by night.

As well as selling fresh poultry, Reg has a range of other products, such as smoked duck and chicken, and he's developing more. He markets a variety of other Northwest produce into London restaurants, too, meat and dairy products in particular.

Everything is run from a Portakabin parked, with the improbable air of Dr Who's Tardis about it, right there in the farmyard. Reg is inside, busy on his mobile phone, a perpetual companion that rings a lot. This time it's Mark Hix, chef director of Le Caprice, The Ivy and J Sheekey. He's ringing from Paris, kidding Reg that the ducks he's dispatched there for an important culinary event will not arrive in time. But Reg is one step ahead. He and daughter, Kara, run an efficient operation, everything has been checked: flight, delivery, the lot. 'That Mark Hix', he grins, 'having me on', and he bounds out of the office, his overall flapping in a self-generated breeze.

Suddenly, we're off on a tour of the plant. Each part of the operation is shown in its totality and explained in detail, starting with the ducklings' nursery sheds. There are four of these, one each for 1 day-olds, 7 day-olds, 15 day-olds and 22 day-olds.

The youngest have a heated shed. It is important to maintain ventilation because, as they grow, the ducklings start generating their own heat. At the fourth shed you can really feel it. They are almost into avian adolescence now and have big beaks in relation to their bodies. 'They shovel food in,' observes Reg, 'that's why they're so expensive to rear. They never stop shovelling it in!'

As they get bigger they are moved again, into much larger barns: 'We provide twice as much room in the sheds than legally required. It's more expensive but I feel better about it. Here they're consistently on clean ground', he says. Reg is hot on hygiene.

At eight weeks they have reached culinary maturity and the end of their lives. 'They're moved out of the barn in small batches, straight into a trailer and across the yard to the plant. They're not stressed. We don't crate them. They're never confined.'

They are killed, plucked and dressed on an automated system, geared up to take 500 an hour on production days. After that, they go into a holding fridge for finished carcasses, prior to delivery. If chefs want particular portions cut, that too will be done.

There is a similar but different system for the corn-fed chickens. They are killed at nine to ten weeks, giving them a 50% longer rearing time than on other farms, but also making them costlier.

The plant processes 2,700 ducks a week; 1,200 corn-fed chickens. It is a far cry from the pre-Paul Heathcote days when Reg inherited the farm from his stepfather, Thomas Swarbrick. Reg remembers: 'We had pedigree Holsteins – a dairy herd, pigs and 20,000 laying hens.' They are long gone and the fields are rented out.

'In the 1980s it was a bit dire in farming. We were producing to a fixed price – we weren't in charge of our own destiny. We had a market stall in Clevely, but even there I realised that, no matter what you did, only a certain number of people ever came into the market. It's one of the reasons we moved in this direction. You have to go out and sell your produce.

'At that time, just down the road, Geoffrey Bond was running Broughton Park Hotel, then privately owned, now a Marriott. He was forward-looking about local produce and in 1987 he got this young chef up from the Manoir aux Quat' Saisons', Reg recalls, '– Paul Heathcote. I've called him a knight in shining armour in a culinary desert! A sound sort of guy.

'He wanted English corn-fed chickens. "Oh aye", I said. They were just names to me. We tried different breeds. We did blind tastings. By trial and error we built up and got it right.'

Paul and Reg experimented with ducks in the same way, finally settling for an Aylesbury–Peking cross. In the process of their endeavours they became great friends. Paul recounts the sterling support Reg gave him in his efforts, how the two would go to London and eat out together and how he would give Reg introductions to chefs such as Albert Roux and Gordon Ramsay.

Reg recalls: 'When I first started to work with Paul, developing the birds he wanted, I thought this is a lot of sweat and trouble – I can't be bothered with this. But when I could see what he saw, I had to do it.

'It's been a great adventure – hard work, but an adventure.'

Immediately you sense the appeal that has for Reg Johnson. He has quick, bright eyes: thinking eyes, an inquiring mind. He communicates a kind of compressed energy, always looking for a new channel of expression, a new endeavour to pursue. An ethos of continual improvement seems to drive him.

A little while ago, he began wondering why cornfed ducks are slightly more moist and tender than their white counterparts. He concluded it must be to do with vegetable oil, told his poultry-diet specialist his thoughts and asked him to look into it. The upshot was a slightly higher level of vegetable oil in the feed. Reg knew he'd effected a marked improvement when a chef in one of Liverpool's top establishments asked, puzzled but approving: 'Have you changed these ducks?'

The phone rings. Fortnum and Mason, this time. It might equally well have been Gordon Ramsay at Claridges, Marcus Wareing at Pétrus, Conran or the Malmaison group. Demand is growing; more expansion is in hand to meet it; new sheds are going up. 'You can't stand still', says Reg. 'If you're standing still, you're going backwards.'

He has expanded the business steadily, upgrading plant and equipment as he goes. 'Farming bores me silly', he says, ' – so much is repetition.' New ventures keep him interested. 'It's when I'm out on my own in the car that I do my thinking: They dread me going out. I plan while I'm driving.' He believes in thinking new ideas through thoroughly though, arming himself against the inevitable pitfalls that go unseen the first time round.

Geese are the biggest growth area at the moment. His are a special breed with a hugely big breast bone. It is the depth of the meat that allows restaurants to make a profit. They take the crown only, and this works in their favour in terms of a shorter cooking time too. The legs are used for confit. 'The fat is worth more than the goose', says Reg, 'so we're looking for a system to produce that and to confit the legs too.'

Recently he has branched out into sourcing Lancashire and other Northwest products for London restaurants. Reg is interested only in the best: 'I want something I can say, hand on heart, this is done the right way, and I'll market it into restaurants.'

One such product is Anne Forshaw's yoghurt. Reg tells the tale: 'She started making it in kits and giving talks to Women's Institutes. By accident, a cousin of mine who worked for her part-time brought me some sample pots. Her yoghurt was completely different. I had to put it back in the car to stop eating it. It's slightly sweetened vanilla. You just can't leave it alone. When a gallon pot first goes into a restaurant kitchen, the chefs just eat it! We supply 60 to 70 gallons a week.'

Reg has a natural talent for marketing. He's been asked by experts where he learned it. 'Well, it's just common sense isn't it?' That's his reply.

But he is in no doubt who deserves the credit for pioneering the renaissance of local produce in the Northwest. Paul Heathcote and Nigel Haworth get Reg's vote – and Eddie Holmes for getting fruit and vegetable growers going.

He muses on the distant past: 1965 when his family came to the farm. He remembers when there would be 20 men threshing and his mum, Winnie, would feed them all. He remembers the hotpots and how, as a kid, he'd eat the burnt bits on the sides of the dishes when the men had gone. He remembers when pigs were killed and people would stagger across the yard with buckets of blood for the black pudding; there'd be pigs' trotters to eat and huge hams hanging in the pantry.

Times have changed a lot since then. Now chefs ring up for his mum's recipes. Her Goosnargh cakes feature in books and her oatcake recipe is used at The Ivy. In 2006, something even more improbable occurred. When Nigel Haworth had his wedding reception, Reg supplied a special contingent of Poulet de Bresse – instead of his own Goosnargh chickens. 'They were good', he concedes, 'but they didn't blow me socks off. Their muscle fibre is much finer, like pheasant, but they've got tough legs. They're overrated. They were no better than mine. I was very disappointed.'

Just now he's got something else on his mind besides chickens. At the suggestion of his brother, Bud Swarbrick, who runs the farm side of the business, Reg is thinking about doing a duck sausage. He might do another one as well: 'A little bit of sage with a light peppery background to the meat …

'Just moving things along', murmurs Reg. 'If it gets boring, I make something happen …'

"We provide twice as much room in the sheds than legally required. It's more expensive but I feel better about it."

Graham Kirkham
Mrs Kirkham's Lancashire Cheese

IT'S A MAGICAL SIGHT: Mrs Kirkham with her hands in the curds, making probably the most celebrated of all Lancashire cheeses – her own. You won't see her doing it so much these days. Her son Graham has taken over the task at Beesley Farm, just outside Goosnargh. Nothing much has changed though. The cheese is still superb, still made in the traditional farmhouse way, and the business is still the small, family affair that it was when Paul Heathcote called at Ruth Kirkham's door twenty odd years ago.

'Paul Heathcote helped to revolutionise food in this country, says Graham Kirkham. 'He uses local produce, and he's done a lot to spread the word. Now we get people turning up at the farm gate with *Rick Stein's Food Heroes* in their hands asking if they can buy our cheese!'

Recognition – that is the one big difference since Mrs Kirkham's own mother showed her the way to make cheese some thirty years back. Since then she has won awards too numerous to mention, including the one craved by all serious cheese-makers, Supreme Champion at London's International Cheese Show. Today you will find Mrs Kirkham's Lancashire Cheese all over the country: on the menus of discerning chefs; in specialist cheese shops; prestigious grocers; famous food halls and at farmers' markets in the Northwest.

All the cheeses are made with unpasteurised milk from the Kirkham's own herd of Friesian Holstein cows which eat specially sown and selected grasses. 'We don't buy milk in', Graham points out, 'and we are quite fussy about what we feed the cattle, because that affects the flavour of the cheese.'

It takes six separate milkings, over three days, to make the cheese. Each contains a mixture of one third of the current day's curd, one third of the previous day's, and one third from the day before that. The three-curd technique, laborious and time consuming, but vital in achieving the unique texture and flavour of Mrs Kirkham's cheese, was developed many generations ago. It dates back to a time when most of the farms hereabouts had only a few cows. Graham explains: 'The cows had small yields, so it took two to three days to get enough curd together to make the cheese, because it takes one gallon of milk to make one pound of cheese.'

A natural starter culture and natural rennet are added to the milk, which causes the curds and whey to separate. When three day's worth of curd has been drained, milled, salted and combined, Graham transfers

it into moulds. These are pressed the old-fashioned way, and once set, they are turned out, wrapped in muslin and then evenly painted with molten butter. The finished cheeses are then matured in a low temperature store for at least six weeks, and some for several months.

Buttering the rind is an important step in securing the essential qualities of this cheese. Most Lancashire is either plastic-wrapped or waxed. The traditional buttered rind allows the cheese to breathe during maturing for a lighter texture and cleaner flavour. The delicate tang is far better tasted than described. 'We want our cheeses to be soft and mild, creamy and slightly crumbly', says Graham. And so they are.

For years, Mrs Kirkham made her cheese in a couple of small rooms at Beesley Farm, but in response to increasing demand the family have expanded their premises. But innovation and enlargement have not altered the traditional hand-made methods. It is hard, physical, time-consuming work. And skilled, very skilled. And instinctive, requiring knowledge that comes only from plenty of experience and an innate understanding of your land and livestock. You can't expect much time off either. The cows don't take a holiday from milk production so you can't take one from the cheesemaking.

Despite the intensive labour of their method, mass production holds no allure for the Kirkhams. 'We are never going to be a monster,' says Graham. 'We still only make a relatively small amount of cheese every day, but this expansion gives us more space and the chance to mature the cheese for longer.'

Small producers are often passionate about what they do, but the Kirkhams are amongst the most dedicated and enthusiastic. Graham hopes this way of life will be a legacy that he can hand down to his sons, and keep alive the tradition of Mrs Kirkham's Lancashire for future generations of cheese lovers.

Robert Kisby
Cock o' Barton
Cheshire

THE CHARMING HAMLET OF BARTON lies enfolded in farmland, twelve miles south of historic Chester, close to the Welsh border. Its pub, homely, black and white, half-timbered, stands by the roadside where it has greeted travellers during four centuries. But oh, what delights await those travellers who discover it today! In this unexpected location they will find a restaurant, as delicious in its decor as its food; animated by the superlative skills of a celebrated chef of great integrity. Robert Kisby, late of Manchester's Le Mont, Bridgewater Hall, and the legendary Midland Hotel; long-standing member of the prestigious Academy of Culinary Arts; winner of numerous awards, has brought his charismatic presence here. The lure? Firstly: the freedom to cook according to his own exacting standards. Secondly: an inspired conversion of this rural inn, done with architectural good manners and great finesse, to create a dining venue of diverse moods. Start at the glittering bar in a spacious, light-filled lounge, all clean lines and cool colours, like a Seattle beach house. Move seamlessly into more formal dining, where Tudor timbering melds with 21st century style. Go further into the original structure and find flickering firelight, claret walls and touches of damask. Or eat outside, in a cosy courtyard under sail-like awnings that act as water sculpture, should it rain. Wherever you choose in this most relaxing of establishments, it is sure to be on Chef Robert's regular round of welcome.

"IN CHESHIRE WE SIT ON A WONDERFUL BELT OF LAND. The dairy pastures on the Plain and the salt underneath give us the county's famous cheese, of course – but there's much more besides. So when I moved here from Manchester, it didn't seem right to just go on using regional produce from the Northwest in general. I decided I'd have to go out and find first-rate producers in this corner of Cheshire – after all, it's from the land we get the flavours of our food.

By the time we opened on the 22nd December 2006, I'd found quite a lot of what I was looking for, helped by Made in Cheshire, which supports the food industry locally. A few more months, a little bit more work, and I had sorted out the provenance of the food to my satisfaction, and developed a menu I feel happy with, one which reflects that superb local produce. I call it a story menu, because it tells you the story of what you're eating and where it comes from.

Our regional food platter is a case in point. The black pudding comes from Andrew Jackson at Gate Farm in Nantwich; the pork rillettes are made from Cholmondeley (pronounced Chumley) Estate Gloucester Old Spot, and the salami is produced by the Cheshire Smokehouse in Wilmslow. Keith Siddorn's rare-breed Hereford cattle at Meadow Bank Farm, a couple of miles from here in Broxton, are the source of our pressed beef brisket and Anne Connelly makes the Federia cheese, a bit further down the road at Larkton Hall Farm. It's just easy-eating food, but flavoursome, wholesome, and with quality.

A large percentage of us now are concerned about what we're eating and where it comes from. Most important to me, and key to having a story menu, is that what I write is what I serve. The majority of our customers – and we have quite a lot of regular customers – know me and what I am. I don't just stay shut in the kitchen, I pass through the restaurant and we have a chat. They know they can rely on the authenticity of the produce. It's an integral part of why they come.

Less than four months after we opened, I had a visit from Trading Standards officers – for the first time in my entire career of more than thirty years! They said: 'We've heard comments about your menu.' They had actually come to verify it. Fortunately, I'd just had some deliveries, so I showed them the boxes, the labels, the invoices – in fact they were overwhelmed with authenticating material. From my point of view that's essential, because if you're going to do what we're doing here, you've got to do it properly. I've recently bought a flock of 450 lambs – that's how far I'm prepared to go to source locally!

The menu is divided into three main sections: our full Wine and Dine menu; a lighter choice, Plate and Glass; and dishes to share, under the heading Platter and Bottle. Customers can eat from any of the menus in whichever of our settings they prefer. There's a wide choice of dishes, and our front-of-house staff are ready to ensure that people feel comfortable with how the menu works and what's on it.

Some things are very traditional, very English: Dover sole, roast beef and Yorkshire pudding; others may be French, mediterranean or have influences from other parts of the world. Our gazpacho, for instance, is a classic, devised by the great Benjamin Urdiain, who did his version of this soup with langoustine at Zalacain, his 3-star Michelin restaurant in Madrid. I have taken the recipe from a Master Chefs of Europe book, and he is duly credited on our menu. Gratin Normande is another classic: cream of onion soup from Normandy, where it is made with cider from the region's famous apples. Here, it seemed logical to use what is, literally, up the road – Eddisbury Fruit Farm's Cheshire Cider.

I particularly like the platters to share. They're something different, and I love the food items and their descriptions. Each has a theme, among them the slightly tongue-in-cheek 'retro' pub platter. This takes its inspiration from old pub-food favourites, so

it has mini-versions of chicken kiev, scampi and chips, gammon and fried egg, sausage and onions and so on. It's a bit of fun – and a talking point for customers who remember the originals! The big difference, of course, is the quality regional produce we use to recreate these dishes.

Ultimately, my cuisine is classical French. Unless you've had that education, I don't believe you can do a menu like this with real substance. Originally, I started out in hotel management at Cambridge College of Art and Technology, but then found I enjoyed cooking. I wasn't necessarily much good at it – and I wasn't the best commis chef when I left! That came in time. You don't go from college through three, four-star British Transport hotels and find yourself, as I did five years later, a junior sous chef in a brigade of 56 under Gilbert Lefevre, unless you're capable of doing it.

We learnt dishes, by their name, according to a bible called *Le Répertoire de la Cuisine*. And we memorised them. There weren't any pictures, not there, nor in *Larousse Gastronomique*, to tell us what they should look like – you had to work that out for yourself! The chef in charge of the menu would just say: 'Gratin Normande', 'sauce Bercy', or whatever it might be. That was all. He didn't explain to you what it was. He expected you to know. Your mind became your recipe book. It's not like that any more in kitchens! Today it's written down, chefs use picture-boards for reference. And that's okay – let's just get it taught!

At British Transport Hotels I had a good training in terms of teaching me to cook, but not necessarily in staff management. It was very much a shout/command scenario in those days. That changed in the early '80s, when I went to work as sous chef for Albert Ulman, at the privately owned Valley Lodge Hotel in Wilmslow. He was inspirational in the way he managed staff. Yes, he shouted at times, but he earned the right. He was respected for the way he worked, how he cooked, the hours he put in, and for challenging the owners when necessary, in order to create an environment of good pay and conditions for everyone. That meant we had very little staff turnover. I learnt a lot from him, and when I left Le Mont, I still had staff who'd started with me

five or six years earlier at the Charles Hallé Restaurant in the Bridgewater Hall. For me that's proof that looking after people, and training them well, works.

Keeping your brigade is key to constructing your business and presenting your food in a consistent way. Most of the inconsistencies in food don't come from being busy but from a constantly changing workforce, who often end up doing their own thing as a result. Your menu should be a statement of the premises and who is cooking. So while acknowledging we all have our own styles, we have a rule in the kitchen that what you have to get on the plate is Robert Kisby! Another rule is no aggressive language. That doesn't mean we don't swear, but it's not aggressive, it's not directed at people – that's the distinction.

It's all about standards. Perhaps it stems from my star sign, Virgo, which means being a perfectionist and striving to do your best. Dress and appearance matter in the kitchen. Hats and neckerchiefs are a thing of the past, but the guys here still wear aprons, white jackets and trousers. You need to feel good about yourself, so be clean, shaven, tidy. It's the same with the way you work in the kitchen: if you work in a mess you will not achieve – your food will be poor. So, be organised – keep your kitchen clean and tidy; keep your fridges the same way and know what's in them; if you spill a little water, get it wiped down quickly. Then, let's go again!

We're open seven days a week, serving food noon till ten. We're doing 100 covers, freshly cooked food, not batch-cooked and held in bain-maries. The chefs are good or they wouldn't be here – in fact the guys in the kitchen are great – and they work hard to ensure the quality of the food on the plate. There are no split shifts. We do four days solid, then have three days off – a day to rest and two to enjoy life – so hopefully everybody's bubbly and cracking on.

It is important how you look after staff. My three basic tenets are: a nice kitchen to work in and all the equipment to do the job; the best ingredients to do the job, and a decent salary. We feed our staff every day with nice food and we encourage them to sit down to it, not stand at a bench and continue working. Good staff management is not about sweet-talking – I'm a stern taskmaster at the end of the day, not a holidaymaker – and there's nothing wrong with a sharp word now and then. But it is about rewarding people and praising them. And it's about celebrating too – at Christmas, on birthdays, when we've received awards or if we've had a particularly good week. That's when I'll buy some champagne or wine to share at the end of service.

It's about creating an environment of support, where staff feel they can share their ambitions with you, where you can advise them, find placements for them, make that first phone call on their behalf when they're looking to progress. That whole approach was instilled in me by Albert Ulman and hopefully, long-term, you are doing the industry good. I'd like to see more of a system through which people can progress in that way. Maybe I'm wrong, but I think that's what catering lacks in its integrity as a profession.

I do my best to put something back into the industry. That's what motivated me to run a Northwest inter-collegiate commis chef competition with the Association Culinaire Française for ten years. In some ways I'm a born teacher, but I don't like teaching in a formal setting, divorced from reality. I like to do it in a practical way. That's the way I work with schools too. I have three as part of the Academy's Adopt a School scheme. I take their programme as my starting point but I also respond to what the schools want.

The Pendlebury Centre is a special school in Stockport. I go there when I'm invited; they've visited my working environment and we've shown them the kitchens, cooked, and eaten together. At Trinity High School, Manchester, in the context of their Food Technology lessons, we did what we called master classes with Years 9 and 10. We'd do a particular product or project, like pastry work, for an afternoon, or even after school, and I'd help judge cooking competitions too.

The main work I do, though, is with Wellfield Infant School in Sale where my wife, Barbara is a classroom assistant. Twice a term, I fit in with an after-school food club. The mothers are invited and we talk about good, healthy eating with kids and balanced diets. I usually have a group of about ten or twelve children. These are only Year 2s, and my part is showing them how to make a fresh soup in twenty minutes. Often it will be tomato. We discuss all the ingredients, the challenges of sweet and sour, and how tomatoes can be both at the same time. I teach them how they taste on the tongue, and where they taste the sweetness and the sourness. We make the soup, with them helping to cut up the vegetables. Then they eat it and we have a thumbs-up, thumbs-down as to whether it's any good. Generally speaking all the kids say it's great because they've bought into it. Then I'll suggest, 'Why not try making that on a Saturday morning?'

It's a little bit similar with apprentices or young chefs, you try to encourage them, make them feel part of things and hopefully, light a fuse in them. There are particular challenges when you open a new restaurant: it's a challenge to work in a new kitchen, to train staff who don't know you or your cooking, and to evolve a culture. To do it successfully is a good feeling. To be recognised for it, just a few months down the road, here at the Cock o' Barton, has been very rewarding.

There were some people in the other night, and as I walked past this guy stood up to shake my hand. I said: 'Please, don't stand up.' He replied: 'Oh, I have to. I've eaten your food a long time. I can even remember dishes you did at Claude's.' Now that's a restaurant I ran in the mid-1980s in Altrincham, with Claude Grossiord, former Maitre d'Hotel at The Midland! Then he added: 'We used to dine at the Bridgewater frequently, so we just thought we'd like to visit you here.'

Things like that are quite warming – and one reason why I don't like constantly changing the menu. You must leave on elements that people who know you are expecting. If friends tell you about a dish they've really enjoyed and say, 'I must take you to the Cock o' Barton so you can try it', and you go and that dish is not available, then you'll be disappointed. What's more, chefs only get good at a dish with practice! And we only get good at a big menu like ours by perseverance, evolving it, developing it.

The consistency of your menu also has an important part to play in building up trust with producers, who need to have confidence in your future intentions. I wasn't using Anne Connelly's cheese when we first opened but now I am, and I've specifically sorted my menu accordingly to include dishes using cheeses that are continental in style. The lady I bought my 'flock' from, Elaine Von Dinther, is passionate about what she does. My butcher had already told me that her sheep were fantastic in form and finish. We tasted her product and Elaine came up here to see what was what. When I said to her that I would buy all her lambs, she had to feel confident she could take me at my word and withdraw them from market.

Now Elaine has her sales assured, I cut out the middleman, save some money and gain enormously in quality. I can pass the benefits on to the customer, and they know exactly where the meat on their plate has come from. They can even go and see the sheep if they want to!

Of course, the seasonality of menus is important. Why would you necessarily want to serve roast lamb for Sunday lunch in February or March when that's not its peak time? It can still be good, if your sourcing and your reliability of product is good, but it's not at its best. People don't see fish as seasonal but it is. I speak to Chris Neve, my supplier, about what's at its best and when. There's no point, for instance, having plaice on when it's full of roe in the spring, or trying to serve John Dory in January.

We strive to deliver quality all the time. You come here, to an old Cheshire inn in the middle of the country and eat great Cheshire produce. It's a gastronome's delight, finding this food in pub mode! Generally speaking, people who come to the Cock o' Barton haven't one iota of an idea of what's going on here. Maybe they've brought their kids, looking for a sandwich – and, no, we haven't got sandwiches – but if they want sausages, there are good wholesome ones – made by my long-standing butcher, Neil Frost – not something full of additives. Or they can have a finger of fish and chips. Let them try a piece of halibut – if they're young kids they've probably never had it before. It's very nice fish. Let them taste it and hopefully it'll be an education!

Robert Kisby, Cock o' Barton, Cheshire 177

Salad of Anne Connolly's Federia Cheese, Cumbrian Air-dried Ham, Cheshire Asparagus and Artichoke

SERVES 4

This is not so much a recipe as a list of high quality ready prepared ingredients that you can put together to form a splendid salad. Feel free to add any of your personal preferences.

Anne Connolly's Federia cheese
Richard Woodall's Cumbrian air-dried ham
Richard Wilding's Cheshire asparagus
Jar of charred artichokes
Vinaigrette dressing

Arrange in your own personal style and enjoy.

Loin of Lamb Wrapped in Chicken and Fresh Herb Mousse with Madeira Sauce

SERVES 4

4 x 100g lamb loin, cleaned

For the Stuffing
300g chicken breast
1 egg
100ml double cream
50g butter
50g shallots
Tarragon, chervil, parsley, rosemary
and general seasoning

For the Madeira Sauce
50g diced onion, leek, carrot and celery
125ml Madeira
350ml veal or beef stock
1 tsp tomato purée
1 tsp flour
25g butter
1 bay leaf
Salt and pepper

Stuffing **1** Finely chop shallots and soften by lightly frying in a hot pan. **2** Remove any sinew from chicken and blend in a food mixer, adding the cream and egg. **3** Pass the stuffing mixture through a fine sieve, add the shallots and chopped herbs, and then refrigerate.

Madeira Sauce **1** Heat a pan, fry the mixed vegetables until they start to brown, add bay leaf, salt and pepper. **2** Add tomato purée and cook for a few minutes, stirring. **3** Add flour to absorb any excess fat. **4** Add Madeira, stirring well to remove any thing left on base of pan, boil until you only have half the amount. **5** Add beef stock and reduce to a sauce consistency. **6** Pass sauce through a fine sieve and check seasoning.

Lamb **1** Place the seasoned lamb in a hot sauté pan and seal. Remove and cool as quickly as possible. **2** Take a sheet of foil, butter and season well. **3** On the foil, spread ½ cm thick layer of stuffing and wrap around the lamb. **4** Roll into a cylinder and refrigerate for 4 hours. **5** To cook, heat a sauté pan and place the meat inside, rolling it around to begin the cooking, before placing in a hot oven and roasting for approximately 12-15 minutes, keeping the lamb pink. **6** Alternatively, if you prefer, you can steam the product for 15-18 minutes. **7** Rest for 5 minutes, before removing the foil and slicing.

To Serve Slice the lamb at an angle, arrange on a plate with your choice of vegetables and pour sauce around.

Chocolate Marquise with Seasonal Orange Salad in Caramel

SERVES 4

For the Chocolate Marquise

2 egg yolks

40g caster sugar

45g dark chocolate (couverture or very good quality plain)

75g clarified, unsalted butter (i.e. melted and solid particles removed from the bottom)

45g cocoa powder

125ml double cream, soft whipped

For the Orange Salad

2 large oranges

50g kumquats

1 Satsuma

1 Clementine

50g caster sugar

100ml water

Chocolate Marquise [1] You can use brick-shaped moulds, such as a mini loaf tin, approximately 8cm x 5cm x 5cm lined with cling film. Alternatively, if you prefer, the mix can simply be turned out on to cling film and shaped into a roll. [2] Chop the chocolate into small pieces and place in a bowl, over hot water, to melt. [3] Combine the clarified butter and cocoa powder. [4] Take egg yolks and caster sugar and whisk over hot water until double in volume. Remove from heat and whisk until tepid. [5] Add the melted chocolate to the eggs and sugar. [6] Add the butter and cocoa mixture to the chocolate, eggs and sugar. [7] Mix well and fold in lightly whipped cream. [8] Turn the mixture out into the lined moulds, or onto cling film and shape. Refrigerate for 24 hours.

Orange Salad [1] Zest large oranges and cut into fine strips (julienne). Peel off pith and segment the fruit. Squeeze juice from the pulp and set aside, with the segments. [2] Slice kumquats and Clementine and place in the water and sugar with the finely cut zest, pouring in the orange juice. [3] Boil until a caramel consistency is achieved. The fruit in the syrup will now have candied. [4] Peel the Satsuma, remove as much pith as possible and pull into segments, set aside. [5] Allow the caramel to cool then add the orange and Satsuma segments.

To Serve Slice chocolate bricks with a warm, thin bladed knife and place on a chilled plate. Arrange the orange salad as you wish.

Elaine Von Dinther
The lady with the lambs
Deemster House, Cheshire

SOME NAMES POSSESS A STRONG POWER OF SUGGESTION. When you hear the patrician-sounding 'Deemster House' and 'Elaine Von Dinther', what do you picture? A country estate perhaps? An elegant chatelaine, impeccably groomed in twinset and pearls, surveying her flocks from beneath a perfectly proportioned portico …

It's a compelling image – but one that only provokes peals of laughter from the real Elaine, as we drink mugs of tea in the modest home she shares with her farrier husband, Allan, and their daughters, three-year-old Heidi and Chloe, aged one. 'This was built as a tied cottage around 1914,' she explains. Its grandiose name comes from the estate which owned it.'

What about that noble 'Von'? 'Allan's father was a German prisoner of war who married a local girl and stayed on. Allan's Cheshire born and bred!' As for Elaine, she's a racehorse trainer's daughter, a Shropshire lass he lured across the border. Now she is a hands-on sheep-farmer, and far less likely to be found in designer gear than clad in jeans, wellies and a waterproof, bouncing over the fields on a quad bike, blonde locks flying.

The family lives in a beautiful part of this well favoured county. Deemster House stands on a narrow, climbing road in Wirswall (pronounced Wurzul). It is a hamlet of scattered farmhouses, set among gentle hills in the south west corner of Cheshire, about a mile north of Whitchurch and the Shropshire border – just twenty minutes from the Cock o' Barton.

Until recently, Elaine used to sell her lambs through the local market – Barbers Auctions at Market Drayton. 'I'd have all the lambs marked up and moved on to the paddock the night before, ready to go. I'd load them up, early in the morning. Allan would get the children up and give them a quick breakfast before he left for work. Then the three of us would be into the car and off. I was lucky – Heidi and Chloe always slept on the journey and we'd have a second breakfast when we got there.'

But she also had – and still has – another string to her bow: selling freezer lambs to friends and locals. 'They're all regular customers. I just pull out the lambs that are ready and take them to Hewitts, a small local abattoir in Huxley. My butcher in Kelsall, Wally Dutton, picks up the carcasses and butchers them – legs, half-legs, chops, occasionally a crown of lamb. Then I'll go out with my little plastic boxes, collect them up and drop them off on the way back.'

One day, the manager from nearby Cholmondeley Castle Estate happened to be in the butcher's. He is Mike Allman, one of chef Robert Kisby's suppliers. Impressed by the quality of the lamb carcasses he saw, he asked who they belonged to and, in quicktime, Elaine found herself hosting a visiting party. 'It was April when they came and we were lambing. The weather was like midsummer. Robert brought his butcher, Neil Frost and they had a good look round. He wanted to know exactly where his lambs were from and how they were managed.'

Elaine took them to her fields at the very top of Wirswall Hill. We are up there today, but in very different conditions. It's late June and the wettest summer for the whole of the United Kingdom since records began in 1914. It's been pouring since daybreak and, not far from here, the main road to Chester is flooded. Every field is saturated and the sheep are huddled back into the hedgerows.

Rain notwithstanding, this is fine country and the view is magnificent. Spread before us is a vast panorama of neat fields; green, lush, undulating; well hedged and husbanded. They are punctuated by trim red-brick houses and barns, church towers of pink sandstone and the softly rounded outlines of trees and groves. Four miles to the north as the crow flies, are the turrets of Cholmondeley Castle, a Gothick fantasy, made flesh in the early nineteenth century. In the distance, are Bickerton Hill, the Peckforton Hills and the dramatic ruins of medieval Beeston Castle.

Elaine's land sweeps down the hill to Deemster House, just visible between the treetops, then up and round to the next village, Marbury, where we seem to be walking in a Constable painting. The pastures slope down to a great mere, fringed by a belt of mature trees. Sheep (Elaine's, of course) graze serenely at the water's edge. Looking down on the pastoral scene stands the village church, crocketed, battlemented and unbelievably picturesque. 'That's where Allan was christened, we were married, and where our children were christened too', says Elaine as we pass.

In all, she has about 140 acres hereabouts, rented from two neighbours who have gone out of farming. Luckily the land is all adjoining which makes managing the flock easier. Much of it is in Environmental Stewardship, the government scheme to encourage wildlife in return for subsidies. That part she leaves to her landlords but grass management is her affair and she is meticulous about it. After all, we are what we eat, and that goes for sheep as well. In general terms, they benefit from short, fresh, clean grazing, especially the lambs whose arrival is timed to coincide with the growth of new grass. Elaine tends the ground to produce those conditions. She doesn't use fertilizers or herbicides. She top-mows any long grass to let through new shoots and young, sweet clover, then waits for it to reach the right length before she brings her animals in. She rests fields, rotates her sheep for optimum grazing and maintains low feeding densities.

'On some fields, under Stewardship, you can only have two sheep to the acre from 1st April to 30th June. If it's a ewe she can have two lambs with her. That means you're not overgrazing – it's better for the ground not to be overstocked. The Stewardship ground has been good for us.'

'Robert wants his lambs fed on grass, as natural as possible. We've got lots of good pasture – not organic, but you can't get more natural. I think that appealed to him, plus the fact that the sheep are close at hand and always being checked and gathered.'

She inspects everything once, if not twice, a day. This morning, while the family slept, Elaine was out at six, as usual, checking on hundreds of sheep and lambs. 'I'm back by eight and then Allan goes out the door. I know everything's okay, and if it's not, then I galvanise the children and off we go. I've got pens in each field where I can gather the sheep and do any work on them that's needed.'

When she first came to Deemster House, eleven years ago, she had no idea of being a sheep farmer. 'I met Allan on a blind date and look what happened!' she jokes. At the time she was working in Gloucester, looking after a little boy with cerebral palsy. Elaine has always worked with children, in their homes and in schools. She began as a nanny at 16, but in her early twenties became strongly drawn to children with special needs, which is where her qualifications lie.

Elaine Von Dinther. Robert Kisby's supplier 187

'When I came here with Allan, I was simply going to work in a school.' But Allan is a keen sheepdog trialler and his Border Collies and a few practice sheep were already installed on the five acres which he'd bought with the house. Soon, Elaine was trialling too. 'The thing is, you train one dog, so you need a few more sheep. You get a few more sheep, so you need another dog, so you need some more sheep …'

The flock began to grow, at first only as far as the limited land holding would allow – to about thirty or forty sheep. Elaine was hooked – but it was just pastime. 'In the early days, if I took some sheep to the livestock auction and sold them, it was a thrill. I had an income from my school work, so it didn't matter that it probably cost me twice as much to get them there!'

It was only when Heidi arrived that Elaine's outlook became more professional. It had to, if she was going to fulfil her intention of looking after her own children full-time. 'The sheep were something I could do from home but, to warrant me not going out to work, I had to make them pay.' She started to rent extra land, build up the flock and concentrate on producing a good quality commercial lamb for market.

Britain has a unique way of doing this, refined over the centuries and known as a three-tier system. It begins with hardy local hill sheep put to a Bluefaced Leicester ram. This breed, easily recognised by its domed forehead and Roman nose, is prized for its high milk production. The resulting cross is always known as a Mule, the name modified by the mother's home-territory: Cheviot Mule, North of England Mule, and so on. The offspring inherit all the virtues of their parents, together with a tendency to grow larger, mature early and lamb prolifically. In the final tier of the system, the Mule ewes are put to a breed renowned for its heavily muscled carcass, usually a Suffolk, or the increasingly popular Texel which originated in Holland. The result is prime lamb.

For her main flock, Elaine has chosen Welsh Mules, noted for their superior mothering instincts. These are not bought in. With quality and biosecurity in mind, she breeds her own, keeping a small flock of about 75 Beulahs for the purpose.

At tupping time she puts the Welsh Mules to Texel rams. This year, over a period of three weeks she lambed singles, twins and triplets from 300 breeding ewes, the most she's ever done. 'We lambed eighty down in the first week – which for us is a lot! But as quick as they lamb down, they're in the pen, mothered up – and even though you've been up all night and you're tired, you know which ewe's had what and you can give individual treatment to the ones that need it.'

At times like these, Allan is Elaine's unpaid helper. For shearing they bring in contractors from Wales, the same people every year. 'Apart from that, we do all the work ourselves', says Elaine. 'Well, primarily I do it. And I can promote breastfeeding at the same time', she adds, bursting into gales of laughter as she tells of nursing her babies in all sorts of locations, from secluded fields, to the queue for washing out trailers at the livestock market (all the while hoping that no-one was going to come and knock on the car window). 'Everything's workable!' she says determinedly. 'My biggest nightmare was that I wouldn't be able to do it, but I persevered with Heidi and I was fortunate. It means you can be anywhere and there's no hassle with bottles – you can just get on with it!'

Both children were summer babies: 'We were out all the time. They were more often sleeping outside holding pens than in a cot!' Now that they're bigger, Elaine has them in a playpen or running around if the weather's nice; in the car if it's not – just as long as they're safe. 'I've got the sheep grouped so that all I have to do is go out and gather them with the dogs. The children know what's going on because they've been used to it since they were days old.'

Heidi is already a practised hand: 'Do you help mummy Heidi?'

'Yes, I sprayed blue dots on the baby lambs.'

'What were they for?'

'It's called their flock mark.'

'What else did you do?'

'I banded the tails.'

'Then what happens?'

'The tails fall off'.

Heidi is brandishing her own, beautifully carved, shepherd's crook while we talk – Chloe has a smaller version. These are presents from Mr Boone, who the family met at at sheepdog trials in Derbyshire. Heidi attended her first – the English National, no less – at nine days of age. It has become an important part of

family life, with Elaine and Allan setting up the Wirswall Sheepdog Society and holding trials twice a year themselves.

There are eleven Border Collies to look after, kennelled in the neat paddock outside the house. Why so many? 'They're all in different stages of training. Two have retired and they just work the flock as and when we need them, all the others are trialling dogs or work dogs. You need a specific dog for trialling and it's not always your farm dog.'

There are also times when you need a lot of dogs to gather your sheep – like shearing. 'One very hot day we must have used seven dogs in relays to move the sheep about. You've got sheep in groups of up to 70; inevitably the lambs get mixed up and have to be sorted out. In addition, you're working against time because the shearers are actually very quick, so the dogs really have to work.'

Does Elaine like sheep? 'Oh I do, I do!' she exclaims. My aim is to have a good stamp of flock, producing a good stamp of lamb. It's improving each year because I'm getting to know more – you never stop learning – and the flock has got stronger. I'm using better rams – I'm more fussy now. Before it was a hobby. We'd go out and work the dogs on the sheep and play about – and yes, we still do that, but my priority is getting those sheep ready for market or another outlet, such as the one which has come up now with the Cock o' Barton.'

For her main flock, Elaine has chosen Welsh Mules, noted for their superior mothering instincts.

Will she miss going to market? 'I like it that my lambs have only got to travel 20 minutes up the road to the slaughter now and there's no stress. I leave here at seven in the morning or even earlier and very often my lambs are first in the queue. So that pleases me. There's only one place for them to go and they go in quick.

'Markets have definitely got their role – the country has to be fed – and what I'm doing now isn't going to suit everybody. Some farmers go out to other jobs, whereas I'm here all the time. If Robert tells his butcher he wants so many lambs next week, all Neil has to do is ring me and I can be out there choosing him some tomorrow. And Robert knows he can come out whenever he wants and bring his chefs with him.'

Is she becoming a business woman now? Not really. 'I'm more concerned with getting the sheep right, seeing the children happy, and concentrating on the house and the dogs than pushing the business aspect. Just as long as it enables me to sustain that little bit of extra income. But, as the children get older, who knows what the future will bring?'

Anne Connelly
Larkton Hall Farm
Cheshire

THE LEVEL PLAINS OF CHESHIRE, could not be more different from the towering Alps of northern Italy. But it is here, in the serenity of the gentle Cheshire countryside, that Anne Connelly has created her superb mountain cheeses, based on traditional Italian alpine recipes.

The cheese, from Larkton Hall Farm near Malpas, is made in the authentic artisan way. The process begins in a tiny room dominated by a sink, and a huge copper vat atop a gas heater. It continues in another, equally tiny, room where the cheese is brined, concluding in a small pantry, where the finished cheeses are left to mature.

As Anne rhythmically stirs the creamy curds in the big copper pan, using what looks like a medieval paddle, she explains the differences between her cheeses. She does two: unpasteurised Federia and Crabtree. They take their inspiration from two Italian cheeses: creamy Scimudin, and Cafera, which means homemade in Italian. Federia is a hard-pressed cheese and, because it takes longer to mature than Crabtree, it has a stronger flavour. 'Chefs rave about Federia', says Anne, 'but we find customers prefer the mildness of Crabtree.' While the taste and texture of each reflects its north Italian origins, the terroir of Cheshire also imbues both. It comes through the milk that goes into them – straight from Larkton Hall Farm's own dairy herd – and the pair of hands that makes them. Together they impart a uniqueness which is characteristic of all artisan cheeses.

The story of how these two outstanding cheeses came to be made at Larkton is a romantic one. Anne, originally from Liverpool, had been working in Italy for seventeen years when she met Peter Clayton, a farmer from Cheshire who had arrived for a skiing holiday. Their romance flourished and Peter persuaded Anne to leave the the little village of Livingo, near the Swiss border, and return with him to England.

She settled happily into her new life on Peter's farm, at Larkton Hall, except for one thing. For someone who had been used to living in a place with small shops, where food was still made by local producers, the world of the big supermarket came as a shock – and a great disappointment. She particularly missed the artisan cheeses which were a speciality of the region in which she had lived. 'I couldn't believe how tasteless the cheese was! So Peter suggested I should try making my own. I was looking for something to do, so I thought, why not?'

Her first step was to enrol on a short course at Reaseheath Agricultural College, to learn the basics of cheese making. When it finished, she was still looking for the right product to make. Then an Italian student who was staying with them, put her in touch with her uncle, through whom she met an Italian farmer and cheesemaker by the name of Beni.

Beni had never left the village in which he was born. There he made his own cheeses, using the traditional mountain methods, handed down through the generations. He was happy to show Anne how to make the semi-pressed and hard-pressed alpine cheeses, so she spent time in the village, learning from him. Beni was generous in divulging his deep and extensive knowledge of cheese-making. Even so, at the end of her stay, Anne was still not confident that she had learnt enough. Certain she was in need of further tuition, she invited her mentor to visit Larkton Hall Farm. 'I never thought he would come', she recalls, the note of disbelief still in her voice, 'but some friends were driving from the village to visit us – and he just got in the car and came with them!'

Beni spent about a month with Anne, and every day they made cheese, perfecting it, and adapting it to suit the temperature, milk and surroundings in which it was being made. She could not have asked for a better teacher. By the time Beni left, his intensive tuition had left Anne well on the way to becoming a skilled cheese maker in her own right. Beni's legacy lives on at Larkton Hall. Anne remains captivated by his passion for cheese and, in making her own, still uses the methods he taught her.

> "If you are passing by on a walk along the Sandstone Trail, I am happy to sell my cheeses from the doorstep,"

Once the cheeses are turned out of their moulds at Larkton they are steeped in a brine bath for twenty-four hours to develop their flavours. It is after this that they are transferred to the cheese pantry, where they are left on its wooden shelves to ripen. During this stage a natural rind forms. Even though she makes cheese two or three times a day, Anne is unable to satisfy the demand for her cheeses at present. Her copper vat holds only one hundred litres at a time. Since there is no room for a bigger one, plans are in hand to create a larger workspace so she can increase the volume of production. Even when this expansion has taken place, Anne still intends to work on her own, making each and every cheese individually, by hand.

She is generous in her praise for other artisan cheese makers in Northwest England, notably the Kirkhams of Lancashire and the Bournes of Cheshire, who have done so much to promote the resurgence of regional cheeses made by traditional methods. And she gratefully acknowledges the vital role they have played in paving the way for people like herself to succeed in the market-place. But she has always wanted to put her own individual stamp on the cheese she makes. 'I wanted to do something different', she explains. 'And when all's said and done, it is worth remembering that this is the kind of cheese the Romans would have made when they came to Cheshire. We know, because we researched it! Without a doubt, they would have used these same methods too.'

Recognition of the quality of her cheeses has come in the form of numerous awards, the most recent, and perhaps the most prestigious, being a Silver Medal in the British Cheese Awards. Closer to home, Anne was voted both the People's choice and the Judges choice in 2007's Wirral Food and Drink Awards. Her Larkton Hall cheeses have won a prominent place in the Northwest's increasingly rich food offering and can be found in several farmshops and specialist cheese shops in the area. But for anyone out Malpas way, Anne offers a warm welcome at Larkton Hall Farm. 'If you are passing by, walking along the Sandstone Trail, call in – I am happy to sell my cheeses from the doorstep', she says.

Anne Connelly's Federia Cheese. Robert Kisby's supplier

Gary Manning

60 Hope Street
Liverpool

NOW IN ITS TENTH OUTSTANDINGLY SUCCESSFUL YEAR, this is the restaurant which raised the bar and set the trend for fine dining in Liverpool, winning award after award for its diverse and witty modern British cuisine. National acclaim came early, but although *The Sunday Times* called it 'a London restaurant in Liverpool', 60 Hope Street has always celebrated its home city, through inspired versions of traditional dishes and a strong commitment to the region's produce. It pursues this quest for taste in the perfect setting: an elegant Georgian house, somewhat grander than its neighbours, in a gracious terrace with theatres, universities and cathedrals for a backdrop. Six wide steps entice you up and in under a filigree fanlight. The prospect of entering such a house, dating from the days when this historic city first leapt onto the world stage, provokes a certain thrill. Walk in and you segue seamlessly from past to present: stylish minimalism, bold colours, refreshingly clean contours. 60 is the creation of two exceptionally talented local brothers, Gary and Colin Manning, responsible respectively for food and front-of-house. Their enterprise operates on three floors: the restaurant occupies the piano nobile; above is private dining; below, a relaxed bar and bistro. Everywhere, careful attention to detail contributes to the enormous cachet this venue enjoys among a starry clientele and regular folk alike.

"THE DAY WE OPENED, I WAS SHAKING. Good restaurants were folding around town. The previous Thursday, we'd driven past one of the very best at eight in the evening and it was closed. I thought to myself: 'What am I doing? Am I mad? It's a desert round here!'

So there we were: two Liverpool lads who'd worked away from home for several years, picked up a shedload of knowledge and come back determined to prove that a restaurant of this calibre could succeed in our city. We were convinced it would work – and we were going to prove it!

At the time, people predicted we'd either fail or quickly drop our standards. Nowadays, they credit us with having had fantastic foresight and say we led Liverpool's restaurant revolution! It's true we saw potential, it's true 60 was a pioneer on Hope Street, but luck had a lot to do with it too. First, we found a beautiful Georgian house in the heart of the city's cultural quarter, a wonderful part of town within easy reach of the business district. Then we were fortunate in having a very successful businessman for a cousin. I pitched the idea to him; we did a formal business plan – based on the location, my cooking ability and my brother Colin's now celebrated expertise in front-of-house – and he invested in us.

He helped us greatly, especially with the purchase and refurbishment of this Grade II listed building. Liverpool still has an extensive network of these fine Georgian terraces – only three other English cities do. No wonder they film so many period dramas round here! The street itself is named after William Hope, a merchant, who built his 'country' house here at the end of the eighteenth century. When our property came into being a few years later, Hope Street was still mostly fields, as you can see from maps of the time. Hard to imagine when you see it now – brilliant, buzzing – and with a cathedral at either end! It's a street like no other in the world. We had to pay tribute to that heritage, so we dropped the name we'd originally chosen for our restaurant and just adopted the address of the private house it used to be. Somehow, it seemed more in keeping.

Inside, we wanted a contemporary look, but in sympathy with the visual values of the period – harmony, proportion, elegance. I designed all three floors myself, using the Georgian colour palette, retaining original features such as the pilasters and fireplaces, but with everything very sleek, very minimal. I was heavily influenced by a Conran restaurant, Le Pont de la Tour, where I had worked for about eighteen months in 1995/96, just when it was reaching its crescendo as a fashionable London venue. Another inspiration was the work of Philippe Starck, in particular a restaurant he had recently finished in Hong Kong. He has a wonderful sense of theatre, which adds so much to the pleasure of eating out. We've tried to capture that here. For instance, customers love the central staircase. I told the architect I wanted it to have that Scarlett O'Hara factor – where you can pause on the top step and make an entrance. Well, it has, and people do!

What I've tried to create at 60 is somewhere I'd like to eat every day – though if I did, I'd probably have to spend more time in the gym! It's just keen, honest food – a little bit quirky – but simple, unpretentious, and focussed on local, seasonal produce. That's been the philosophy from the beginning. When Mathew Fort came with Paul Heathcote shortly after we opened, he gave us fourteen and a half out of twenty in his *Guardian* review. He gave Gordon Ramsay sixteen the following week. So I was quite happy with that! We set a new standard in Liverpool. No-one had seen a poached egg the way we did it – people used to think it was mozzarella! It was little touches like that which set the food apart.

We wanted to use local produce, but oh, it was so hard at the beginning to get suppliers. They'd say: 'We don't come to Liverpool' or 'We only come once a week and we want cash on delivery'. So I'd invite them to come and meet me at the restaurant. When they arrived and saw the investment, it was: 'Wow, this guy means business', and they'd start supplying us.

Quality was the next hurdle. At first, some suppliers were sending us absolute rubbish. 'But that's what we deliver to so-and-so down the road', they'd tell me. And I'd say: 'Well, you can deliver this to them as well. In fact, I'll take it down myself. I'm certainly not accepting it, because I want the person who comes in here to taste the best they've ever had.'

Eventually, we got there. With the help of North West Fine Foods, which was created to promote the region's producers, we made some very good connections. Now, more often than not, the difficulty is making the choice between products, because there's just so much good quality available. Recently, I was judging twenty different entries of bacon for the annual regional awards, and I'm thinking to myself: 'Now, that one would be great on a butty, but that'd be great for breakfast; this'd be great with some liver; that'd be great wrapped round some kidneys; this one would be great with some scallops …' It was virtually impossible to pick the best one!

Why am I so loyal to local produce? Well, I could be really hip and cool and say it's all about green miles – and that is an element. But there are other reasons to do with taste and quality and freshness and reflecting the region we're in. That's what inspires our menus.

When people come here they need to taste local food. There's so much to enjoy – Wirral asparagus, Southport potted shrimps, meat from the Cumbrian fells, sea trout from the River Dee – and guests want to see all of that on the menu. If you went to Normandy, you wouldn't expect to eat ratatouille. Oysters, apples, cider, cream and butter – yes. These are the products the region is famous for and these are the ingredients you would go there to eat. It depresses me to see the current trend for national chains of restaurants that are quite soulless, where the chefs become clones. There's no real creative effort, no real passion going into the food, because it all has to look like the same – in Manchester, Bristol, London, or wherever. Human beings want individuality. If everything is the same everywhere, what's left to discover?

Ours is a totally modern British menu, incorporating cultural influences from around the world, but we include some very local dishes too. We've taken Liverpool's traditional boiled ham with pea whack and created a restauranty version of it. And we still serve some old favourites from when we first opened, like our jam butty – a deep-fried jam sandwich with Carnation Milk ice cream. It's a bit of fun, very popular and not something you're going to see on many other menus!

High quality is key to whatever we do, so we continue to get certain produce from France, Italy and Spain. In a shrimp paella, for instance, the rice will be from Spain but the shrimps will be from Southport. We still have foie gras on the menu – it's one of those ingredients that some guests expect to see – but we encrust it in gingerbread and serve it with Goosnargh duck breast and rhubarb. So we mix and match with local ingredients.

To find there's fantastic food on your doorstep, to realise there are people with the same passion as you producing it – and they want to supply you – that's a wonderful feeling. A few weeks ago, I took some of our staff up to Cumbria to visit one of our meat suppliers, Lakes Speciality Foods. They took us to see a flock of sheep and lambs being born, a herd of beef cattle too. They pointed out the qualities of different beasts, and explained how to tell which ones are ready and which will give the best meat. We talked to the farmer about breed and feed, about the impact of BSE and foot and mouth disease, and the changes that have followed. We discussed the changing requirements of restaurateurs too. It was very interesting, very instructive and really useful for all concerned.

Afterwards, we visited the butchers, where the carcasses come after slaughter, and saw beef being hung and aged. The fillets we use in our restaurant are dry-aged on the bone in this way. Twenty-five years ago, when I started my career, sides of meat would be hung in the kitchen to mature – not something today's chefs are likely to experience. So it was good for our guys to actually see the process by which beef slowly but surely gains flavour and tenderness. It is vital to understand the importance of this process, rather than just open plastic bags with pieces of bright red meat inside, which may look lovely to the eye but don't necessarily eat well.

Next, carcasses were appraised for quality. We watched skilled practitioners divide them into the various cuts, and it gave us the chance to appreciate the craft that still exists in butchery. This is another thing that young chefs tend not to see any more. Meat, like fish, comes into the kitchens of today ready-cut to requirements. In the past, we would prepare a beef carcass ourselves; the bones would be used for stock, the skirt for stews, or braised, sliced cold and put in a terrine, and so on. If you put a side of beef in many a kitchen nowadays, no-one would know how to deal with it. They'd throw away more than they'd use.

It's important to stem this erosion of skill and knowledge. That's why we like to use the traditional brigade system at 60, and to train new staff, take them out to meet producers and see products in their raw state and being prepared. Understanding all of that also plays a vital part in fighting food waste in this disposable society of ours. I always remember the reaction of one of our staff when he saw a young chef wasting food in the kitchen. He pulled me aside and said: 'Gary, do we live to eat or eat to live?' Those few words struck a chord with me. They seemed to put the whole issue of food into perspective. It's here to sustain our lives, to keep us healthy and make us strong. It reminded me of my grandma, and seeing her larder full of home-made preserves and herbs hanging up to dry for Christmas stuffing. Nothing went to waste.

My grandma sparked my interest in cooking. She taught me proper respect for food, to appreciate the seasons and traditional dishes that made full use of good, wholesome ingredients, including those we often disregard today, like offal. That's why you'll find kidneys on our menu.

My dad and mum ran a fruit and veg shop but they were really bad cooks. So from the age of fourteen, I was sent home to get the dinner. I started with roasts, then spaghetti bolognese – cooked from raw mince – before branching out into curries and Chinese food. It was just trial and error. I always remember cooking veal à la crème. My dad got me some veal from the butcher and I did this Brian Turner recipe. I thought it was great, though I expect it was awful – there was no actual stock in it!

At school, I did Home Economics for two years and because I was good at that, they urged me to go to catering college. I felt pushed into it at the time. I didn't really understand that this was something I could excel at. It was my teacher who saw that. I thought: 'If it doesn't work out, at least I'll know how to cook and I'll have a skill I can use for the rest of my life.'

Half-way through my second year at college, I got bored. I left and began waiting on and cheffing in a very busy suburban restaurant. It was the mid 1980s – a low point for this city – and I left after twelve months to join my brother in the Channel Islands. I worked in Jersey for about eight years, on and off. It was there I acquired my respect for, and knowledge of, seafood and fish, which is something we have a good reputation for here. I also spent a year in Australia, where I learnt a little about fusion cooking.

When I came back to England, I worked at a number of well-known London restaurants, but it was Le Pont de la Tour that showed me how to run a business. It had the work ethic, the knowledge that goes behind the food, the staff training, and the brigade system of running a kitchen, with the various ranks of chef and everyone responsible for their own section. It was quite a slick operation. There were 36 chefs producing high quality food and easily capable of doing 180 covers in an hour. On the busiest night we ever had, there were 288. I was standing at the pass, controlling the whole business and thinking: 'Hell, it's all down to me tonight!' I've got six commis standing behind me with silver trays: 'Right: table two; table ten …' Bang, bang, bang! 'Take that back! Where's the food?' I take my hat off to the people who do those jobs.

After eight years cooking full-time at 60 Hope Street, I handed over the reins to my Head Chef, Sarah Kershaw. We work closely together and I think the secret of our successful relationship is that Sarah knows I have full confidence in her and her ability to lead a busy kitchen. Sarah was in charge on the evening that Gordon Ramsay ate here. It was great to see the buzz it gave her when he asked to compliment her personally after his meal – scollops and Southport shrimps followed by foie gras and lamb.

Like me, Sarah comes from Liverpool. She trained at Southport College and worked in the south of England, before joining us, initially as chef de partie. Her work-rate and her ability to multi-task is phenomenal compared to anyone else's, including mine. She knows how to manage herself and the kitchen – and she doesn't lose her temper.

It's harder for women to survive in this industry. It's such a male environment, so competitive that, in order to succeed, female chefs are forced to prove themselves far more than men are. It takes a certain personality, because a lot of women wouldn't put up with all the male bravado and the laddishness, which does get pretty wearing at times.

In fact, the easiest part about being a chef is the cooking. That's because it's a natural ability. The hardest part of the job is getting in on time, being hygienic, meeting deadlines, working with other staff, then coping with the stress when it gets busy. The customer has come for fantastic food and a fantastic experience and it's your business to deliver that to them, no matter how bad your day has been. My brother, Colin, is very passionate about food and wine and service. We place a great deal of importance on front-of-house, on understanding how to look after the customers, and on having the knowledge to be able to tell them about dishes on the menu and wines that will best complement them. I think that emphasis and our hands on, family-run approach helps set us apart from other restaurants.

Kids see the celebrity status of chefs on television, but I think they also see that it's a tough industry to be in. You've really got to have the passion to be a chef. It's in your blood, it's in your heart. You can't teach that. When a guy comes into the kitchen, straightaway you know whether he's got it or not. You know from the respect he shows for the food, the way he handles it, the way he uses his knife. A chef needs plenty of good, common sense too – plus a sixth sense for putting flavours and textures together, an innate understanding of which ingredients will combine successfully and which ones you would never, ever, put together. People ask me if I find it hard to get chefs. The answer is no – but I do find it hard to get good chefs.

The other reality of the restaurant business is you have to make money! The discipline which that entails can sometimes come as a shock to a college-leaver. Tutors try to be positive with students who mess up – 'That's okay, never mind, try doing it this way.' But in the workplace it's definitely not okay, because mistakes are expensive and we have staff to pay.

The business side occupies a lot of my time these days. We run a second restaurant now, The Quarter Café Bar. From the doorway of 60, you can see its pavement tables set out along the cobbled Georgian side-street opposite. Our idea

was to evoke that simplicity you find in little places in France, Italy and Spain – the simplest, most fantastic tasting food, local produce, a glass of wine, a cup of coffee. Relaxed, comfortable, friendly.

Will I open more restaurants? I am doing so, but I have a huge emotional attachment to what we do here, my heart will always be at 60. This place was always, and is still, our flagship and sets the standards. Every meal that goes out is part of me, even if I'm on the other side of the world, because I employed the people to do the job. It's very personal and I'm still passionate about it. If you lose that, standards start to decline.

With 60 Hope Street I've achieved my goal of a fantastic restaurant, a fantastic team of people, a fantastic customer base. *And* we're in Liverpool, a most amazing, unique world city, European Capital of Culture 2008, and now growing bigger, attracting more and more people back to live in the city centre. In my personal life, I'm quite a retiring kind of guy, but when it comes to all of that I can't help getting pretty enthusiastic!"

Gary Manning, 60 Hope Street, Liverpool **203**

Pea Whack Soup

SERVES 4-6

1 ham hock
2lts water
1 whole head celery
2 medium leeks
500g carrots
500g red lentils
Large sprig thyme
3 bay leaves
6 whole black peppercorns

1 In a large saucepan place water, herbs, ham hock and peppercorns. **2** Bring to the boil and simmer for approximately 2 hours – skimming if necessary. When the ham begins to fall away from the bone it is cooked, remove and put to one side. **3** Add the lentils and all remaining ingredients to the pan and bring to the boil. Then lower the heat so that the mixture is just simmering (just below boiling) for about 1 hour until the lentils and vegetables are cooked. **4** Crush the lentils and vegetables with the end of a rolling pin in the pan, being careful not to get splashed. **5** Flake the cooked ham hock into the soup, then taste and season as required.

Serve with crusty bread and butter.

Seared Treacle Beef with Sweet and Sour Carrot Salad

SERVES 4-6

For the Beef
1 kg rump of Cumbrian beef, trimmed and cut into a rectangle
1 x 250g tin treacle
1lt water
1 red chilli, roughly chopped
125g grated fresh ginger
6 star anise
2 cinnamon sticks
Olive oil
Salt and pepper

Beef 1 Bring water to the boil, add treacle and mix well. 2 Return to the boil, turn off and add the spices, then leave to cool. 3 Once cold place beef in the mix and submerge – seal and cover and place in the fridge for 1 week. 4 Remove and drain liquid – the beef will look like leather. 5 In a large sauté pan heat a little olive oil on a medium heat. Seal beef off (brown) on all sides for approximately 5 minutes on each side – keeping it rare. 6 Leave to cool and rest. 7 To serve cut into very thin slices – carpaccio style.

For the Carrot Salad
500g carrots cut into very thin strips (julienne)
100ml white wine vinegar
Brown sugar to taste
4 cardamom pods, crushed
Olive oil
Sea salt

To Serve
Shavings of Croglin Cheese or pecorino

Carrot Salad 1 In a saucepan, gently heat the white wine vinegar, add the crushed cardamom pods and infuse. 2 Add carrots, stirring all the time to coat with the mixture, not to cook them. Carrots should still have crunch – al dente. 3 Add a tablespoon of brown sugar to the carrots, taste and add a little more if required. 4 Drain the carrots, season and chill before serving.

To Serve Arrange slightly overlapping slices of beef in a ring on the plate. Fill the central space with some of the chilled carrot salad and top with a scattering of cheese shavings.

Liverpool Tart

SERVES 4-6

For the Pastry
500g plain flour
250g butter, diced
150g icing sugar, sieved
4 egg yolks
100ml water

Pastry ☐1 Rub diced butter, flour, and sugar together using fingertips, add the egg yolks and enough water as needed to bring the mixture together to form a dough. ☐2 Cut the dough into 2 even pieces, wrap in cling film and leave the dough to rest, ideally for up to 8 hours in the fridge or for 1 hour in the freezer. ☐3 Take one of the pieces and roll on a floured board to fit a 25cm tart tin. The remaining dough can be put in the freezer and used at a later date. ☐4 Line the tin with the pastry and bake blind by placing scrunched baking parchment over the pastry and placing baking beans on top. ☐5 Bake for 20 minutes in a pre-heated oven 150°C / gas mark 2. ☐6 Remove paper and beans and allow to cool.

For the Filling
6 eggs
60g dark Muscovado sugar
1 lemon – juice and zest
200g Brioche breadcrumbs
Golden syrup a generous amount

Filling ☐1 Whisk the eggs and sugar to sabayon (just leaves a trail from the whisk) then add lemon zest and juice. ☐2 Fold in the breadcrumbs. ☐3 Pour the mixture into the cooked pastry cake. ☐4 Cook in a pre-heated oven at 180°C / gas mark 4 for approximately 15 minutes – until firm to the touch. ☐5 Once cooked brush the top with hot golden syrup, repeat this process twice.

For the Ice Cream
6 egg yolks
300ml cream
300ml milk
300g Halewood honey

Ice Cream ☐1 In a saucepan heat cream until boiling. ☐2 Remove from heat and pour over the eggs and honey whisking well. ☐3 Return to the heat and cook until the mixture coats the back of a spoon. ☐4 Pour into a bowl to cool and add the milk. ☐5 Mix well and place in ice cream maker, or freeze in a flat dish stirring every 30 minutes to keep the ice crystals small and the ice cream smooth.

Paul Hevey and Dan Weston
Lakes Speciality Foods
Cumbria

PAUL HEVEY AND DAN WESTON ARE HIGH CLASS BUTCHERS to the catering trade – with a modicum of retail on the side. These are the men who find the farms, who compute the costs, who cut the cuts, who work out the mind-numbing nitty-gritty of product-flow, so restaurants don't have to. Their calling is indispensable to the hospitality industry. It ensures that chefs can get the top quality meat they want at one end of the supply chain, and specialist livestock farmers can stay in business at the other. Doesn't sound like the kind of undertaking you can get all fired up about? Don't you believe it.

Enter the premises of Lakes Speciality Foods in the idyllic Cumbrian village of Staveley and you'll encounter professional fervour second to none. On the ground floor, in the clinically clean environment of the meat-cutting plant, a squad of men, smartly attired in claret coats, white caps and red-and-white striped butchers' aprons, are chopping, boning and trimming with deft strokes and practised precision. Upstairs, in the office, they're taking orders: two men, two women, glued to their phones, stock strands of conversation merging and diverging:

'… so you want loin chops, pork loin steaks. Loin steaks at four fifty. Okay boss. Lamb chops? Right. Take care, bye, bye.'

'… no sir, I'm sorry, Kendal Rough Fell lamb is only available between November and May …'

'… racks of lamb, mmm. Gammon steaks, pork fillets, yeh. Strip loins, braising steak pieces, two cases of our Cumberland sausage. Yes sir. I'll tell you what I'll do, I'll send you the whole lot tomorrow and invoice it for Wednesday …'

Between fielding calls, Paul and Dan, the company directors, take it in turns to talk about their business, dovetailing into duologue when the phone traffic subsides, and finishing one another's sentences like a happily married couple. They are a contrasting pair: Paul is fair, slim; exuberant, effervescing with ideas; Dan is dark, more heavily-built; relaxed, equable, analytical. 'There's one or two similarities, but not many', says Dan. 'We're quite opposite really, aren't we?'

'Age, I'd say Dan', quips Paul with a mischievous twinkle.

'Yeh, he's older than I am. He thinks he looks younger.'

'Dan is my rock!'

'Paul's like a spaniel, I'm like a labrador. He's very, very fast and moving quickly all the time, whereas I'm more coming along steady behind. We sort of bash ideas off one another. It's fun.'

Paul agrees. He launched the company in May 2004 and Dan joined him in October 2005. They come from opposite ends of England and from different working backgrounds, but as business partners they're a perfect match.

Paul is Staveley born and bred. You can hear it in his drawn-out Cumbrian vowels, his detailed knowledge of the surrounding country, the way obscure local place-names trip off his tongue. He started in the meat business as a butcher's boy at the age of fourteen, set up on his own in due course, and in one shape or form he's been in butchery nigh on thirty years.

Not so Dan. 'If I cut meat we lose customers', he chortles. He's a Devon man from a farming background, a chartered surveyor by trade. 'I was on the building side, involved in abattoirs, and then I went into the meat industry. I've worked for most of the big boys, like MacDonald's, Waitrose, Tesco, all the big buying abattoirs. But I came to a point in my life where I started asking myself: why am I earning my money here and spending it over there? I don't believe you can be poacher and gamekeeper at the same time, so I decided to join Paul. We knew each other, we'd shared ideas before, and the thought came: why not work together?'

Since then their complementary skills have taken them from strength to strength. Dan's very keen on production protocols and producing the meat. Paul's very good on the butchery side and selling it. They specialise in what's local and seasonal, with a distinct penchant for naturally reared, native British breeds like Swaledale sheep, Saddleback pigs and Galloway cattle.

'But just because it's local doesn't mean it's good', Dan warns. 'You want the quality to be right first. So we set our own specifications to start off with: breed, age, growth-rate, weight, size, type of fat cover, where it's grown –'

'– and then we work closely with the farmers to help them achieve it', adds Paul. 'Together we're all supplying the catering trade, prestigious establishments, and they require products that are consistent in quality and uniform in shape and size.'

The next step in their strategy is to link the parties at each end of the supply chain. Lakes do a lot of farm tours with chefs, and with catering students who will be the next generation of chefs. They believe strongly in the value of having front of house staff along too, so they can talk knowledgeably to diners about meat on the menu. Dan: 'We look at live animals, showing them how to judge quality. Then we look at carcasses hanging, and in the cutting plant, and explain the difference between high quality meat and poor quality meat. There's a massive learning curve out there, and I think that sharing knowledge up and down the supply chain, and with the public at large, is very important.'

By looking at the meat, their visitors also learn how to tell what cattle have been eating, which is important, not only from a health point of view (ours and the animals') but for flavour too. Dan explains: 'A carotene diet – grass, silage, hay – is forage-based and forage makes yellow fat. If an animal is fed on an ad lib diet of cereals and straw, it has very white fat. You can see it quite distinctively. Now, we don't want that, so we don't buy bull meat or white-fatted beef. We buy steers and heifers, slower grown, traditionally reared.'

Not every animal comes off the fells of Cumbria. They tell you straight that they'll go to the rest of the Northwest and beyond for the right product. But they buy only British beef and lamb: reared, slaughtered and boned in the United Kingdom. 'Most of the catering industry in the UK is driven by foreign meats', Dan points out, 'because it's very price-sensitive.' In fact, according figures published by the former Meat and Livestock Commission, a whacking 60% of meat served in restaurants, cafés, pubs and fast-food outlets in the United Kingdom comes from overseas. 'If someone's selling steak and chips for £4.99, it ain't British!' says Dan.

Paul swivels away from his desk: 'We don't buy imported', he states crisply. 'We made that decision as a company. There's two types of supplier out there: a local meat supplier or a supplier of local meat.' He adds tellingly: 'You can slice Danish bacon in the UK and call it British sliced bacon. We could supply a pub down the road with Argentinian strip loin and they could describe it quite legally on the menu as 'locally sourced'. We could, but we don't. It's hard fighting with one hand tied behind your back, but we're keen on where meat comes from. Traceability is big with us.'

The complicated and confusing field of food labelling exercises the passions of these men. It's little wonder. To date there is no legal definition of 'local' and no clear, straightforward way for the consumer to judge the quality, age, or provenance of meat from the words on a supermarket packet, or the description on many a menu. Yet consultations by the Food Standards Agency have repeatedly shown that consumers want transparency on the origin of food – particularly meat.

When it comes to judging quality, probably most of us, including chefs, don't know what first-rate meat should look, taste or feel like, because we have never been taught about it and rarely, if ever, seen or eaten it. And what we've never had, we're never likely to miss. On that premise approximations of the 'real' thing flourish freely. It's a bit like stolen identity perpetrated on food.

'Bear in mind', says Dan, 'that most chefs aren't like Gary at 60 Hope Street, and before they have understood about types and cuts of meat, or seasonality and locality, they've probably rung up 3663 and cases of something you can get 365 days of the year will be delivered by 10 o'clock the next morning.' He's referring to Britain's largest foodservice company (the numbers spell out 'FOOD' on the phone-pad), which supplies the country's commercial kitchens with a vast range of products, some fresh, most frozen or pre-prepared. These even include an extensive range of heat-and-serve ready-meals, from low-budget lasagne to luxury lamb confit, plus starters and desserts, which make it possible for a chef to function without ever cooking anything from scratch at all.

Dan would like to see a greater appreciation of seasonal food, with more of us enjoying the pleasures of 'eating our way round the calendar', as he puts it. 'Supermarkets are fantastically successful businesses, bringing us a huge variety of produce from all round the world, all through the year. But I think sometimes they're wrong. Sometimes they should be saying no – no, you can't have strawberries at Christmas because they're out of season and they'll be pretty tasteless. Try these apples that we've stored from the autumn harvest instead.'

Lakes aren't afraid to tell their customers no. They see it as a positive response, because they plan carefully to ensure there's always a tip-top, in-season alternative. Take lamb for instance. Paul has created a 'lamb calendar' for the whole of Cumbria, going from flocks at sea level to those on the high fells. 'Down here', he explains, pointing to the south east of the county on the map behind his desk, 'they'll be lambing early, and as you go up the hills the lambing season gets later. That gives us a year-round supply, moving with the grass and with the farms. That way we're not just getting lamb, but lamb at its very best.'

Dan takes up the story: 'This year, we've been on lambs from Crooklands, just south of Kendal; on salt marsh lamb from around the coastline; then our flocks round here, then Kendal Rough Fell, on to winter Swaledales between December and March – and then the cycle starts again. We believe in a sustainable supply chain and we've built up a helluva database to give us that. Whereas a supermarket might buy 1,600 sheep to get the 1,000 that meet their needs, we've gone out actively to the farmers, brought them in here and explained our

requirements. So we can take out all that wastage that Mr Supermarket gets – wrong size, wrong weight, too fat, too thin – and get exactly what the chefs want and exactly what we want to cut.

'We like our lambs to be 42 kilos live weight. So we make sure every farmer has a set of scales – if you can't measure it, you can't manage it! The farmer will ring when he has twenty or so lambs ready, all weighing between 42 and 44 kilos. If he tells us he has some more at 40 kilos, we know they will be ready the following week, because they put on about 300–400 grams a day maximum. Whereas, if you went to market and bought a batch, they might *average* 42 kilos, but individually they might go from forty to fifty. That means you'd get massive saddles off some, little ones off the others, and so on with the other cuts. That doesn't give our man in the restaurant the consistency of cut or portion control that he needs.'

Good relationships with farmers matter to them. Sometimes it hits them in the pocket. That's because the meat market is very volatile and, although downward price-swings are rarely reflected in the supermarket chill cabinet, they frequently put farmers out of business, especially the small, local kind that Lakes tend to work with. But even in the face of a collapsed market, Paul and Dan have maintained their price because they know that a farmer who is raising slow-grown lambs is highly vulnerable, and they value his product. This way they ensure that both parties are there for each other – and us – in the following year.

"When farmers who sell us their lambs say they'd like to do a bit of retailing on their own account, Paul will tell them how much to charge, how much it will cost to cut and so on."

Other times, a bit of advice is all it takes. One chap was running all his lambs together when they first started with him, until Paul pointed out that his single lambs would grow faster than his twins and triplets because they were getting more milk off mum. Now they're kept on different parts of the hillside – we can see them from the office window. 'The farmer hasn't got to disturb them or stress them by moving them about – he can just go straight to the batch that's ready', Paul explains. 'He's improved his efficiency by talking to us and we've improved ours by being supplied by him.'

'One of the things that amazed me about Paul when I first met him was his encouragement for others', says Dan. 'When farmers who sell us their lambs say they'd like to do a bit of retailing on their own account, Paul will tell them how much to charge, how much it will cost to cut and so on.'

'There's plenty of trade for those who are doing it correctly', comments Paul, 'because there's norra 'nough of the proper stock to go round anyway.'

However, to succeed in this business you must secure markets for *all* the meat from a carcass – not just the prime cuts – before you can move on. With lamb that's not too problematic and, with pork in particular, you've got the sausage trade. Lakes make their own gold medal winning range – from old favourites like Cumberland (of course) to the pork and black pudding variety that saw Paul crowned National Sausage Week champion in 2007. Beef gives them the most headaches. There's such a lot of meat to sell on a big body of beef: the forequarters, where most of the cheaper, stewing and braising cuts come from; the hindquarters where most roasting joints and steaks come from. In weight, both are fairly similar but in monetary worth there's a big discrepancy.

'Beef has been the downfall of many a business', says Paul. 'You're looking at an initial outlay of £700-£800 per carcass.' Then there's hanging to develop tenderness and flavour.

'Do people truly understand what hanging beef for five weeks actually does to finances? Say you hung twenty bodies of beef for five weeks and you wanted to guarantee a five-week turnover. If a body of beef costs £700, that's £14,000 you've shelled out in week one. You've got these twenty bodies of beef hanging and, remember, you've got to take them up to week five before you can sell them, so you've got to have five lots of twenty before you can sell one. That's £70,000 hanging in the fridge. It's a lot easier to hang fifty lambs for two weeks!'

Most meat in the commercial market is not hung, mainly due to cost and capacity. Dan provides another example. 'Suppose a restaurant wants a beef carcass weighing 300 kilos hung for three weeks. You might find that, twenty-one days later, you've lost seven to eight per cent of the carcass weight – just evaporated in what they call drip-loss and shrinkage.

'So when people talk about receiving a premium for their three-week hung beef – well, they bloody well need it, compared to your fresh beef which will be perhaps four to six days of age from a supermarket or butcher. That will be good quality meat, but it won't be in the same league as three-to-five-week hung beef. It's not the loss in weight that makes the price difference, it's the cost of running the chiller and the space the carcass takes up in it. If it's a rib of beef hanging up, there's about three foot of air above and three below. That means one piece of beef is taking up a whole seven foot of space. So it's quite an expensive exercise.'

Fortunately, Lakes has Paul's wife, Kirsten, looking after the money side of things – and keeping them both on their toes. But buying the best is what they're sticking to. Dan sums it up: 'As an old butcher told me once, the sweetness of a cheap price never makes up for the bitterness of poor quality. Come and meet one of our suppliers. His name's Bob Day and he produces some of the best beef going.'

Bob Day
High Chapel Farm
Cumbria

THEY LIFT THEIR HEADS AND LOOK AT US WITH INTEREST and inquiry. There are six of them, dark-bodied in an isolated grove of oaks, where they have come for coolness on this sun-drenched afternoon, the last of July. We draw closer. They stand their ground sturdily; assess us steadily with long-lashed eyes of velvet brown. Then with a few flicks of their bear-like ears, these furry, curly-coated cattle resume their grazing. It could be a painting by Stubbs.

In fact, these engaging beasts belong to a herd of Galloways and Blue Greys that Bob Day is rearing on eight hundred acres of majestic Lakeland country not far from Shap Summit. At present we are standing on the crest of a hill, roughly midway between the picturesque villages of Orton and Tebay. A protective windbreak of conifers lies to the north. Beyond, the long, gentle swell of blue-green fells enfolds the horizon. Where our vantage ground sweeps down to the south, we can see the weathered grey stone of High Chapel Farm, Bob's home, nestling in a sheltered dell. It's a canny spot, well chosen by the folk who built his house 200 years ago, and as neat and trim today, with its new barns and sheds, as ever it was in the past.

'Aye, you can't work in a better environment', remarks Bob softly, smiling his calm, ready smile as he surveys the glorious landscape and takes a deep draft of the grass-scented air. He begins pointing out some features of the fells and, as soon as you hear the rising lilt of his accent, you know he's that rarity among Cumbrian farmers: a man from somewhere else. He was raised on a hill farm in Teesdale, County Durham – in Mickleton where his dad lives still. It is barely thirty miles away yet, in many ways, another country. He came here, fresh out of Newton Rigg agricultural college in 1985, as a shepherd, intending to stay just a couple of years. He never left.

In the intervening period the farm has grown and now Bob is manager. It's the unflagging interest of the work that's held him, for which he thanks High Chapel's owner, John Dunning, a man whose entrepreneurial flair has made him a bit of a legend in these parts.

To sketch in some background: when the M6 motorway was scheduled to cut through their farm, the Dunning family responded by bidding to run a service station right there, on the affected land. It opened in 1972, the only one in England to be built and operated by a small, locally-owned company. The family business, Westmorland Limited, has since added other ventures to its portfolio, including an hotel and Rheged Discovery Centre near Penrith. But perhaps the most ingenious Dunning brainwave of recent years was to bolt a couple of classy farmshops onto their already startlingly good motorway service stations at Tebay Northbound and Tebay Southbound – yes, farmshops at motorway service stations! Ironically, it was compensation following the 2001 foot and mouth crisis that helped pay for them, because although High Chapel was free of the disease, it was contiguous to infection and culled out just the same.

Since they opened in 2003, the farmshops have been nationally lauded and awarded – the fine quality and range of food could give Fortnum's a run for its money. Bob supplies to these and other Westmorland enterprises, not only beef from the Galloways but also lamb from High Chapel's flock of 1,450 ewes. He supplies local butchers, pubs as well: 'Selling direct to customers is what we like doing', he says, 'because you can see where your end product is going and it's nice to hear the positive feedback, particularly with these Galloways.' Being a forward-thinker, Bob is always on the look-out for good outlets for his products. That's how he happens to be a supplier of Lakes Speciality Foods and – for chefs like Gary Manning and his staff who come to gain a deeper understanding of the meat they're serving – a bit of an educational resource to boot.

It was in 2001 that Bob started keeping Galloways, switching to them from the larger, faster-growing continental cross cattle that have been so popular in Britain for the last fifty years. So why did he make the change? What's their big attraction? And why can't top chefs get enough of them?

To begin at the beginning: Galloways are one of our oldest native breeds, so old that no-one knows quite when they first appeared. We do know where though – not far from here, in fact – just across the Solway Firth, in Galloway, south east Scotland. You might say the hillside is their natural habitat. Hardy and robust, they thrive outdoors in rugged terrain – and rugged weather – purely on grass and what they can forage. That makes them ideal for exposed hill farms like Bob's where the land, however beautiful, is officially designated 'disadvantaged.' 'They make very good use of very poor quality vegetation', Bob explains, 'and you'll see them grazing whether it's raining or blowing, they're not fazed by any sort of weather at all.'

Nor is it excessive fat which gives them insulation against the elements – it's that shaggy coat, second only to the buffalo's in density. Even so, because the climate is very wet at High Chapel, Bob brings his cattle indoors about Christmas-time, feeding them on simple grass silage. Last year, though, he left almost half his yearlings out – with interesting results. 'We have a really good cattle shed and you would say that those inside it had a better environment, better rations, better care – but those outside wintered better! By spring they looked fantastic. They just like being outside.'

The Galloways' special magic is the way they convert a natural grass diet into high quality beef. Unlike big breeds, they have no need of concentrated commercial feed or grain, high in price, high in energy-costs and hard on the

planet. As Dan says: 'You can't grow cereals up here so why keep cattle that need it?' These smaller, native breeds are economical and sustainable to farm. Also, because they are slower maturing, and because their meat has a choice marbling of fat, the beef has a remarkable richness of texture and flavour. As early as the sixteenth century it was famed as 'flesh right tender and delicious'. Today, chefs prize it for the same reason.

And the Blue Greys? Where do they fit in? They are the result of a 19th century cross between Galloway cows and a Whitebred Shorthorn bull (another native breed and a rare one too). Sharing most of their pure-bred 'Scottish' cousins' characteristics, they even look like them in shape and size, and in being naturally polled or hornless. Where they differ is in colour. While Galloways may be black, dun or red, – or even sporting a bizarre white band around the middle if they're Belted Galloways – the Blue Greys are as their name suggests, dappled roans, resplendent in steely blue chiaroscuro. They are increasingly popular for conservation grazing, and particularly on hill farms like this, where all the land is in one Environmental Stewardship Scheme or another.

'Both breeds are good to deal with', says Bob appreciatively. 'The Blue Greys

Bob Day, High Chapel Farm. Gary Manning's supplier 221

are very placid. The Galloways are known for being a bit highly strung, but we find them no problem at all. The only downside that you have with these is, if you go round their back end, and they know you're in range, you'll get a kick every time!' He laughs. 'It's just a breed trait. Other than that they're grand.'

But is there a difference in the beef produced by these two breeds? Bob turns to Dan: 'Can you tell, Dan, which is which when a Galloway carcass is hung up next to a Blue Grey?'

'No sir!'

'And does it cut any different Dan?'

'No sir! If anything I'd say the Blue Grey actually has a better confirmation than the Galloway. See that one, walking down there …'

And they fall to discussing the finer points of individual animals: which has more rounding at its back end, which will yield more meat, which will be better in the primary cuts. There are about 200 beasts of different ages in the herd at its annual peak. When the time comes for slaughter which, post-BSE, is just before each one reaches thirty months, they go to the abattoir at nearby Hawes. Bob takes them himself, four or five a week. 'You've to go carefully with livestock in the back', he warns, 'you don't want to bump and bang them about, and round here the roads are murderous, especially in the wet.' He appreciates the importance of minimising stress, not only because stressed animals produce tough meat lacking in flavour, not only because of the pride he takes in managing his livestock, but also out of innate respect for each and every beast. 'You need to understand them', he says firmly, 'and treat them accordingly.'

> "Selling direct to customers is what we like doing, because you can see where your end product is going and it's nice to hear the positive feedback, particularly with these Galloways."

There's something we all need to understand about these fine animals, as more of us discover this beef and demand continues to rise. Like almost everything else that's worth eating, they are seasonal and we must pay our dues to nature accordingly. Bob spells it out: 'The most difficult thing about farming these cattle is that people do want them twelve months of the year. But they're a seasonal animal. They grow like blazes in spring, when the days start to lengthen, and then they do fantastically well from about July to September. They have these little growing spurts, and then they do nothing.' It's not a matter of food either: increase the amount or the richness and they'll get fat – but stay small, because they're storing energy to see them through the winter. 'You've just to work with the animal', says Bob simply, 'and accept they're not going to do much at that time.'

222

Bob's talent for livestock is something he's passed on to the younger of his two daughters, Jane, who's come to get him in for tea. At ten and twelve both his girls are pretty handy round the place, although they don't get to do much farming – it's a bit of a health and safety nightmare. But last lambing time he found Jane with nine sheep lambed down and her strategy for managing them all worked out too. 'She's superb, a brilliant aptitude for stock', he says. 'I think you're born with it.'

He hopes she will work in something to do with livestock but he doesn't want her to be a farmer – too hard. Dan and Bob debate some of the calling's perennial problems, as Jane reels her dad in. 'If only farmers would work together', sighs Bob, listing the savings co-operation could bring, 'but famers are individualists …'

'Ah well', says Dan, 'as an old fella said to me years ago, if you want to get three farmers together, you have to shoot two!' At the astute insight of this mischievous remark, difficulties dissolve into laughter. We go our separate ways. The cattle have moved on to pastures new. Perhaps they've found a cooling beck to plodge through.

Bob Day, High Chapel Farm. Gary Manning's supplier 223

Robbie Woods
Halewood Honey
Merseyside

BARELY TWENTY MINUTES DRIVE south from Liverpool's teeming city centre, sheep graze the fields and apples, pears and plums weigh down the orchard boughs. This is Yew Tree Farm, in Halewood Village, where chef Gary Manning came across the honey for his ice cream. It's one of a wide range of local products, which farmers Ann and Graham Lund sell in their nicely converted 17th century hay barn. But they don't make the honey. That's in someone else's hands.

On a nearby smallholding, Robbie Woods tends his gently humming hives, a dozen of them, sheltered by oak, elder and dog-rose. Bees have always fascinated him, but ten years ago he went on a course, took the plunge and started keeping them. 'Bees have been around far longer than us, more than 150 million years', he observes, 'and have the perfect, symbiotic relationship with nature.

'They're fascinating just to watch, and then there's the honey they make. It's an incorruptible product – even after two thousand years, it would still be edible.' Evidence comes from an excavation among the temples of ancient Paestum, in southern Italy. In 1954 archaeologists found eight magnificent bronze vessels, dating from around 500 BC. They were filled to the brim. A taste revealed the contents to be honey.

Down the millennia, mankind has valued this golden gift of nature as sweetener, energy-provider, preservative, versatile cooking ingredient and health-giver. But today, its manufacturers – honeybees – are struggling against very serious threats to their own health. In addition to pesticides and habitat destruction, they are now under attack from the varroa mite, which can wipe out whole colonies. It arrived in Britain from the USA in 1992 and now has global reach. According to the UK's National Bee Unit, set up to protect our honeybees, British beekeepers lost 14% of their colonies in 2007. Now a deadlier syndrome has appeared. As yet little understood, and simply named Colony Collapse Disorder, it has been identified in the USA and Europe but not, so far, in Britain.

The British Beekeepers Association (BBKA) and the Government are deeply concerned, because without bees, not only would honey disappear, but perhaps a third of all our food, since it is largely dependent on bees for pollination. To a great extent, the nation relies on people like Robbie to save our honeybees. Wild colonies are virtually non-existent and nearly 90% of all others are kept by small-scale, part-time enthusiasts like him. As Defra figures show, there are some 44,000

beekeepers in the UK maintaining some 274,000 colonies. Of these around only 300 are commercial bee farmers, keeping just 40,000 colonies.

A hive will produce from 25lbs to 60lbs of honey, in excess of the bees' own needs to feed the colony. The only treatment needed is to filter the honey to remove any wax debris that has come away from the comb during the extraction process. There are no additives.

Honey flavour is deliciously variable, depending on the flowers the bees visit. Since bees fly within a four-mile radius of their hive (and few go that far) this factor can be simply monitored or strictly controlled. A mix of different blooms will tend to produce a light, delicate flavour, as will a single crop of lavender or borage. These honeys are good to use with salads, cooked fruit and desserts. Stronger, darker honeys, such as heather and chestnut are better for more robust dishes.

People often wonder why some honey is clear and runny, some opaque and set. Once again, the answer is in the flowers. Garden flowers, for example, tend to produce the first kind; bright yellow oil seed rape (to which bees are very partial) the latter. Some clear honey will set naturally in the jar after a few weeks and all will crystallize eventually. But as Robbie points out, it hasn't 'gone off', and if you want it to be runny again, just warm it up gently.

World wide production can't keep up with the demand for honey and, to make matters worse, in 2007, Britain's rain-soaked summer prevented bees from foraging and resulted in a disappointingly poor honey harvest. Nevertheless, more people are keeping bees and membership of the BBKA has shot up by nearly a third in recent years. As for Robbie, 'I don't think I will ever give up keeping bees', he says. 'It gets into your blood.'

Robbie Woods, Halewood Honey. Gary Manning's supplier 227

Simon Radley

The Arkle Restaurant

The Chester Grosvenor and Spa
Cheshire

TO STEP INTO THE CHESTER GROSVENOR is to step into undiluted luxury. There can be no doubt: from the moment you walk through its enfilade of Corinthian columns and cross its chequered marble pavement; from the moment a doorman, impeccable in frock coat and cockaded tophat, ushers you into the lustrous, mahogany-panelled foyer. Built in 1865 in the very centre of the city by the Grosvenor family, and owned by them ever since, this internationally renowned five-star hotel is currently in the hands of the 6th Duke of Westminster. Naturally, there is a gourmet restaurant – the Arkle. Naturally, it has a Michelin star – retained for the eighteenth consecutive year by Executive Chef, Simon Radley. His exquisite dishes change with the seasons and use the finest produce in what seems like an infinity of innovative ways. They are served by the most accomplished of staff in a dining room of serenity and grace. Its style is modern neo-classical, complemented by the angular elegance of chairs in the style of Charles Rennie Macintosh. Portraits of Arkle, the greatest steeplechaser of all time, adorn the walls. The décor subtly blends yellow, black and gold, the racing colours of Arkle's owner, the late Anne, Duchess of Westminster. Behind the scenes, Simon Radley's intense and productive energy is at work. Always there is a fresh project, a new challenge he has set himself, something to be created, something to be sourced. His words pour out at the speed of a Superpendolino. It is difficult to imagine him wasting a moment.

"THERE IS SUCH AN ETHOS OF EXCELLENCE AT THE CHESTER GROSVENOR, so many different styles of cooking required in so many different settings, and so much freedom to express yourself, that it's a real privilege to work here. We have the Arkle restaurant, we have the hundred-seater La Brasserie, we have The Library lounge for coffee, afternoon tea and light meals, as well as a

great variety of private dining in the function suites upstairs. There's always such a lot going on that it can never, ever, be boring.

I first came here as chef de partie in 1986, when I was 21. Less than a year later, the hotel closed for major refurbishment and I went on secondment for twelve months, working with Paul Gayler at the former Inigo Jones restaurant in London's Covent Garden. That experience was very influential. I think it was the start of my real interest in food.

When I was at school, I didn't know what I wanted to do. I'd always been interested in food but never with a view to taking it up as a living.

I was born in Manchester. However, because my father's job took us to the south of England, I grew up at Tring, in Hertfordshire. It was when we moved north again, this time to Congleton in Cheshire, that I decided on a fresh start and I decided that fresh start would be cookery. It took me to college in Crewe where I did a catering course.

Funnily enough, I started off as a waiter. I went to France, and it was while I was there – working as a waiter – that I realised I was far more interested in making food than serving it. As soon as I returned home to Cheshire, I got a job as a commis chef at the Belfry in Handforth, before moving to The Chester Grosvenor.

That's how it all began. Then, after my stint in London, I came back to The Chester Grosvenor in 1988, to the Arkle, my own brigade and a fairly free hand to experiment with the food – just as long as I was successful. I was 23 at the time, so it was a wonderful opportunity to have at that stage in my career. Fortunately, we were successful and the Arkle was awarded a Michelin star in 1990. The following year I found myself on the other side of the globe, spending some time as The Chester Grosvenor's ambassador at two of the best hotels in the world – the Peninsula in Hong Kong and the Oriental Bangkok.

After six and a half years as head chef at The Grosvenor, I felt it was time for a move, time to widen my experience. In 1994, I went to another Small Luxury Hotel, New Hall in Sutton Coldfield, where I was executive chef. Soon, a development of a different kind brought me back to Cheshire – I got married. My wife, Joanne, comes from Wrexham, just twelve miles from here in North Wales, and we wanted to be in this part of the country. First I moved to Nunsmere Hall at Oakmere, then I returned to The Chester Grosvenor in 1998.

The fact that the Arkle restaurant has retained its Michelin star every year since first achieving it, is a great testament to the quality of what is done here, both by the excellent brigade we have in the kitchen and the exceptional team in the dining room. Anyone who has held a Michelin star knows exactly how tough it is to maintain the high standards needed. Without doubt, it is a great system to show how quality restaurants measure up to one another. However, the star should not be your main driver: you must never forget that the most important thing is the excellence of the food. Your goal must be to create great dishes. It's about always working to high standards – and making sure you reach them – while continually raising your sights and those of your staff to get the very best result.

Given those provisos, you are free to express your culinary self in any shape or form at the Arkle – not something people are going to be able to do in many other places.

We are constantly developing new dishes, new sensations of taste and texture, new flavours. Inspiration comes from all sorts of sources and we run ideas across one another in the kitchen all the time. For example, one day, we were talking about watercress while we were doing a dish with crayfish and we came up with a new composition involving two snails, two crayfish tails, two deboned frogs' legs and aerated watercress. This dish is so dainty in its execution! Anyway, someone made the throwaway comment 'pond life' – but I didn't throw it away. Although it's not strictly accurate, the name Pond Life stuck and it turned out to be a very popular starter, as well as adding a touch of humour to the menu.

In some ways, I can be quite pig-headed about dishes – if I think it goes, it goes. But don't get me wrong. I listen to customers' comments and I ask them what they think. It is important to experience the dish from the customer's point of view. You get blinkered sometimes – because you're fixated on the taste you can let presentation go by the board. Once we served a dish in what was basically a glass jar. Customers didn't know how to approach it – should they empty it out onto the plate or should they eat it straight from the jar? It's no good coming up with imaginative

Simon Radley, The Arkle Restaurant, Chester 231

ideas if you end up confusing people. We altered our service accordingly.

Presentation is a very important factor, even more so today than in the recent past. Fifteen years ago you would have had just one dinner service in a hotel. Now we have a choice of fifteen or twenty different styles of plate here. So, immediately, you are thinking about presentation when you create a dish. How is that going to look on black granite? How would it look on glass?

If presentation is the finishing point for any dish, the starting point must always be selecting ingredients of the finest quality. Our menu changes seasonally, with the emphasis on using the very best fresh local produce. Consequently, we are always looking to form partnerships with producers in the area – but they have to meet our strict standards and the five-star ethos we have here. They must be consistent too. After all local, of itself, doesn't necessarily mean better. That said, nine out of ten products are great.

We take quite a lot from Lancashire, also from North Wales and Cheshire, and we get the pick of the crop. Paul Heathcote and Nigel Haworth have done a lot for Lancashire produce. It's their input that has helped the producers get their heads round the commercial side of it.

We're getting there in Cheshire too – catching up fast now. Recently, I did a 'grand tour' of the Cholmondeley Food Hub which is made up of farms surrounding the Cholmondeley Estate, about twelve miles from here in south Cheshire. It was a pleasure to see grass, with herbs growing in it, free of pesticides and fertilizers; sheep and cattle growing naturally to maturity – and that's what you want. Watching Gloucester Old Spot pigs foraging in woodland, you immediately start thinking that this should be on the menu – you have a mental picture of what you're getting.

But, it's not just a case of showing you round the land and showing you the animals, of course. You can talk about all of that, quite literally, till the cows come home. Produce is not enough. It's about getting it out there in the marketplace and getting it to you. It's no good if you phone up and you have a hard time trying to get the product. The middleman, the guy who's going to get it to your door, has a crucial role to play. If someone contacts me and tells me about a product – and it's top quality – I'm your man, but I need service! The effort there needs to come not from the chefs but from the other side. Chefs should be in the kitchen cooking.

A good example of a supplier who understands all of that, and delivers on it, is Pugh's Piglets. I've used them for years and they're really on the ball, bang on the mark, every time. Fortunately, pig usually features quite heavily on our menu. We use their suckling pigs and their porchetta joints. Lancashire is where their business is based, but they source from farms in neighbouring counties too. In fact it was a farm in Cheshire, near Tarporley, that raised the suckling pig which Pugh's Piglets supplied for my main course in this book.

Quality is all about discipline, and producers have to have the discipline. Take a recent case of a guy phoning me up about asparagus. The first thing he tells me is how expensive it is. What is the point of that? High cost is not necessarily an indicator

of quality and it certainly doesn't impress me. Anyway, he sends it in and the heads have all gone to flower. It's rubbish. An obvious example of what not to do.

Despite that type of bad experience, it has to be said there is some fantastic stuff out there and some fantastic people supplying it who really care about quality in every aspect of their businesses. Bowland Forest Foods whose lamb we use, and some of their beef, are a really good case in point. They are a group of farmers who formed themselves into a co-operative to supply top quality, great-tasting, naturally reared meats direct to the customer.

The Duke of Westminster, who I'm lucky enough to work for, gave them a helping hand to get their wonderful products to the market place. They are actually based in the Home Farm Office on his Abbeystead Estate in the Forest of Bowland in Lancashire – which also happens to be somewhere we've had venison from.

Bowland Forest Foods have gone from strength to strength. They don't just stop at rearing the animals, they also make sure the meat is handed on to high quality butchers who are capable of preparing and packing the products to first-rate standards. It's food like that – which we've got coming in from all directions here – that is such a stimulus to inspiring ideas for dishes.

Simon Radley, The Arkle Restaurant, Chester 233

Being able to source ingredients and match them to other things on the menu is one of the joys of my job. I source the products for most of what is listed in the Arkle and La Brasserie, each of which has its own distinct style of cooking and set of menus. La Brasserie offers relaxed dining and an à la carte menu which is essentially classical French but with a lightness of touch and a mixture of other influences. Alongside it there is a light bites menu which includes a lot of items from our in-house bakery. We make everything ourselves – a selection of breads, biscuits and so on. Yes it's labour – you could say we make a rod for our own backs – but there's no choice in the matter if you want to offer the selection and the quality we do. We are very fortunate to have the facility.

In the Arkle, the style of cooking could be described as French-influenced modern British. It is a gourmet restaurant and treated as a separate entity when it comes to sourcing produce. Suppliers are handpicked for every product on the menu. I don't take the same products week-in, week-out. There's quite a bit of variation, especially with seasonality.

Catering for meetings and events is different again. We offer private dining for up to two hundred and fifty guests, in a variety of elegant rooms. Customers want bespoke menus and, of course, when events are booked as far ahead as many are, it is impossible to be spontaneously seasonal. What you can do, though, is inform them what's likely to be good and what's not.

So cooking at The Chester Grosvenor is really diverse. Every week is completely different. There are twenty-eight chefs and three mealtimes, seven days a week, with the same ethos and the same quality product throughout. To deliver that you've got to be a ball of energy. You've got to do tasks yourself in all parts of the kitchen in order to be able to get others to do them. And you need good, like-minded people around you.

Nothing pleases me more than bringing on a young person here and seeing them become my sous chef. We have an in-house training scheme called Total People and we get fantastic students on placement here too from Coleg Menai in North Wales. I believe in catching people young and keeping them interested. Let them go away and broaden their horizons, work in London, and then come back – you'll really benefit as a result. Here at The Grosvenor, though, they do have to be absolutely certain that working in a five-star establishment is what they want to do.

One thing I would like to see is more women coming into the industry. We have one female pastry chef and another who works part-time. I think the situation is improving and the greater interest in food that there is now is raising awareness generally.

There are still a lot of people who don't know where their meat comes from or how – or, indeed, where a great deal of their food comes from. There are a lot of worrying products out there, too – I still can't believe the amount of salt there is in some of them, ready meals, snacks, tinned food. I was shocked, horrified. But at least supermarkets and manufacturers are providing a lot more information about the contents of their products now. On the whole, I do see standards rising, across the board.

The Chester Grosvenor is continually evolving and advancing. That's an inspiration for the whole team. You need a new project all the time or else things get stale. We've just had a £3m refurbishment of our meeting and private dining facilities which has really stimulated ideas in the kitchen. My calendar is so full, it can be difficult to get out but I set targets and that helps. The more complicated the work gets, the more interesting it becomes. Bring it on! It's all changing for the better."

*The Arkle restaurant has now been sympathetically refurbished and renamed 'Simon Radley at The Chester Grosvenor' in honour of its highly respected Executive Chef.

Chilled Pumpkin Vichyssoise with Ravens Oak Kidderton Ash Goats Cheese

SERVES 4

1 small pumpkin
1 flowering courgette
300ml chicken / vegetable stock
1 clove garlic
3 shallots
2 sprigs thyme
Pumpkin seeds
Pumpkin seed oil
Kidderton Ash goats cheese to taste
100ml cream
30g butter
Chives, tarragon, watercress to taste
Olive oil

Pumpkin Vichyssoise [1] Peel and dice pumpkin, crush garlic and chop shallots. [2] In a thick bottomed pan, add a splash of olive oil to the butter and melt. Cook pumpkin, garlic and shallots slowly, without a lid, until all liquid has been evaporated, add thyme. [3] Half way through the cooking, moisten with small amounts of stock and season with salt and pepper. [4] When soft, add cream, then place in food processor, blitz until smooth. Pass through a fine sieve and check for consistency and seasoning. Chill.

Garnish Pick the chives, tarragon, and watercress, tear courgette flowers, slice courgette into wafers and cook in olive oil until soft, toast pumpkin seeds.

To Serve Pour vichyssoise into cold bowls, crumble goat's cheese to taste, arrange garnish. Drizzle with pumpkin oil and scatter with seeds.

Pugh's Cheshire Suckling Pig with Sticky Cheek and Piccalilli

SERVES 4

1 suckling pig
4 pork cheeks
Rosemary
Rock salt
4 large cloves garlic
500g peeled Cheshire new potatoes
150ml double cream
100g butter
1 carrot
Stick celery
2 shallots
4 bay leaves
4 sprigs thyme
200ml red wine
1 lt strong meat stock

For the Piccalilli
1 small cauliflower
2 shallots, chopped
$^1/_2$ cucumber, peeled and diced
150ml white wine vinegar
75ml malt vinegar
85g sugar
6g ground turmeric
8 button onions, peeled
English mustard
Cornflour
Red chilli, chopped
Salt

Piccalilli [1] The piccalilli should be made well in advance. [2] Salt florets of cauliflower, chopped shallots, peeled button onions and diced peeled cucumber and leave to draw in a colander for 1 hour. [3] Bring to the boil the 2 vinegars, sugar, turmeric, chopped chilli and English mustard to taste. Thicken with cornflour. [4] Wash salt off vegetables and add to thickened liquid. [5] Chill and reserve.

Suckling Pig [1] The night before rub suckling pig with rosemary, garlic and rock salt. [2] Place the pork cheeks under cold running water for 30 minutes. [3] Place carrot, celery, garlic, thyme and bay leaves in a thick bottomed casserole and lightly colour, add wine and reduce. [4] Add stock and place cheeks into casserole, cover with lid and braise slowly for $1^1/_2$ hours at 150°C / gas mark 2. When cooked a knife should pass through with no resistance. [5] Remove cheeks, allow to cool slightly, then remove any excess fat while still warm. [6] Pass liquid through sieve and reduce, skimming as you go, until you have a rich gravy. [7] Place cheeks back into finished sauce and leave. [8] Roast suckling pig on a trivet at 180°C / gas mark 4 for approximately 45 minutes. [9] Boil potatoes and make a Cheshire potato purée, enriching with plenty of butter and double cream, salt and pepper.

To Serve Warm cheeks and carve pork. Place a generous portion of potato on warmed plates with a sticky cheek and a slice of suckling pig, pan juices and piccalilli.

Caramelised Eddisbury Pear Tarts with Smoked Almond Frangipane and Iced Pear Nectar

SERVES 4

4 Williams Pears, ripe
1 sheet all butter puff pastry
1 pod vanilla
150g sugar
10g butter
Smoked almonds
Lemon juice

For the Frangipane
100g smoked butter
100g sugar
1 egg
80g ground almonds
15g flour

For the Iced Pear Nectar Sorbet
60ml milk
125ml Eddisbury pear juice
125g sugar
125ml water

Iced Pear Nectar Sorbet ☐1 Place the milk, pear juice, sugar and water in a pan and bring to the boil, cool and churn in an ice cream maker, or freeze in a flat dish, stirring every 30 minutes until set. Store in the freezer.

Frangipane ☐1 Cream the butter and sugar; add the egg, ground almonds and flour.

Pears ☐1 peel and core the pears, cut two in half for the tarts and dice the other two. ☐2 Place the diced pear in a pan with a scraped vanilla pod and a squeeze of lemon, pinch of sugar, splash of water. ☐3 Cook until soft and purée.

Tarts ☐1 Heat a pan, place the sugar in directly. Stir until the sugar turns to caramel (be careful!). Take pan off the heat and add butter. Quickly place pears into caramel and cook for 2 minutes. ☐2 Using a foil case, pour some of the caramel in and place the semi-cooked half-pear on top. ☐3 Place a ball of frangipane in the core recess then cover with pastry, cut to size, tucking underneath. ☐4 Bake in a hot oven 200°C / gas mark 6 until pastry is golden.

To Serve Turn out tart onto plate, garnish with pear and sorbet and a scattering of smoked almonds.

Barry and Gillian Pugh
Pugh's Piglets
Lancashire

WHEN PIG PRICES PLUMMETED and the cost of feed rocketed in the mid-1970s, a young couple called Barry and Gillian Pugh looked at the two thousand pigs on their farm and wondered how on earth they were going to make a living. They put their heads and their skills together and came up with a novel idea: they'd sell direct to restaurants and what they'd sell them would be suckling pigs – a far from inexpensive product.

It was bold thinking over thirty years ago when the nation had yet to display much interest in food at all, let alone anything as challenging and earthy as suckling pigs. But Barry is a man with marketing flair and he'd spotted a promising niche. 'We started with Chinese restaurants', he explains. 'The pig has a symbolic significance in Chinese culture as a thrifty, happy, healthy animal, busy, and benign towards everyone. So when there's a celebration, Chinese people like to put a whole pig on the table.'

To drum up business, Barry went knocking on doors in Soho where London's Chinatown was beginning to burgeon. 'He's very good at cold calling', says Gillian, 'and, slowly but surely, business built up.' Before too long he'd captured the entire market, only to spot the economic tide turning again. Cheaper, foreign imports were starting to chip away at the Chinese trade. It was time to find additional custom. 'We already supplied one or two embassies', Barry recalls, 'a couple of Portuguese restaurants, and a few places down and around the King's Road who were ambitious enough to take on suckling pig. We decided to widen our horizons to other, european-influenced restaurants.'

They were uphill years. 'We had very few funds and very few connections. How we did it I don't know really, but we started here in Lancashire with Paul Heathcote when he was head chef at Broughton Park Hotel. Then there was Nigel Haworth at Northcote Manor and now we supply places all over the country.'

In fact the delivery rosters of Pugh's Piglets read like a roll-call of Britain's top restaurants and best known chefs. The Ivy, Le Manoir, The Ritz, the Boxwood Café at The Berkeley, The Devonshire Arms at Bolton Abbey are just a few of the regulars. Michel Roux, Marco Pierre White, Aldo Zilli, Mark Hix, Anthony Worrall-Thompson … they're all on the books.

What attracted such top-flight names in the first place probably owes a lot to the re-entry into Britain's contemporary haute cuisine of those robust and all-but-forgotten traditional dishes from the rural past. After all, for centuries, no self-respecting feast or festival could be complete without a suckling pig: recipes appear in cookery books from ancient Rome to nineteenth century England. However, what keeps such customers coming back to Pugh's Piglets, again and again, is clearly satisfaction. Barry understands their needs and makes it his business to meet them.

'Take Simon Radley at The Chester Grosvenor, who we've supplied for six or seven years. Like any other chef, if he rings up for a product, he wants exactly the same high quality every time and he wants it delivered on time. If he knows he can count on that, he can put his effort into doing what he does best, which is preparing and cooking the meal. He doesn't want to be worrying, chasing up products. He wants reliability.'

That reliability starts with the pigs. Nowadays, you'll not detect sight, sound nor smell of one at Bowgreave House Farm, the family home where the business is based. Instead, Barry has some fifteen farmers in Cheshire, Lancashire, Yorkshire and the Welsh Borders, supplying him with over 250 piglets a week, personally selected by himself and his team.

Of course, Barry knows a thing or two about pigs. Among those he chooses most often are the tastier rare breeds: Middle Whites with their distinctive 'squashed' snouts, Saddlebacks, and the increasingly popular Gloucester Old Spots. 'Every piglet is paid for in advance', he says, 'and every one is fully traceable from the farm to the customer. They go to our own slaughterman at Tarporley, in Cheshire, then back here to our little factory. We take photographs all the way along the line, so people know they're getting what we say. The piglets are sorted out here, according to size and breed, and prepared according to customers' various requirements. Then they are distributed throughout the UK, door to door, by us or by courier.'

From Edinburgh to London to Southampton, you'll see Pugh's delivery vans making their rounds – but suckling pigs are not their only cargo. 'Fine Food Specialist' it says in flowing red script on the side of their wagons, and what they specialize in is a range of high quality, hand-crafted, oven-ready products. These include gourmet lamb and assorted sausages, as well as a particularly delicious development of their original product – porchetta.

That most succulent of Italian specialities, boned and rolled suckling pig, prepared plain or stuffed, is now a best seller for Pugh's Piglets. Anyone who has been lured by the nose in Lazio, or the Campagna, to a roadside stall selling thick slices of this hot, fragrant, melting meat will understand why. It's irresistible and unforgettable. But what is it doing in Lancashire?

Simple really. One day, when Barry was delivering to a local Italian restaurant he met Giovanni Maticheccia, boning out pigs, and hankering after a job with more sociable hours so he could spend more time with his children. 'Why don't you come and work for us?' Barry asked in his inviting way, and in no time at all Pugh's Piglets had acquired their resident chef.

Gillian takes up the story: 'The porchetta was Giovanni's brainwave. He completely bones out a young pig, then before it's rolled and strung he adds various seasonings. The main one he does is from the Rome area – fresh bay leaves, fresh rosemary, fresh garlic, salt and pepper.' The customer roasts it until the skin is crisp, and the result is a luscious little bit of Italy.

Before long Lancashire came nipping at the heel, demanding its own version. Ecco! Giovanni created porchetta stuffed with R. S. Ireland's multi-award winning Real Lancashire Black Pudding. There's a Somerset recipe, too, with caramelized apple, ten-year-old Calvados, fresh nutmeg, fresh sage and breadcrumbs to bind.

It seems almost too tantalizingly cruel to tell of others but, 'To make things more exciting', as Gillian puts it, 'we do a Christmas Fruits porchetta with apricots and mixed spice, orange and lemon rind, caramelized apple, breadcrumbs and brown sugar.' Or a chef can have a recipe individually made for his restaurant. The Ritz has one with sage and fennel seeds.

'Giovanni works to a very high standard', says Barry. 'When he first started here, I got him some garlic paste, to save him time peeling and chopping garlic.

"Oh, I'm not using that!" he said.

"Why not Giovanni?" I asked – me being a bit of a philistine.

" Because", he said "it's rubbish!"

'This is the standard he set when he came here fourteen years ago. So we provide him with quality meat that we think is the best from the farms. He then adds all the fresh ingredients, and if somebody isn't happy with what they get, Giovanni is very concerned. Like all artists, he cares very keenly about his work.'

Barry's well-founded admiration for the food culture of Italy has generated another creative association, this time with a fourth-generation Sardinian butcher, settled in Lancashire. Giovanni Bassu is now producing Sardinian, Sicilian, and Gloucester Old Spot sausages for Pugh's Piglets.

'The Italians are a very cultured people', says Barry. 'Art, architecture, fashion, food, they have a wonderful flair for whatever they put together – and they care deeply about food. Food is very much part of culture, it can't be missed out.'

For Barry and Gillian, sitting down to a freshly prepared meal with the family is an important part of life, and running the business as a family is part of the same picture. There are about fourteen staff on site at Bowgreave House Farm. The place they work in is as spick and span and good-looking as any townie could wish a country enterprise to be. That doesn't just apply to the family home either. The mellow-stone outbuildings in the yard with their terracotta window troughs of red pelargoniums make as picturesque an office as you're likely to see. The preparation plant, the chill room, all neat as a new pin.

That's the physical setting. On the human front there's a palpable warmth about the place, a sense of everybody joining in, and enjoying what they do. Gillian: 'We've got a marvellous team here. They all work so hard and, hopefully, everyone is happy. We don't talk of people working for us, but working with us, which is how I'd like to be treated myself.'

Even through the hard times, the glue sticks. During the last devastating

outbreak of foot and mouth disease, Pugh's kept the whole workforce together. They did odd jobs – they painted the office – but disbanding was not on the agenda.

The future of the family business will rest with Richard Pugh, who joined his parents in the firm seventeen years ago. A seasoned worker, now as wedded to the enterprise as his parents, Richard began with a rather different attitude. 'I thought I'd get a cushy number as the boss's son, but after a couple of weeks I got a rude awakening', he confesses with the wry smile of a man remembering the boy he used to be. 'I was sixteen when I started and there were people here twice my age who had all the knowledge and all the experience. I had to knuckle down, do as I was told and earn people's respect – which was a very good thing!'

Authenticity, consistency, high standards, in their products and service, are the key factors in the enduring success of Pugh's Piglets, and they guard their reputation with care. They are selective over who they supply: no catering butchers, no wholesale establishments, no supermarkets. 'I once knew a guy who had the same attitude as we have now', says Barry, 'and I used to think, what a vain man, thinking he can control his product like that. And here I am, doing virtually the same!' But private retail customers need not despair. Restaurants and corporate events are not quite the only outlets. Pugh's Piglets have developed a range of similar products, available from online gourmet food company Forman and Field.

Barry and Gillian have relished their business odyssey – even if it was blind Fortune that drove their fate in the first place. 'I wasn't trained for this kind of business', Barry points out. 'My family were country people, I went to agricultural college, became a farmer and just happened to make a successful transition into marketing.'

> "Every piglet is paid for in advance and every one is fully traceable from the farm to the customer."

As for Gillian: 'I never thought I'd marry a farmer – never! You meet someone, you fall in love with them, it doesn't matter what they do. I was quite prepared to be a farmer's wife. I only drove a tractor once. It was disastrous! I didn't have the strength. I had to stand on the pedals to stop it!'

You can just see her. A slim youthful figure, attractive, vivacious and fashionable, she must hardly have changed in thirty-five years of marriage. 'People say to us, "Oh crikey, and you work together too!" We're probably the most boring couple going, because all we talk about is work! But it's the most enjoyable job, the most enjoyable.

'I can remember, years ago, here in the office one Saturday afternoon and the phone rang. I picked it up and a voice said: "This is Gary Rhodes", and I very nearly said, "Yes and I'm the Queen of England", but it *was* him. We've met a lot of really lovely chefs and eaten in some wonderful restaurants. In Soho, we could walk down the centre of Gerrard Street and we'd meet more people we knew than in Garstang. At Sale e Pepe, behind Harrods, the manager, Tony (Corricelli) used to shout across the street to me, "Hello, Miss Piggy". It's things like that which have made it all such fun.'

Not that they have any, thoughts of retirement just yet. They're still up at 4.30 in the morning, so Barry can get on the road. Then Gillian will be in the office about eight. 'Both of us are getting older, though', she says with a twinkle, 'and we do want a bit more time off and a few more holidays.'

'And if we want cheering up on a dark winter's night in east Lancashire we go to a nice restaurant', adds Barry. 'That always make you feel better.'

While they're there, what's the betting a major topic of conversation will be Pugh's Piglets?

Michael Dykes
Eddisbury Fruit Farm, Cheshire

NEAR THE VILLAGE OF KELSALL, where Cheshire's beautiful Vale Royal skirts the edge of Delamere Forest, lies a cluster of buildings surrounded by orchards. This is Eddisbury Fruit Farm. In spring its fields froth with blossom. In summer and autumn the boughs of its trees and bushes are bowed with a sweet harvest: apples and pears, in red, green and gold; clusters of blackcurrants, whitecurrants, redcurrants; raspberries, gooseberries, strawberries, tayberries; ruby damsons and purple plums with yellow flesh ...

The cycle of growth, fruition and renewal has been continuous here since 1936. In that year, Leslie Haworth converted an existing dairy farm into a fruit farm. Thirty-five years later, he passed Eddisbury to his son Colin who still runs it today, alongside his wife Monica, and stepson Michael Dykes with whom he went into partnership in 2001.

Fruit growing remains the main focus of the business but new developments have grown from it in recent years. What makes the Eddisbury enterprise stand out is what happens to the fruit after it is picked. The bulk of the entire fruit crop, hard and soft, goes into a variety of products. There is a range of apple juices and ciders, fruit liqueurs and preserves – all made on the farm using freshly picked fruit from field and orchard. None of the fresh fruit from the farm is supplied to wholesale markets, and the surplus is sold in the Eddisbury Farm Shop. As a model of how a farm should be run, and how our food should be produced, it would be difficult to find a better example than Eddisbury.

Michael established Cheshire Apple Juice in 1996 and has continued to grow the brand ever since. Production has increased every year, from the modest 3,500 bottles initially, to 70,000 in 2007. Eddisbury is well placed for this particular venture. They grow upwards of 25 varieties of apple – old and new, sharp or sweet – and with such a variety of flavours that each merits individual sampling. Their unique characteristics transfer to the juices – Russet, Howgate Wonder, Gala, Bramley, Cox ...

The juicing process begins as soon as possible after picking, when the apples are taken to the washroom to be rinsed, before being sucked up into the mill, where they are crushed to a pulp. The pulp is then dispensed by hand into cloths stretched across wooden frames. These frames, or segments, are stacked on top of one another and are then placed under the press. The juice which is extracted during the pressing is collected in trays, where L-ascorbic acid (Vitamin C) is added to stop discoloration.

After bottling, the juice is then pasteurised to give it better keeping properties and a shelf-life of two years. Finally, the attractive labels with their distinctive red border are applied and the apple juice is ready for the shelves of the Eddisbury Farm Shop, or any one of the many other outlets through which it is sold. Smaller bottles, which are particularly suitable for restaurants and cafés, are also produced.

And that's it! Nothing else is added – no artificial flavours, colours, or preservatives, just one hundred per cent pure apple juice. Alternative flavours are produced by combining the apple juice with soft fruits from the farm or by adding spices such as ginger or cinnamon. Eddisbury's Cheshire Cider – sweet, medium or dry – is produced from both culinary and dessert apples and is aged in oak casks to develop flavour and aroma. It is sold in bottle and draught forms and because it is very good for cooking, it's in particular demand with local chefs.

Of pears, four much-admired varieties are grown at Eddisbury: the plump, russet-flushed yellow Comice; the sweet and juicy Williams; the tapering green Conference and the sweet Beurre Hardy with its hint of rosewater. Says Michael: 'Apples and pears go together like fish and chips, so it was only natural to grow both.' Predictably, plans to produce an Eddisbury Perry are afoot. Now what a delight that would be!

Using only fruit from the farm, Colin's wife makes all the jams and jellies in small batches, by hand and sells them under her alternative identity of Granny Haworth. Since she recently retired, the family have decided to keep Mrs Haworth busy by encouraging her to open a tearoom. Generously stocked with homemade cakes, scones, sandwiches and panini, the tearoom has now become a very popular destination in its own right.

In addition to their farmshop, the family also hosts its own FARMA-certified farmers' market every third Saturday of the month, from ten o'clock until two. For those who don't live locally Eddisbury also sells via the internet.

"Apples and pears go together like fish and chips, so it was natural to grow both."

Eddisbury Fruit Farm. Simon Radley's supplier 251

Simon Rimmer
The Earle Restaurant
Hale, Cheshire

STYLISH, EGALITARIAN AND JUST A LITTLE BIT GLAMOROUS: Earle bears a remarkable resemblance to its begetter, Simon Rimmer. A graduate in fashion textiles, he is a self-taught chef, restaurateur, prolific television presence and best-selling cookery author, who still remains the friendly guy next door. Creativity bubbles in his blood. His talent translates onto the menu as eclectic, seemingly simple food that you and I could cook. Yet here it is executed with such expertise and brio as to leave a wannabe waiting in the wings. The stage on which he first found fame was Greens, his celebrated Manchester restaurant which made vegetarian dining mainstream. At Earle, his acclaimed second eaterie, this always accidental vegetarian is catering for carnivores, so widening his scope, both as an inventive cook and a passionate promoter of local produce. The pleasant little town of Hale, on the outskirts of Manchester, provides the location. Earle's tables spill out invitingly onto the pavement. Inside, a laid-back restaurant unfolds: open and hidden spaces, made enticingly atmospheric by clever plays of light. Cool colours and smooth surfaces are warmed by wood and roughened by brick; gilded mirrors shimmer with beguiling reflections and the discreet glitz of crystal chandeliers. Despite a punishing schedule, Simon still finds time to cook here. Fluent, fast-talking and funny, he puts a zing in the air with his persona and a zing on the palate with his food.

"I'VE ALWAYS LOVED RESTAURANTS. Within a week of working in one, I knew: this is what I want to do. I never meant to end up cooking, though. That was going to be someone else's job. I'd be the host with the most, drink wine, swan round talking to customers and chat up girls! It was simple necessity that turned me into a chef.

It all started when I got a part-time job as a waiter. By day, I was a freelance designer, and doing all right, but it was quite a lonely way of life – and I'm a

253

massive people-person. From my first night working at the Steak and Kebab Restaurant in West Didsbury, Manchester, I couldn't believe what a brilliant, brilliant industry I'd got myself into. It might be long hours at unsociable times but it's an incredibly sociable job – and you're actually doing something that makes people happy. I teamed up with another waiter there, Simon Connelly, and we decided to open our own place together. It took us two years, but we did it.

We'd had our eye on a sort of hippie veggie café, nearby. It was small but had a great location, and looked like somewhere we might actually be able to afford. Then, one day as I was passing, I saw a 'For Sale' sign going up. It was an incredible opportunity. We made an offer, got a bank loan, and moved in three months later. We were both in our twenties, full of enthusiasm – and pretty clueless. It was only when we did our sums we realised the awful truth. We couldn't afford a chef. We were going to have to learn how to cook.

But what were we going to cook? We wanted to keep the existing customers, and they were vegetarians. On the other hand, back in 1990 when we opened, veggie restaurants were almost more about making a political statement than they were about making food. Well, I'm a devout carnivore and, to be honest, when I first started, I was cooking food I didn't particularly like – things like nut roast and vegetable lasagne. So I had to find a way of making food that I'd enjoy. Apart from any other considerations, I was earning £100 from Greens for a 100-hour week, so I couldn't afford to eat anything else.

I researched, I practised techniques, I experimented. I learnt by the seat of my pants. The big mistake a lot of people still make with vegetarian food is they try and recreate meat dishes using vegetables. Veg and two veg doesn't work. My starting point was always those cuisines that had brilliant veggie food: Mediterranean, South East Asian, Middle Eastern, African. I'd steal ideas, combine elements from different cultures and then source interesting produce for the dishes I'd dreamed up. Because I'm not trained, I had no preconceptions of what veggie food was. There was no stigma attached to it for me, and I didn't see it as a pain to prepare compared with meat-based cookery. It was how I was going to make my living, so I had to be naturally creative about it.

I've got a dogged, stubborn streak. I can't let go of things unless I feel they're resolved. That's quite a driving force with me. I think I'm an obsessive person really and I have a desire to be good at what I do. So, if I'm going to cook, I want to be a really good cook. If I run a restaurant, I want it to be a really good restaurant.

After two years, Greens was full – and not only with vegetarians. Nobody else was doing food like ours. People found it exciting. We began to get noticed in the national press and win awards, including Manchester Restaurant of the Year – no 'vegetarian' tag attached – and an AA rosette. We'd expanded from 28 to 48 covers and we were still having to turn away a couple of hundred people a week. Since I competed to cook for the Queen's 80th birthday on BBC2's *Great British Menu* in 2006, it's been more like 600!

I still love Greens, but when I decided to open Earle I wanted to do something

different. This time I wanted to create a place where I wanted to eat – a neighbourhood restaurant that could be all things to all people. They do that really well in the States, particularly New York. In this country, you either have to be a posh restaurant or a café-bar.

I think restaurants should be classless really. Every year I go to New York, where the industry is very exciting, and I research restaurants and bars non-stop. One of my favourites is The Spotted Pig in Greenwich Village. You can go in there and have a burger and chips with a glass of water if you want, or you can have fantastic food with a bottle of champagne, or any combination of those things. I felt that was the ethos I wanted to create – and, incidentally, if you want to drink a £240 bottle of Cristal champagne with a £9.95 burger at Earle, you can!

When I thought about what food we would serve, I asked myself: 'What would I like to have if I was going to eat in a restaurant?' I read an interview with Gordon Ramsay saying all he wanted when he went out was steak and chips or a nice piece of fish. Well, that's true of all chefs. We purveyors of the trade want good ingredients, we want people to respect those ingredients and cook them simply. And that's what we do at Earle.

Simon Rimmer, The Earle Restaurant, Hale, Cheshire 255

The menu is very straightforward. We serve modern brasserie food and we don't mess around with anything we cook. The final factor in the equation is the provenance of the ingredients we use. Most are local: all the meat; as much as possible of the fish, fruit and vegetables, depending on the seasons; all the cheeses, with the exception of a little bit of ricotta.

My home is in Manchester, I grew up in Wallasey, on the Wirral. I love the fact that I live in the Northwest of England and that we have some of the finest produce in the world here. We are blessed with incredible dairy, incredible beef, incredible lamb and some of the finest cheesemakers you could wish to find.

A lot of the people who come to Earle are really clued up about all of that and I try to make sure we don't ram it down their throats so it becomes preachy. At the same time, I try and ensure that all of our staff have all of the knowledge and all of the stories of who our producers are. It makes for a little bit more of an interesting journey when people eat out.

The Northwest is just full of funky entrepreneurs who do things you don't expect to happen – like Andy Holt, this tremendous black pudding maker, working from a little place in Lancashire, who one day suddenly decides he's going to make a veggie version of his black pudding. Basically, just to provoke people. I love that mentality!

How did I discover his product? He came up to me at the Tatton Park Food Festival in 2005 and said: 'I've made something for you.' I used it at Greens, and it was so good that I decided to use it on the *Great British Menu*. That's when things went kind of crazy for Andy and his veggie black pudding. It could have stayed as a little novelty item that made up a tiny percentage of his business. Instead it's become a cult product, his output has soared and deservedly so.

I'm hugely proud to have been a catalyst for that. He has incredible passion for what he does and a real chef's approach towards it, continually trying out recipes and producing fantastic flavours. It's his product and I can't take any credit for it, but it's lovely to be in a position where you can showcase producers like Andy, who most people would otherwise never get access to.

That's why, of all the things I've done on telly, ITV's *Grubs Up*, about regional food and producers, is a real labour of love for me. We're on our fifth series now and every single producer who's been featured on it says it's made a positive difference to their business.

It was while I was filming for *Grubs Up* in Cumbria that I discovered damsons. I knew we produced them in the Northwest but it wasn't till I met Michelle Partington at Savin Hill Farm that I learnt about their history and the 'damson trail' that links farms and communities. I'm a sucker for a good story, and that's what drew me in at first. Then I realised what great fruit this is to cook with. I've put them in all sorts of recipes, savoury included. In this book I've used them in cheesecake – cheesecakes are a complete obsession of mine, and I think you'll find this is a really good one.

You don't just have to turn Northwest produce into traditional fare like Lancashire Hotpot. I enjoy using it to create dishes that sound as if they come

Simon Rimmer, The Earle Restaurant, Hale, Cheshire 257

from somewhere else entirely. My starter of sea bass on potato rösti with tomato and avocado salsa doesn't sound remotely local but, in season, we're getting the sea bass and the potatoes from Lancashire's Fylde Coast and we're using Southport tomatoes for the salsa – that's at least 75% of the dish.

I regard all the components of that dish as being equally important, by the way, which is possibly what makes our food slightly different. A lot of people, not so much chefs, still work on a meat-and-two-veg philosophy, where meat or fish is cast as the main player, with the other ingredients in a supporting role. If you do that the result may be nice, but it's nowhere near as nice as what we do at Earle!

A word of warning about local produce: there is a danger now of people just jumping on the bandwagon. Some establishments might well be buying from local farmers, but that's not the point if the product is rubbish. From the consumer's point of view, there needs to be a lot more to provenance than 'from within a 30-mile radius'. Produce should never be local at the expense of quality. We still buy things from outside the region and always will.

Also, quality must be present at every stage of the process. If the animal husbandry on a farm isn't particularly magnificent, or storage or packing is poor, you're better off buying something from France. We had to stop using one beef producer because, although it was beautiful meat, the butchery was terrible. It was a real shame. He couldn't sort it out and I couldn't afford the cost of having to throw away two steaks out of every batch.

Sourcing produce is actually a very exciting thing to do these days. Fifteen years ago, if someone had rung me up and said, 'We're a small company producing herbs, are you interested?' The answer would probably have been, 'No, we're a busy restaurant.' Now there's a hugely sympathetic ear from chefs. 'Bring 'em in, let's have a look', is more likely to be the reaction.

At Earle, myself, together with Craig Kirk and Steve McLoughlin, my joint head chefs, are constantly sourcing produce. We work as a team. I'll never hand it over – I like it too much! The producers are on my mobile and we talk. It's great to have that kind of relationship and, also, to be able to ring up sometimes and just say thanks for a brilliant product. For instance, Jim Curwen at Bowland Forest Foods supplies our lamb, and it's always good quality, but one week it was particularly beautiful. It was really lovely to be able to call him, tell him how much we'd sold and the way everyone had said how amazing it was.

Great ingredients are a real inspiration. One of the best things that ever happened for Greens was when cheesemakers started using vegetarian rennet, post-BSE. Suddenly, we had a whole new palette of ingredients at our disposal. Before, you'd get a bit of veggie stilton or cheddar. After, you got magnificent artisan cheesemakers who, without realising it, were turning out brilliant cheeses suitable for vegetarians. And right on our doorstep.

That's how I developed our Cheshire cheese sausages. By popular demand, they've been on the menu at Greens ever since. If you can do a great sausage and mash in a vegetarian restaurant, you get blokes like me coming in and eating there

Simon Rimmer, The Earle Restaurant, Hale, Cheshire 259

out of choice – carnivores in their thirties and forties who'd run a mile from a lentil! They've been a real success here at Earle too. We do a version with Lancashire cheese, a smoked cheese and date sausage which is superb, and we're doing a new one for our next menu.

In fact, they are much, much better now than when I first did them. How come they're so 'meaty'? Well, you learn about the texture over time, and if I were to rewrite the recipe in my first book, *The Accidental Vegetarian*, I'd add that you need to work the mixture for about twenty minutes before you attempt to cook them. You want it to be like plasticine – really, really worked – so that, when you roll them, they're tight.

I wish I'd included them on the *Great British Menu*. I think that series was one of the biggest turning points for me. I'd just sort of slipped under the radar for all of my cooking life. Then, all of a sudden, I was competing against Michelin-starred Marcus Wareing of Pétrus and The Savoy Grill. So there's me, self-taught, running a 48-cover veggie restaurant in West Didsbury, in the arena with one of the best chefs practising in the UK today! It was terrifying but great, and I think it gave me a huge amount of confidence to open Earle. We've had very good notices in the national press as well as being named number-one celebrity-chef restaurant in the Northwest, which is something I'm particularly proud of though I hate that expression. I'd rather people just judged us by the food.

All the same, I love doing the telly work. My wife, Ali, tells our children, Flo and Hamish, that I get paid to show off! One of the things I worried about when I first started, back in 1999, was that you end up becoming a caricature of yourself. But I feel reassured by the fact that, to the best of my knowledge, no-one has ever been afraid to come up to me at cookery demonstrations or wherever and say hello. I'd hate to be unapproachable.

260

However, running two restaurants, cooking and doing a lot of telly does mean my life is hideously complex. I have to be hugely organised and tremendously focussed. Tonight, for instance, after I leave Earle, I'll drive to Birmingham to do fifteen hours filming tomorrow on the BBC2 series, *Recipe for Success*. That's the programme where amateurs take over the running of a restaurant for a day. We film three days a week and, in between, I come back and cook, pretty much a day each, at Earle and Greens.

Let's see, what's the time now? Ten to seven on a Thursday evening and I'm in my fifty-seventh hour of work this week. I never do less than eighty hours, plus a thousand miles travel a week – and my phone rings non-stop. Ali is really supportive. She's been area manager for a pizza chain and a head chef, so she understands the industry, and what it is to be a restaurant widow. Like me, Ali's self-taught – we're both stubborn Taureans.

Without our fantastic restaurant staff, I couldn't do what I do. Craig was with me at Greens and he and Steve run a really tight ship. They do everything I want them to; they're excited by the producers, they share the passion I've got, and the same determination.

I'm a big believer in empowering your staff. If you give them knowledge and a sense of pride in what they do, they'll fly. In Greens, my second and third chefs both started as kitchen porters. They've been with me over ten years now. I like starting people and bringing them on if they show an interest in what they're doing. It's the same with front of house. One lad's only previous catering experience was a night a week at MacDonalds, but he was really nice, so we gave him a try as a runner. Within months he went from being the rawest of raw recruits to someone with loads of his own customers and the power to instill real passion in them too.

If staff are in charge of a job, I don't interfere. Fundamentally, they all know that I'll back their decisions, even if I don't necessarily agree with them. They'll get the customers' plaudits for their achievements, not me, and rightly so.

I can't decide whether to open more restaurants. I'm thinking about a pub. I love what I do, but I'm still driven, and ambition can be a horrible bedfellow a lot of the time! I've got this theory that I've got five years of boundless energy left. If I haven't got the sort of choices I hope to have then, it won't be through lack of trying!

I think I'm that rare breed of male who is quite good at multi-tasking. I've always got projects on the go. At the moment, I'm just following up my second book, *Rebel Cook* with a third, *Lazy Brunch*, from the BBC2 Sunday morning show, *Something for the Weekend*. I'm designing an extension to our house and thinking about what I can do to make my kids' lives more exciting. I've got various bits and pieces for telly in the pipeline – and I'm reinventing the nutloaf! It's had such a bad press, I'm going to recreate it and make it fantastic. I'm three-quarters of the way there …

Whatever else I do, I'll always be a chef first.

Sea Bass with Potato Rosti

SERVES 4

For the Rosti
2 large baking potatoes
3 finely sliced spring onions
1 clove crushed garlic
Salt and pepper

For the Sea Bass
4 x 100g sea bass fillets
Olive oil for frying
Salt and freshly ground black pepper

For the Salsa
1 small red bird's eye chilli
About 20 cherry tomatoes cut into quarters
1 tbsp chopped coriander
$^1/_2$ ripe avocado, chopped
1 tbsp sherry vinegar
4 tbsp extra virgin olive oil

Rosti **1** Boil the potatoes in their jackets for exactly 7 minutes, drain and allow to cool then peel. **2** Grate coarsely, add the onion, garlic and lots of seasoning. **3** Divide into 4 and mould into circles about 10cm across, chill for 20 minutes, then fry over a medium heat for 4 minutes on each side, until they are crisp and golden. **4** Drain on kitchen paper and keep warm.

Salsa **1** Simply combine all the ingredients, leaving the avocado until just before serving.

Sea Bass **1** Pre-heat the oven to 200°C / gas mark 6. **2** Season the fish well and fry in the oil for a couple of minutes, skin side down, then flip over and put in the oven for 2 minutes.

To Serve Place a fillet of fish on top of a rosti, spoon over some salsa.

Smoked Cheshire Cheese Sausages with Mustard Mash, Onion Gravy and Vegetarian Black Pudding

SERVES 6

1 vegetarian black pudding, cut into slices
450g of mashed potato
50g whole grain mustard

For the Sausages
600g grated or crumbled smoked Cheshire cheese
200g fresh breadcrumbs
6 spring onions
30g fresh thyme
30g fresh chopped parsley
3 whole eggs
3 egg yolks
50ml milk to bind
2 cloves of garlic, crushed
Salt and freshly ground black pepper

For the Onion Gravy
3 large onions, sliced
2 cloves garlic, crushed
1 tbsp brown sugar
75g plain flour
75ml gravy browning
500ml stock
Olive oil

Sausages [1] Mix all the ingredients into a big bowl, season it and use your hands to mix it really well until it feels like modelling clay. [2] When you taste it, you will probably need to over season it by about 15%, so it's a bit more salty and peppery than you'd normally expect to have. This is because the mix seems to loose a bit of its power as it chills and cooks. Let the mixture chill for a couple of hours.

Onion Gravy [1] Fry the onions and garlic in a little oil with the sugar until golden – a low heat is needed. [2] Sprinkle on the flour and cook for 3-4 minutes. [3] Add the gravy browning and stock, bring to the boil, season and simmer for at least 20 minutes.

To Serve [1] Mould the chilled sausage mix into sausage shapes. You should get about 12 decent bangers out of the mix, depending on how big you like your sausages. Deep fry for 6-8 minutes until crisp and golden [2] Shallow fry the black pudding in a little butter until crisp. [3] Mix the mustard into the mashed potato, check the seasoning. [4] Serve a dollop of mash with 2 sausages on top, gravy and crisp black pudding.

White Chocolate and Damson Cheesecake

SERVES 12

250g shortbread biscuits
125g melted butter
600g full fat cream cheese
600g ricotta
150g white chocolate
6 eggs
150g caster sugar
2 vanilla pods, scraped
400g damsons
150ml clear honey

Whipped cream to serve

[1] Halve and stone the damsons. [2] Place them cut side up on a tray, drizzle with honey, then roast at 180°C / gas mark 4 for 25 minutes. [3] Crush the biscuits and add the butter, press into a 23cm spring form tin. [4] Place the chocolate in a bowl over barely simmering water (make sure the water doesn't touch the bottom of the bowl) and leave until just melted. Don't stir it, as this ruins white chocolate. [5] Pulse remaining ingredients, except the damsons, in a processor until smooth. Then fold in about 200g of the fruit. [6] Spoon this mixture on to the base and cook at 180°C / gas mark 4 for about 1 hour until springy to the touch.

Serve with the rest of the damsons and a neat spoonful (a quenelle) of whipped cream.

Andrew Holt
Knight of the Black Pudding
Lancashire

HE'S A CHAMPION BLACK PUDDING MAKER is Andrew Holt. In every sense. He makes great black puddings *and* he's collected a legion of prizes for them all over Europe – from Best in Britain to the international Grand Prix d'Excellence. And he wins them again and again. In France they've made him a Knight of the Black Pudding – Chevalier du Goûte-Boudin. In a grand ceremony, he swore his solemn allegiance to the black pudding, promising to uphold and promote it to the best of his ability.

And what an ability! It was a very lucky day for this product when Andrew Holt walked past the premises of black pudding maker R.S. Ireland in 1993 and saw a hand-written notice in the window advertising the business for sale. Andrew just happened to be looking for a new venture for himself. As a fully trained butcher he had considered opening a butcher's shop, but since they were closing down in large numbers at the time, he needed an alternative option.

So he knocked on the door. The firm's owner, Dick Ireland, was hoping to retire but, when Andrew took over the company, he agreed to stay on for a couple more years and show him the ropes. Andrew was not a total novice: he had made black puddings years before as an apprentice butcher. But Dick was able to make him two invaluable gifts: firstly his considerable expertise, and secondly his original, highly prized Bury black pudding recipe of 1879.

As soon as he took over the business, Andrew realized that his customers were mainly older people and he would have to do something to bring black pudding into the limelight. 'We knew we had to raise the profile and make it more popular. So we started entering competitions and getting ourselves into the media as much as possible.' As a result he began to get converts among the younger generation. But there was another hurdle to clear: 'There is a misconception that black puddings are full of junk. So the other thing we've had do is to change the image of the product in people's minds and let them know that it's quality food', he explains.

'We were selling at a lot of farmers' markets and we couldn't help noticing the expressions on some people's faces as they passed our stall. Far too many of them would walk past quickly, without even trying our puddings.' These impressions were confirmed by research which showed that only about forty per cent of people would ever consider buying black pudding. Andrew knew that something more had to be done to get people interested if the business was to thrive. A radical move was required. So Sir Black Pudding took up arms.

His tactic was to create the Vegetarian Black Pudding. Now, everyone knows that black puddings are made from blood, so this caused quite a sensation. 'We assured customers at market that there was absolutely no blood in the pudding and it became a good talking point', he recalls.

His approach was to replace the blood with liquidised beetroot, caramel and soya. The fat was supplied by using solidified pine kernel oil, and a synthetic casing was used instead of intestine. But for chef Simon Rimmer, who chose the vegetarian black pudding when he competed to cook for the Queen on BBC2's *Great British Menu*, it was the depth of flavour in this new product that was so exciting. The secret, according to Andrew is in the seven different herbs and two spices that he uses: oregano, thyme, allspice – he's not prepared to divulge any more!

Simon was so delighted with the veggie black pudding that he personally championed it, featuring Andrew making it on his *Grub's Up* TV show. That really helped rocket the 'V-pudding', as it's known, to fame.

Traditional black pudding is one of the oldest dishes in the country. Paul Heathcote re-acquainted the nation and fine dining with it by making his own version in the 1990s. Today it enjoys a still wider resurgence. It is now valued as a British regional delight. No longer confined to the full English breakfast, it has burst out as a full and versatile player in all manner of recipes and main meals.

Pop a sample into your mouth and savour its rich and creamy texture and slight peppery tang.

At The Real Lancashire Black Pudding Company it is made with the best of ingredients in the traditional way, with no short cuts contemplated, even though production has increased dramatically. There is an extensive range to choose from (white puddings too), in natural or synthetic casings and in various shapes and sizes: slicing sticks, rings and chubs. The method is much the same for all, but let's concentrate on one: the traditional Bury (pronounced 'Burrie') black pudding, familiar in these parts for more than 150 years.

The Bury looks quite different from its counterparts. Each one is a small, round individual pudding in the shape of a hoop - you can slice it in half, a bit like a bap, if you're so minded. Because each pudding is individual, they retain their moisture during cooking, so that they stay soft and present well on the plate.

The process of making them starts with the cooking of pearl barley and oatmeal. To these are added blood, pork back-fat, onions, rusk, and flour, plus herbs and spices. The ingredients are mixed thoroughly, loaded into the filling machine and, in the case of the traditional Bury run out into casings of ox-intestine and tied by hand into small, round, hoops – the traditional shape. They are then simmered for about half an hour. When they emerge, they look rather grey and unappetizing, but as you watch them cool, they take on their glorious deep black colour and characteristic dull shine.

As you would expect, the eating quality of these and of all Andrew's puddings is exceptional. The black puddings are meltingly tender, very far removed from infinitely inferior, common-or-garden offerings. 'If you haven't tasted this Lancashire delight', says Andrew, 'you haven't lived.' When you try a sample, you taste the difference immediately: creamy texture, rich flavour and a slight peppery tang. A real treat.

Andrew is also evangelical about the health properties of his traditional black puddings and points out that, contrary to what some people believe, they are ninety-six per cent fat-free. The oats which they contain, as well as providing fibre, are absorbed slowly by our bodies, which is beneficial for blood sugar levels.

The black puddings of the Northwest are renowned but do we know where they originated? Strictly speaking, the answer is probably 'no'. One theory has it that monks brought the recipe with them from France. And so they may have done, but Andrew believes they first arrived with the Romans. 'They had a camp up here near Ribblesdale', he says and there were a lot of Hungarian troops in the garrison who liked spicy sausages. It's reckoned that's where the recipe spread from – it's well documented that the Romans were expert in preserving meat in sausages and salamis.' Andrew who now has an encyclopaedic knowledge on the subject of black pudding, points to the spread of the blood sausage throughout the lands of the Roman Empire: the boudin noir in France, the morcilla in Spain and the biroldo in Italy.

His own Lancashire-made black puddings now regularly invade the ancient boundaries, picking up a plethora of medals, shields and cups in competitions throughout Europe. Despite all the awards, Andrew prefers his reputation to rest on his product. After all, as he is keen to point out, the proof of the pudding is in the eating.

Real Lancashire Black Pudding Company. Simon Rimmer's supplier 271

Michelle Partington
Savin Hill Farm
Cumbria

AROUND SEVENTY YEARS AGO, in spring, charabancs would take trippers from all over Lancashire to visit the Lyth Valley in Westmorland. The sight they came to see was short-lived but stunning: the entire valley under a drift of snow-white blossom, as the damson trees came into flower in every farm and hedgerow.

From late summer and into autumn, the small violet fruits, with their firm amber flesh, were eagerly harvested. They were a common sight, piled up in carts, in greengrocers' shops and on roadside stalls, destined for jam and pies and puddings and drinks. But in particular it was the jam they went for – by rail to the big jam-making factories of northern England. Whole families would come from the cities and be paid for the picking. Then came war in 1939, and soon there was no sugar for the jam and no pickers for the fruit either. The damson went into deep decline. Until recently, that is.

Now damsons are back in fashion. In the intervening period the county of Westmorland has been officially excised, absorbed into the new, bigger administrative area of Cumbria. But strong affinities persist, and in 1996 the Westmorland Damson Association was formed to encourage people to use the fruit, so as to ensure the survival of existing orchards and promote the planting of more.

One of those involved in the Association is Michelle Partington, and when Simon Rimmer decided on damsons for his cheesecake, he was adamant that they had to come from her. Michelle and her brother Shaun run Savin Hill Farm, better known for the excellence of its traditional and rare breed pork and beef than its damsons. But when the Partingtons set up business, here in the Lyth Valley, fourteen years ago, they took good note of the numerous damson trees on their land and determined to put that bounty to good use at some future date.

Meanwhile, they put their energies into their main purpose: preserving three traditional and rare native breeds: British White cattle, Middle White and British Saddleback pigs. They do this by rearing them, breeding them and selling the fine food that comes from them. Says Michelle: 'My brother always wanted his own farm and a herd of cows and pigs that originated in the UK. You do get a very good quality of meat from these breeds. The animals just take that bit longer to grow.' With their passionate devotion to the old English livestock breeds, it seemed a natural step to campaign on behalf of beleaguered local damsons as well.

They now use damsons in their own products: beef olives with damson purée, and a very popular Middle White pork and Lyth Valley damson pie. Their

creative approach has demonstrated the versatility of the fruit, showing that it can be used in both sweet and savoury dishes. Of course, damson gin and damson jams, jellies and chutneys are still firm favourites. As a member of the Westmorland Damson Association, Michelle is also helping to put damsons back on the map in a number of different ways, including an annual Damson Day and Damson Feast, held in September.

It's thought that damsons were originally brought to England in the middle ages from Damascus (hence the fruit's name). However, they are known to have been popular with the Romans, who planted them around their forts and settlements, as archaeological evidence shows. Today they are grown throughout the United Kingdom, but it is the slightly smaller varieties from the Lyth Valley in Cumbria that are acknowledged to be the best. Damsons love limestone, so it is hardly surprising that the limestone-fringed Lyth Valley should be a favoured spot for their cultivation. They have been grown here in South Lakeland since at least the 1700s. During that time they have cross-pollinated with wild bullace and sloe, which has given them a distinctive taste, at once sweet and light. 'I think it is to do with the climate here too, says Michelle. 'They have an almondy flavour which is unique to Cumbria. Do try them. They are very versatile and go so well with meat and game.'

Marc Verité
The Warehouse Brasserie
Southport

TUCKED AWAY IN AN UNPREPOSSESSING SIDE STREET, behind the grand boulevard of this handsome Victorian seaside resort, lies a gem of cosmopolitan style and cuisine. Despite its inconspicuous location, diners of all kinds flock here, celebrities among them (including celebrity chefs). Some neither know nor care that the Warehouse Brasserie holds a Michelin Bib Gourmand. They just come for the food and the atmosphere. The chef director, Marc Verité, is Southport born and bred – and half-French. Though his accent is local, he talks about food like a Frenchman: with passion, joy, infectious excitement and a pronounced sense of terroir. Simple dishes and local produce are his particular delight. He brings them together in an internationally inspired menu, perfectly complemented by the urbane surroundings in which it is served. Deftly designed in the international style of the 1930s, this is Art Deco at the height of its streamlined glamour, resonant of Raymond Chandler's Los Angeles. There's a masculine feel to the easy comfort: plenty of wood, glass and metal; warm tones of russet, tan and yellow; a soothing geometry made by tables and low pendant lights. To one side, the gently curving bar, its neat bottles bathed in a creme-de-menthe glow; to the other, tantalizing surrealist images by Salvador Dalí. At the far end, an entirely mirror-clad wall, doubling the spacious interior. In the air, a tingle of anticipation.

"THIS RESTAURANT BUZZES. People go away excited about what we do here and we get excited doing it for them. The dishes are quite diverse, quite cosmopolitan. You could have Malaysian-fried halibut, say, or a foie gras terrine; a spring vegetable risotto, or bangers and mash. Whoever comes in, we want them to find something they like on the menu. We want people to enjoy themselves, from the minute they arrive to the minute they leave. We want them to be able to say: 'We went to the Warehouse Brasserie last night, had a fantastic time – good atmosphere, good food, good service. We'd recommend it – we'll definitely go back.'

That's how we've built our business. We've never advertised. The only publicity we've had is through giving interviews or when our chefs win competitions. Even so, the Brasserie has developed quite a following since it opened in 1996. But I have to admit, back then, when I first saw the premises, I thought to myself, there's no way this is going to take off. I had to eat my words! At the time though, this building was a near-derelict warehouse. It was Paul Adams, the Brasserie's owner, who had the vision to see what it could become. He travels a lot and saw the opportunity to bring something new to Southport – a restaurant with an international theme. He transformed the place into what you see today.

We've never wavered from the original format, because it works so well. We keep a mainstay of classic dishes, but change the menu every two to three weeks. Our food is very eclectic. I'm always reading books about the cuisine of different countries, and if I see a recipe that looks interesting, I'll try it. I love experimenting, inventing new dishes, tweaking old ones and I encourage the lads in the kitchen to do the same.

Last Saturday, we did a mixed fish sashimi, with tuna, organic salmon and scallops, served on long slate beds with soy dip and wasabi. There's Moroccan chicken on the menu at the moment, like a tagine, with coriander rice and lime crème fraîche, served in a little stone pot. American food I'm not really into, but you'll always see something on the menu, like smoked-bacon-wrapped tuna with herb velvet potatoes, or you could try our homemade cheeseburger or beefburger.

I like the diversity of this restaurant. It's good for the customers because it offers plenty of choice, and it's good for the people who work here as well, because it means we're not pigeonholed in what we do. There's plenty of scope for ideas, and I ask everyone for suggestions – including the sixteen and seventeen year-olds. A typical scenario took place yesterday. I said: 'What do you want to put on the menu for tomorrow's special – fishwise? Give me some ideas.'

One of the young lads said: 'When I was in Spain with my mum and dad, we had hake with chorizo. Don't ask me how they did it, but it was great.'

So we all talk about it: 'Was the fish crispy or soft-skinned? Fried or baked …?'

We teased out the details, came up with our own version and it went on the menu.

I've got lads working here from Spain, Portugal, other countries. Everyone has an input. I think it's important, in that the food here is not just about Marc Verité. Obviously, I am at the head of the team and I can lead everyone in the direction they want to go, but it's more than just me at work. This morning, for example, we were discussing the menu for this book. One of the lads had made a fantastic egg custard tart. It was perfect, it was gorgeous. So, I said: 'Right, I think that would be a good dish to put on this menu. We just need to incorporate a little extra something of Southport.'

'Okay, well … what do you think?'

'I know, Southport honey!'

'Fantastic!'

Rightaway, I was on the phone to order the honey from John and Lorraine Bryan who keep bees about five miles from us, in little village called Banks.

I always try and utilise local produce as much as possible, purely because I find it better. It seems to be trendy now, but I've been doing it for years. I haven't really got a philosophy on the subject. To me, it's just common sense. We're right at the heart of West Lancashire, a great agricultural area, great fruit, great vegetables. We struggle in winter, of course, and if I can't get something locally I have to do what every other chef has to do and buy the best I can elsewhere. But whenever anything is in season, you're on a roll in Southport. So buy local, get it used!

Take our famous Formby asparagus – excellent quality because it's grown on the fine, sandy soil of the local dunes. It's only available for about six weeks, starting at the end of April and finishing mid-June, but it's the best in the world in my opinion. The Brooks family of Larkhill Farm have been growing it for generations. So why would you buy asparagus that's come all the way from Chile when you can get it freshly cut just up the road? Alright, it may be a little bit more expensive because it's labour intensive and not mass-produced, but for the taste, the texture, the freshness it's worth it, every time.

Another local delicacy – and a perfect complement to the asparagus – are Southport shrimps. When they come into season, I can't get enough of them. They're the most popular starter on the menu! Unfortunately, there are are hardly any people going out to catch them these days and the trade is in danger of dying out. Otherwise, Fleetwood is about as local as we can get round here for seafood and fish, apart from a little locally-caught seabass and mackeral.

Have you tried seabass with sampy? A beautiful combination – I'm cooking that for my main course. You don't know what sampy is? It's samphire. Sampy's always been the name for it round here. My mum wouldn't know it as anything else. When I was a kid, I used to live in the Marshside area of Southport and I'd go down to the beach, out onto the salt marsh and pick sampy with my French grandma. We'd come home, wash it, cook it for a couple of minutes in boiling water and serve it with vinaigrette – a little bit salty, a little bit crunchy and absolutely delicious! I was only six. At that age you don't realise how lucky you are to be gathering your own food, fresh from the wild. It's only when you're older you appreciate it.

I suppose that was a formative experience for me in developing the love of food. The love of cooking came to me later, when I was about twelve or thirteen. That's when I started working with my dad in his pâtisserie and outside catering business.

My father, Claude, is French, a pâtissier by trade. Originally he came over here to learn English. That was in the early 1960s and, like a lot of young people at the time, he wanted to come to the place where the Beatles were. His boss in Paris organised the work placement for him and, instead of finding himself in Liverpool, my dad ended up in Southport! Funnily enough, he worked directly behind this building in a bakery-confectioners on Lord Street called Mellors. He was only supposed to stay for three months but he met my mum, got married, had kids, and opened a pâtisserie in Churchtown, just north of here. He ran that for twenty-five years.

I was never really interested in the confectionery side, I wanted to get into a kitchen and cook. So I studied catering at Southport College, got a lucky break and started my career with Nigel Haworth at Northcote Manor in 1989. Of all the chefs that I have worked for, he is probably the one who has influenced me most. Even then, he was busy trying to get produce that was as local as possible – and growing his own, too. He instilled those values into you. We used to gather salad leaves from the kitchen garden, including things you would never see for sale, like salad burnet which has that lovely, delicate cucumber flavour.

Nigel's was a very good training kitchen. I stayed for eighteen months, and then left for France. My dad never spoke French to us as kids and I wanted to learn the language. I stayed for just over two years, working in all kinds of places – charcuteries, pâtisseries – and for twelve months at Le Vieux Logis, a lovely four-star Relais Chateaux hotel, with a gourmet restaurant, at Tremolat in the Dordogne.

I came home briefly, then, it was off to Belgium with my wife-to-be, Michaela, to a job as sous-chef in a Michelin-starred casino. I stayed two years in Belgium and gained a lot of good experience, but I kept being drawn back to Southport. When I finally came home, I'd been away so long I didn't know where to start. I was working in a four-star hotel in Lancashire, Kilhey Court at Standish, when this opportunity came up.

I will never forget my first day at the Brasserie. No sooner was I in the kichen, than I got a phone call to say Michaela had gone into labour with our first child. Now we have three boys, 12, 10 and 4 – and like me, they love food. They've got muscles coming out of their ears!

Cooking food that people will enjoy – good, wholesome food that's as fresh as can be – is a pleasure to me. When you're a chef in your early twenties, there's a tendency to try and impress too much when you cook. When you're a little bit older, you see things differently. With maturity, you realise food doesn't have to be messed around and fussed over. Keep it simple, treat it with respect. Cook your vegetables correctly; don't smother your ingredients with other flavours. Let them speak for themselves.

Take potatoes. People think of them as just part of a roast dinner. They don't realise how good they are in their own right. But, oh, when you get them straight from the soil, rinse them, cut them, cook them, they are absolutely delicious. That earthy taste! Wonderful! You can't get anything better.

There's a potato grown near here, in Scarisbrick, which they harvest from the middle of May. I first had them at my mother-in law's – straight out of the ground that morning, boiled, seasoned and served with butter. Ahh … I can still taste them! That was all I had on the plate. It was the best potato I'd ever had in my life – better than Jersey Royals.

They're a first early called Ulster Prince and, every year, when they come into season, I like to put them on the menu. I do a starter of these, on their own. People who know the variety get the idea. Others don't. They'll say: 'Why have you got potatoes as a starter?' Well, because you've never had anything like it! The taste, the fluffiness, the creaminess – everything about them! They're just beautiful.

Every chef has a different way. I like the simplicity of things. I like the excitement of the seasons, the anticipation, the suspense of what's to come. You know what it's like in your own garden. Spring, summer and you're out there wondering, 'What's coming through now? Lovage, runner beans, beetroot …' Already, you're creating meals in your head … and you have to stop yourself: 'No, leave those beans a bit longer; don't pick them yet.'

I've got a Victoria plum tree at the back of my house. I watch the fruits growing over the months, and when they ripen, I'm out there, knocking them down, gathering them in. You just get excited don't you? Why do we do it? Because it's natural, it's life itself.

I'd love to have a little vegetable and fruit garden close by the Brasserie. Imagine, having someone looking after it, going down there, seeing how things are

doing, picking out your produce. Maybe one day, you never know … I just got some wild garlic leaves in this morning, from Preston way. It's taken me two weeks to get hold of them and I was all excited! They have such a subtle savour. I use them in a starter: rare-cooked fillet of beef with wild garlic leaves, dressed with a little horseradish cream. Very popular.

Now, fresh horseradish is difficult to get hold of but, if you are lucky enough to grow it in your garden, I would recommend making your own horseradish cream, rather than buying it in a jar. As soon as you get the root out of the ground, wash it, grate it, put some lemon juice on it and leave it. Come back a bit later, add your cream and a touch of mayonnaise. A word of warning: horseradish root is very, very hot when it first comes out of the ground. I did some horseradish Yorkshire puddings a couple of years ago. I only grated a little bit of horseradish into the batter, made the pudding, put some in my mouth and ...whew! So be careful!

I do think people are gaining more confidence in using fresh produce, and taking more pride in what is produced in their own region. But we've got to stop it being taken away from us! We've got to start utilizing it, the way they do in France. Tremolat, where I worked, was just a little village but every Wednesday they had a market. You'd see produce there to stop you in your tracks: gorgeous local fruit and vegetables; ducks hanging up; someone selling their own homemade sausage or goats' cheese – proper artisan food. And bread. It was bread that had just been baked – straight out of the oven, into the van, on the stall and on sale. My father and I ran a bakery here for a few years until he retired in 2006. We used to deliver to local shops, hotels, restaurants and sell to the public, here in the Brasserie. There's nothing like good, fresh bread – and croissants of course – properly baked.

People want to see more of this kind of food in Britain. If you go to a farmers' market, like the one we have here in Southport, you can chat to producers, discover wonderful products – like Banks tomatoes. Vibrant-red, little plum tomatoes, grown just up the coast from here. Beautiful! We want to get away from buying everything in supermarkets. It's important, it really is.

A lot of our customers in the Brasserie are local, and they enjoy it when the produce on their plate comes from a farm they know. I like to know my customers and give them what they want. Many are regulars, including some who travel quite a distance. One guy loves foie gras and when I see his name in the bookings, I just get it ready and surprise him with it as a little intermediary course. Steven Gerrard comes in for our duck rolls. Another customer comes solely for the soup. 'It doesn't matter what soup you make', he says, 'you always make a good one.'

We are consistent in what we do here, both the food, the service. That's why we've got a Michelin Bib Gourmand and two AA rosettes and why we have customers coming back to us again and again. If a customer comes in one week for fish and chips and comes back for it again the week after, she expects it to be exactly the same.

Your staff team has a big role to play in achieving that. We're very lucky in having great longevity in ours, both in the kitchen and front of house. Darren Smith, for example, who is our head chef, started with me when he was 17. I don't know what this phenomenon is down to – not me! Perhaps it's due to the fact that we close on Sundays – always popular with staff! Or perhaps it's because we don't take ourselves too seriously. We work hard but we enjoy it.

This is a fun restaurant, somewhere customers can feel relaxed. The waiters are knowledgeable about dishes and wines, but the service isn't in your face. We're a brasserie and we don't pretend to be anything more. People know that the food is going to be good and they're going to feel good. It sets them up for a great night out.

Southport Shrimp Salad with Warm Formby Asparagus, Saffron and Ginger Dressing

SERVES 4

225g Southport shrimps
1 tbsp fresh mayonnaise
1 tsp crème fresh
1 avocado
12 Formby asparagus spears
Juice of 1 lemon
Zest of 1 lemon
Salt and pepper

For the Dressing
Pinch of saffron
Juice of 1 lemon
1 tsp finely chopped ginger
150ml extra virgin olive oil
Pinch salt and sugar

For the Garnish
A few peashoots

Dressing **1** Warm the lemon juice and saffron strands together, add the chopped ginger and leave to infuse. **2** Whisk the olive oil in slowly, along with a pinch of salt and sugar.

Asparagus **1** Peel the asparagus, but not too far up the stem. Trim each spear to an overall length of about 9cm cutting diagonally, using a sharp knife. **2** Bring a pan of water to the boil with a good pinch of salt and cook the asparagus, in batches, for 2-3 minutes. **3** Plunge the cooked asparagus into iced water to stop the cooking process. **4** Remove from the water and reserve until needed. **5** The asparagus should be served 'al dente', that is just tender but with a little crunch left.

Salad **1** Mix the cooked Southport shrimps with the mayonnaise, crème fresh, a squeeze of lemon, and a touch of lemon zest. **2** Check the seasoning, adding a little black pepper if required. **3** Peel the avocado and remove the stone. Roughly chop the flesh, add a squeeze of lemon to stop any discolouration, add seasoning to taste.

To Serve **1** You will need a metal ring approximately 7cm deep and 5cm in diameter. Press the shrimps into it about three quarters of the way up, topping up the remaining space with the avocado. If no ring is available simply pile the ingredients carefully to form a tower. **2** Warm the asparagus through, under the grill with a knob of butter. **3** Arrange 3 spears on each plate around the Southport shrimp tower, drizzle with saffron and ginger dressing as desired. **4** Garnish each plate with a few peashoots.

Locally Caught Sea Bass with Sweet Potato and Rosemary Purée and Garlic Buttered Marshside Sampy

SERVES 4

4 sea bass, skin on, scaled and pin boned (ask the fishmonger to oblige)
3 sweet potatoes
Small bunch rosemary
250ml milk
Bunch of freshly picked samphire
Knob of garlic butter
Sea salt
Olive oil

Sweet Potato Purée ☐1 Warm the rosemary and milk together, add the sweet potato and cook slowly until the potato just gives. Remove the rosemary. ☐2 Using a food processor, blend the sweet potato until it takes on a nice sheen. ☐3 Remove from processor and reserve in a small saucepan until needed.

Samphire ☐1 Simply blanch in boiling water – NO SALT – for a couple of minutes, then plunge into iced water to stop the cooking process. The woody stalk at the centre of the samphire is easily removed once blanched.

Sea Bass ☐1 Score the sea bass fillet skins to stop the fish curling up, season with sea salt crystals and brush with olive oil. ☐2 Place on buttered greaseproof paper on a baking tray and cook in the oven for 10-12 minutes at 180°C / gas mark 4.

To Serve ☐1 Warm the purée and swirl in the middle of the plate, place the sea bass fillet on top, skin side up. ☐2 Quickly sauté the samphire in the garlic butter and arrange around the plate.

The earthy flavour of the rosemary and sweet potato complement the fresh moist sea bass and samphire.

Baked Egg Custard Tart with Southport Honey

SERVES 4

For the Sweet Pastry
You will need a 20cm flan ring and baking beans
1 egg
225g plain flour
110g diced butter
50g caster sugar

For the Egg Mixture
9 egg yolks
500ml whipping cream
3 dsp Southport honey
30g caster sugar

Sweet Pastry 1 Rub the flour and butter together until the mixture resembles breadcrumbs, then mix in the sugar. 2 Make a well in the centre and add the egg, mix until the pastry comes together. 3 Place on a lightly floured surface and knead until smooth. 4 Place in cling film and refrigerate for 45 minutes. 5 Once the pastry has been rested, roll out and line the flan ring (any excess can be left hanging over the edge and trimmed once baked to ensure an even finish). 6 Line the pastry case with greaseproof paper, put in baking beans and bake for 15 minutes at 180°C / gas mark 4. 7 Once cooked remove from oven and carefully lift out greaseproof and beans.

Chef's Tip You can now brush egg wash (egg with a little water or milk added) all around the inside of the case and return to the oven for a couple of minutes to ensure that the case will not crack when the egg mixture is added.

Egg Mixture 1 Bring the cream to the boil. Mix the sugar and egg yolks together. 2 Pour the boiled cream onto the egg mixture and stir well, now add the honey and pass through a sieve, skimming any froth from the surface. 3 Pour the custard mix into the baked pastry case. 4 Turn the oven down to 120°C / gas mark 1 and bake for 30-40 minutes until the custard is just set. 5 Remove from the oven and allow to cool to room temperature before serving.

This is beautifully fragrant dessert which can be served on its own, but I like to serve it with locally grown fresh strawberries or poached rhubarb.

Christian and Tuk Peet
Gone shrimping
Merseyside

ACT I: OUT TO SEA

Shortly after seven one fine July morning, four of us set out from Southport on the ebb-tide to catch the brown shrimp which are local to this coast. For Christian and Tuk Peet of Southport Seafoods, the only husband-and-wife shrimpers hereabouts, it's a daily occurrence. Their living depends on it. For the photographer and myself, it's a voyage of discovery, and we both scent adventure in the salty air as we clamber aboard.

We're not on a boat but what the shrimpers call a wagon, an amphibious vehicle which defies comparison with any other sea-going craft. It is faintly reminiscent of a World War Two DUKW. With angular lines and squared-off front – you can't call it a prow – these shrimping wagons look anything but yare: more home-made, constructed from a sturdy garden shed and a trailer, mounted on lorry wheels. Nonetheless, they are well adapted to their purpose, and a new one, like Christian's, can set you back fifteen grand.

We trundle down a windswept dune onto the beach, a vast empty tract of watery sand, and begin heading north-west, across the Ribble estuary, towards an infinity of merging sea and sky. We are not quite alone against the huge horizon. Two other wagons are on the move behind us. Just two: and one of those is being driven by an 80 year-old, working on his own. 'Years ago it was a thriving business', observes Christian in his steady, mellifluous baritone. 'When my great-grandfather went shrimping with his horse and cart there used be as many as a hundred fishermen going out. There's hardly any now. When I pack in, that'll be it – because I am definitely the youngest person doing the job at the moment.'

Except, that is, for Tuk. She met Christian when he was holidaying in Thailand. They fell in love; eighteen months later her visa came through, and now they're looking forward to their third wedding anniversary and awaiting their first-born. As soon as she arrived in her new home, Tuk, a slight, willowy figure, insisted on coming out shrimping with her big, brawny husband. Does this mean she likes it, then?

'I love it!' she declares fervently, her merry eyes dancing with delight. 'From child, I love fishing. In Thailand the rainy season lasts three months and we catch fish, shrimps, crab, so I'm not scared.' She laughs. Her voice is lilting and she speaks English with an engaging accent: part Thai, part Southport. Elfin-like and lovely, in huge buttercup-yellow dungarees, Tuk sits on the tailboard, the breeze ruffling her jet-black hair, her face upturned to the already-hot, eight o'clock sun. She is clearly relishing every minute of the ride out.

Suddenly, we sight a wreck. It looks like the brown, barnacle-encrusted ribcage of a dinosaur, immensely long, embedded irrevocably in the rippled sand. Christian tells us about The Mexico, a 400-ton iron barque, which foundered here in 1886, and occasioned England's worst-ever lifeboat disaster. Of the three lifeboats that rowed to her rescue, two capsized, drowning 27 of the 29 crewmen. We grow momentarily silent. It is a daunting reminder. The sands here may look serene but they are treacherous, constantly shifting, riven with changing channels; continually revealing and concealing the remains of hundreds of ships that lie scattered along this stretch of coastline.

By now, Southport is a mere mirage in the blue-grey distance; our tracks have disappeared under an ankle's depth of sea and we have reached the Pinfold Channel, where our fishing will begin. Because the shrimp live in surface-burrows in the sand, to catch them you must work in shallow water, on the last wave of the ebb-tide, on the first flood of its successor.

Christian calls to Tuk from the wheelhouse and, in a flash, she has taken over from him. He strides to the back of the wagon to swing out the nets. 'Straighten up love!' he shouts back to her. 'Which way you want to go?' demands Tuk.

The deep-down throb of the diesel engine smothers their voices. Christian has put out two nets but one is not sitting right in the water. 'A nuisance that', he says mildly. 'I'm going to have to spin it round'. The wagon stops. He jumps off the tailboard into the sea and begins to heave at the unwieldy gear. This is hazardous. In a trice, Tuk has joined him and together they straighten the net, heavy with the weight of sand and water.

Then they are back up on board, dashing past us to the wheelhouse. 'Sorry', says Christian, 'but wagons tend to get stuck in the sand if you stand still too long, and then you can't budge them.'

Meanwhile, our companions have caught up and are moving in on us. 'Because I stopped, I've lost my little slot now', he begins (there's clearly an etiquette involved here) – then: 'Watch! You'll see the shrimp jumping.' And we do. A shower of luminous little bodies, every which way. 'That's a good sign – means there's plenty here. But it also means we've missed them – they've jumped over the side of the net.'

The engine roars in the now oppressively hot wheelhouse; the deck vibrates. The drag of the sand on nets in this shallow water must be incredible. 'I'm only fishing in first gear at the moment', he explains, over one shoulder. 'The reason is so as not to catch too many small fish because we have to sort out those out later.'

Christian dons his waterproof dungarees and prepares to haul in the nets. His strong arms and capable hands move with power and assurance. It is wet, salty,

Southport Seafoods, Marc Verité's supplier **293**

tricky work. He tosses a wriggling mass of life on deck, shakes the glistening net, propels it back into the water and we're back in the business of catching again.

The air is exhilarating; light and water dazzling. Activity becomes intense. Tuk starts to sieve the haul with practised skill. 'Alright darling?' asks Christian. 'A lot of fish', she answers, shaking her head. We see exactly what she means. Little flapping flounders, tiny plaice, the odd crab and a lot of whiting are mixed in with the shrimps. The whiting come specially, they love eating shrimps.

For those who have never seen them live, it might come as a surprise to know how straight brown shrimps are. Their segmented bodies are like translucent torpedoes, on delicate, filigree legs. Close-to, they look strange, primeval, sci-fi creatures: from fan-shaped tail to feathered face, black boot-button eyes and long, fine-drawn antennae. A kind of fawn colour, mottled with minute dark spots, they can lighten or darken to blend in with their backgrounds. Aficionados prize them for their flavour, rejecting the commoner pink kind.

Cast, catch, haul. Empty, sieve, separate. The work is repetitive, unremitting and, like everything to do with shrimping, physically demanding. Now Christian and Tuk are at the workbenches on either side of the open wagon, sieving back-to-back. Concentrating intently, they work in total harmony; quickly, silently; Christian's big, powerful fingers as nimble in this task as Tuk's slim, tapering ones. Any remaining young fish are individually removed and returned to the sea to live.

I try my hand at this last task. It's not as easy as it looks to grasp the slippery, somersaulting, bodies. 'Watch out for weever fish', warns Christian anxiously, pointing one out. They've got poisonous spines on the dorsal fin. 'If it pricks you in the finger it's not so bad. If the spine goes down your finger nail, you break-dance!'

Seagulls teem in, screeching, wheeling round the stern, diving for the spoils. The glittering water is so shallow, some wade. Then, as abruptly as they came, they depart, rising in a confused mass. The fishing is over for today.

Now it's time to cook the shrimps. Christian pours fresh water into the boiler and salts it. As well as being cleaner than sea water, this gives the shrimps a lighter look and a better taste, he says. While the boiler heats up, Christian and Tuk sieve, tidy, scrub, sweep up. Once the shrimps go in, they keep vigil, checking the flame, adjusting the gas. Cooking in the open, at sea, needs constant attention – even in the shallows – and Christian likes to cook his shrimps slowly, for 20–25 minutes, to retain flavour, colour and the right texture for peeling.

When the lid is raised an intensely pungent smell of salt and sea-flesh fills the air. Christian scoops them out onto cooling trays. Steam rises. Tuk and he swiftly peel some and hand them round. Hot, sweet, meltingly tender. Addictive! 'I know', says Christian, 'whatever you do to them later, they never taste so good as now. I have to watch her or there'd be none left!' Tuk laughs, 'I love them!' And we peel some more …

This is the first catch in the new wagon and it's been good – four baskets. Shrimping is a hit and miss affair, impossible to predict. Christian recalls one magic morning, ten years ago, when he was out with his dad: 'There wasn't a cloud in the sky, yet it seemed to be raining. I looked up and realised it was shrimps – shrimps jumping everywhere. We brought home seventeen basketfuls that day. Never known before, or since. The next morning I went back on my own and got a bucketful!'

Tomorrow, they will leave the wagon at home. It's a lower tide so they will take a tractor and work further out. They use three different vehicles in all, depending on conditions. The third is a quad bike, ideal for working in very shallow water. 'We take a trailer with us to put the baskets of shrimps in. We've had some very good catches at night.'

'You get black on the quad bike', puts in Tuk, grinning delightedly.

'Shrimping is hard work', reflects Christian 'and not always rewarding. Sometimes it's cold and miserable –'

'In the winter, it's crazy out here', she agrees. 'I wear about ten jumpers and I can hardly move!'

'But on a day like this', he asks the company in general, 'where would you rather be?' Nowhere else, that's for sure. They smile at us with the contentment of people completely happy in their work.

But already we're on the juddery ride back. Christian washes down the deck, parks up and transfers the cooked shrimps to his refrigerated van. These must be peeled and others must be potted. It's back home now for the second half of the day's labours.

ACT II: POTTING UP

We drive two or three miles north to the Marshside area of Southport, once a fishing village and, for many years, home to the Peet family, who have a long association with the sea. Through his grandmother, Christian can claim kin with the leader of the mutiny on The Bounty, Fletcher Christian. Like her, he too came from that old Isle of Man family.

Marshside is still a place full of character. The local pub is called The Shrimper. Not far from it, is the tellingly named Shellfield Road, where, years ago, nearly every resident was involved in the shrimp trade. Among its Victorian villas are far older, fishermen's cottages. At back of the Peet family house, invisible from the road, is an even more remarkable survivor: a nineteenth-century shrimp 'factory'. Painted gleaming white and no bigger than a cottage itself, it has two storeys: upstairs for peeling; downstairs for potting.

That is the venue for the afternoon's work, and after a delicious alfresco lunch of tea and mighty shrimp sandwiches, we are ready to begin. Before entering, everyone must put on whites and cover their hair. 'Cleanliness is the most important thing', insists Christian, as he leads us into the modern, stainless-steel interior. Although it is absolutely spotless, his first act is to clean all the surfaces again. He is preparing to make a product which can be traced back at least to the eighteenth century and one for which Southport has long been famous – potted shrimps. In antique shops, you can still find the little china ramekins in which they were once sold in, decorated with the producer's name and address.

Not all the shrimps Christian catches go for potting. A proportion will go, simply boiled and peeled, to restaurants, like the Warehouse Brasserie. The peeling is too time consuming a job for Christian and Tuk on their own. They have a team of peelers, their efforts co-ordinated by Mr Peet senior. 'When I was a kid', comments Christian, 'I used to have to peel shrimps when I came home from school, and I hated it, because all the other lads were out playing football. It's how I got very, very fast at the job. I used to help my dad, now he helps me. In fact, I couldn't do without him.'

But cooking shrimps for potting is entirely Christian's province: 'Only I do this.' First he heats up a large stainless steel wok on a gas brazier. He puts ground mace, ground nutmeg, salt, cayenne pepper and lemon-juice to sizzle in butter. When he judges the mixture blended, he stirs in cooked and peeled brown shrimps. This 'stews', to use the traditional terminology, for about twenty minutes until the flavours are absorbed. The aroma is intense and intensely pleasurable.

When they are done, the golden-brown shrimps are spread out to cool. 'They really are lovely', says Christian, 'you can taste them in a minute.' We do. And they are. A perfect marriage of ingredients.

Tuk then pots them: a mountain of shrimp to her left, plastic pots in the centre, electronic scales to her right. She works with wordless concentration, at lightning speed, checking the weight of each filled tub and demonstrating uncanny accuracy in the process. The only sounds are the click of her spoon on the stainless steel counter and the hum of the microwave, where Christian is softening oodles of butter. He tamps down the shrimps ready to receive their buttery cap. Then he pours in the whisked, molten gold that will seal them.

> "I used to have to peel shrimps when I came home from school, and I hated it, because all the other lads were out playing football. It's how I got very, very fast at the job. I used to help my dad, now he helps me."

And there you have that rare and desirable delicacy: authentic, brown, Southport potted shrimps. 'I think I'm the last one doing it from beginning to end of the process', muses Christian. 'I love what I do and I'm quite proud of it. I catch and cook them myself; I help peel and pot them myself, and I deliver them myself. You can't get more genuine than that!'

It is, you might say, a true cottage industry. On average they will do 300–500 pots a day. Most of Christian's business is wholesale but he has internet retail customers too, all the way from the Outer Hebrides to the Channel Islands. Right now, they are working flat out, but in February they will go to Thailand for a month, as usual, visit Tuk's family in the countryside where they grow rice and vegetables. Then they will sail down the River Kwai and stay in their usual hotel. 'I absolutely love the place', he says. 'It's life as we used to live it. You come back a different person, a better person.'

'At the end of the day, this job is about love, not money.' He turns to Tuk who is putting the lids on the pots. 'You're a great wife, you know that?' She smiles back at him, playfully.

A good catch. In every way.

*The Peets now have a son, baby Jack Christian, who they hope will carry on the family's shrimping tradition.

Picking samphire by the seashore

MARC VERITÉ RINGS: 'Do you fancy picking some samphire?' We're both fans of this wild-growing seashore vegetable. Sometimes known as sea asparagus, it's piquant, juicy and crisp. Marc likes to serve it with fish at the restaurant and he likes to pick it for home use too.

The name is a corruption of Saint Pierre – St Peter, the patron saint of fishermen. It was called after him because it grows mainly on the seashore. There are two main kinds of edible samphire, quite different species with distinct tastes: rock samphire (crithmum maritimum) is rare; only marsh samphire (salicornia europaea) – sometimes called glasswort – is readily available. It's the second sort we're after, known round here as sampy.

We meet at the Warehouse Brasserie and follow Marc (on his easy-park Vespa scooter) out of bustling Southport and along the unspoilt coast. He leads us to an empty stretch of salt marsh, so extensive that we can't even see the sea. Only the distant outline of Southport pier bears witness to its presence. Samphire is a robust coloniser of mudflats. Able to tolerate high salinity and tidal inundation, it prepares the way for other plants to follow. On this shore, it has played a key role in creating more land. 'When I came here with my grandma, about 1976, this was beach, with just a few patches of greenery – purely samphire, no other plants.'

Snaking towards the endless horizon nowadays is a man-made sandy causeway. There waiting for us is Marc's father, Claude, unmistakable, standing next to his Citroën deux chevaux van. Although he has lived his whole adult life round here, Mr Verité senior has never before picked samphire. Marc takes us three novices down onto the marsh. Our feet squelch with every step – a deep, satisfying squelch on springy turf.

At first it all looks like rough grass, with water glistening at the roots. But, after a swift lesson from Marc in plant identification, we each begin to get our eye in and realise there's samphire everywhere, among the sea purslane, asters and other flora. It looks like branching, emerald-green coral and it tastes as salty as the sea. You can crunch the jointed, fleshy stems between your teeth, and feel them pop like bubble-wrap. Eating it becomes compulsive and, soon, nobody can get enough.

Marc shows us the woody core of the stem and explains how you can easily pull it out after blanching the stalks in boiling water and letting them cool. 'I usually just serve it with butter after re-warming, but you can make a sweet pickle with it, which I used to do in the past.' And he begins to talk of wonders with green pesto, sweet red chilli jam and a balsamic reduction …

But if you stand talking in one place for any length of time, you find your feet are in two puddles. We disperse in search of more samphire, four hunter-gatherers on the saltmarsh. It is early July, the perfect time of year for this occupation. Samphire is reaching its peak (by September it will be finishing). The afternoon is brilliantly sunny, though barely warm in an onshore breeze. In the azure sky, clouds are swirling out like spun silk. We forage to a magical accompaniment of trilling birds; photographer Colin alerts us to a skylark (the Marshside nature reserve is close by).

"I usually just serve it with butter after re-warming, but you can make a sweet pickle with it."

All done, carefully clutching our bundles, we turn back. Marc has most – 'My three lads have more eye for sampy than me' – and he shares it with us. 'I will cook this tonight, when I return from playing tennis', says Claude in his enchanting French accent. We are each looking forward to a feast.

Marc Wilkinson

Fraiche
Oxton, Wirral

MARC WILKINSON'S INTIMATE AND SOPHISTICATED little restaurant, in the conservation village of Oxton, comes highly recommended. It is the first on Merseyside to be awarded three AA rosettes, as well as being named a rising star by Michelin. Here, modern cooking techniques are used to create a light, contemporary French cuisine which takes diners on thrilling adventures in taste, texture and temperature. Three skilfully composed, fixed-price tasting menus are the guide to subtle and complex dishes that surprise and delight. Only the best ingredients satisfy this chef-patron, who is as attentive to the creation of a beautiful eating environment as he is to the creation of beautiful food. Soft lighting bathes the warm sandy tones of the soigné interior, with its sensual suede chairs, specially commissioned artwork and fine tableware. Or you can dine al fresco to the soothing sound of a water sculpture. Art, architecture and design are important interests for this many-layered man, but food is his raison d'être. He devours the latest books, especially those on the science of food (often reviewing them for the catering press), and carries out his own action-research in great restaurants like El Bulli (returning with menus for guests to browse). Unassuming, immensely hardworking and gently humorous, Marc Wilkinson is lauded at every turn, for the dazzling quality of his cooking and the delicious originality of his food.

"WE TRY TO BE DIFFERENT AT FRAICHE. We try. It's very difficult to be original about everything, but we try to have our own touch, our own twist to things. The highlight of cooking for me is when you create a new dish. Take our Shot of Pesto. It's so good – one of my best amuse bouche! You take pesto and deconstruct it: put all the ingredients in front of you – or just picture them in your head – and then reconstruct them in a different format. What I am doing is a basil and lemon sorbet, with fresh parmesan shavings, and pine nuts with extra virgin oil. Close your eyes and you've got pesto there. But it's so fresh! – because the basil isn't cooked. It's raw in the sorbet so, when it hits, you get that floral depth which I love.

Of course, sometimes, you arrive at things by accident – like using rice as part of my seasoning for fish. It happened when I was making puffed rice. That's where you blow wild rice at 200° C until it puffs, a bit like popcorn. I just started experimenting, and found that if I crushed it, and mixed in liquorice, sea salt and orange-powder, I got an interesting crust on the skin of the fish.

At the moment, I'm working on rice pudding, which I like a lot. I began by cooking a classic version, like grandma used to make, with skin and everything, just to get back to the roots. Since then, I've made five more, one with rhubarb through it. The final version will look like a classic individual rice pudding in a copper pan – but it will taste quite different. In my head I know what I want to create, but it's translating that into reality that takes the time. Some dishes come quicker than others. The rice pudding is going to take a while ...

There's always a new dish in the back of my mind. I suppose that's what drives me. I know money makes the world go round, but Fraiche isn't money-driven. It doesn't give me sufficient incentive. I'm one of those passionate people who are a bit stupid in the head, who aren't that interested in financial gain. Ideally, money would be nice to have. Then I'd go and eat at Per Se, Thomas Keller's restaurant in New York. I suppose everything revolves around food with me!

My friends call me obsessed ... I am obsessed! But to be good at anything, I don't see how you can't be slightly bonkers about it. Take Salvador Dalí for example. I love Dalí – I've visited his galleries in Figueres. I think he was slightly mad, bless him, but look what work that produced!

Ferran Adrià, the most influential chef in the world, is another instance, but he's reaching the heights because of it. I met him at his restaurant, El Bulli, which is regularly voted the best in the world. He and his brother Albert, and the rest of the team, refuse to accept the same parameters as other people. It's the only way to break new ground.

The problem is you tend not to switch off. I normally work seven days a week at Fraiche. I do fifteen or sixteen hours straight in the kitchen, except Sundays and Mondays when we're closed. Monday is my day for meetings and job-runs, Sunday for any other tasks. So, now and again, when I need a break, I fly somewhere for a day. I go to Barcelona a lot. I love the architecture in Spain, especially the stunning modern buildings – the Guggenheim in Bilbao is better than the art inside! In particular, I love Catalonia – my second home. I leave on a Sunday from John Lennon Airport, Liverpool, have dinner at a good restaurant, then maybe a lunch somewhere else the next day, on my way back.

That's what I'm doing this weekend. I'm going to Barcelona and eating at Sergi Arola on Sunday and at Hisop, which is so exciting, on Monday. You *know* the food is going to make you sit up in your chair. It's not going to be a fishcake, lamb shank, or confit duck. You can eat food like that closer to home and it can be well cooked, substantial, comforting or whatever. But, for me, it's not *excitement*. It's not sensual, it's just sustenance.

I need these little breaks, just to fire me up. It's definitely important to eat out. Not enough chefs do. But I'd never go into a restaurant and copy a dish, just like for like. That's so lazy, and so unfair on the chef and restaurant that you've just visited. But they do it! Gordon Ramsay's lobster ravioli, Marco Pierre White's lemon tart, Michel Bras' chocolate fondant – you'll find them everywhere. The trouble is, when things get copied, they sometimes end up far removed from the original. For instance, Beefeater restaurants have chocolate fondant on the menu now, but it's a completely different entity from the fantastic dish invented by Bras in Laguiole.

Certain techniques, certain principles of cooking might come from something you've seen elsewhere, but sometimes, the ideas you pick up in places are nothing to do with the food. In Padua, at Le Calandre – which I think is the best restaurant in Italy – it was something about the service which stuck in my head. In Barcelona, at a restaurant called Abac, it was handbag hooks. I thought, why didn't we think of that? So, before I jumped on the plane, I went into El Corte Inglés bought two dozen, came home and installed them.

I designed Fraiche myself, on a seaside theme, inspired by views from my former home. We had to take this 1850s terraced house back to the bare brick and start afresh: new floors, new walls – the lot! Hard work, most of which I did myself. The thing is, you have this vision, this dream which drives you on. But it's fun too, especially working with artists who convert your ideas into reality. I'm a big fan of glass, so we have six pieces of wall art commissioned from Liverpool glass artist, Jenny Barker, and we've just taken delivery of water glasses, which are unique to Fraiche, by local artist Charlie MacPherson. Our glass plates are by two London artists I found through Heston Blumenthal at the Fat Duck, where I used to eat when I lived nearby. The 'moon' over the bar in the back room is by Paul Cocksedge, a fantastic lighting designer, who I came across at the V & A.

I go on evolving the restaurant in various ways, whether by adding new artwork, special tableware, or an outside eating area. It's all part of the pleasure, the theatre of dining out. I like guests to be able to relax in comfort, to be pampered. So I put a lot of emphasis on front of house. When you come here, you are always greeted and welcomed in. Even though you might have had a rough day at work, when you shut that door, you can just switch off. Sometimes people come in stiff as ice, but then friendly staff bring them some amuse bouche, they have a drink and start to melt. If we can make you smile, relax you, entertain you, surprise you, warm up your spirit by giving you something that tastes wonderful … that's what drives me too, I guess.

How did I start in this business? I was fifteen, I was poor, and I wanted a bike! So I got a job as a chef's donkey in Anglesey, North Wales, which is where my family had moved to from the Wirral. The restaurant was in a three-star hotel. Scampi, fillet steak, sole meunière – this food was all new, all exciting. It's cringeworthy now, but back then I didn't know what these things were. I'd never eaten out in a restaurant as a kid. It was unheard of. A packet of crisps in the back of the car was the scenario – we never actually went into any of these places.

Things are much better now, and if I had children I would definitely, definitely bring them up dining in restaurants. It opens the palate – and opens the mind to so much more. Hopefully, they wouldn't have tunnel vision for MacDonalds and eating chips. I'd be gutted if a child of mine turned out like that. I can hear it now:

'Oh dad, how can you eat this rubbish? You never take us anywhere nice!'

And I'd growl, 'Shut up and eat your foie gras!'

Anyway – back in Anglesey – I got my bike. The work just seemed to click with me, and I was rapidly getting more responsibility in the kitchen. So there I was, plodding along, when a programme came on TV called *Take Six Chefs*. It turned my world upside down. I watched it in awe. I was absolutely gobsmacked at what these people did with food!

Suddenly, I realised I wasn't even scratching the surface of what was out there. The world of fine dining was where I wanted to be. So I asked my father to take me to a Michelin-starred restaurant for my eighteenth birthday. He did, and I was hooked. Once the addiction kicks in, it's a one-way street: the more you experience, the more your palate is opened up, the higher your expectations become, and the higher your standards rise.

So I got myself a job in a classical French kitchen, at a restaurant run by a French family in Yorkshire. It was a good solid foundation. I did everything:

butchered the meat, plucked the birds, boned the fish, shucked the oysters ... It was a hard time, but an awakening.

Next, I spent two years in the Michelin-starred Arkle restaurant at The Chester Grosvenor, followed by a spell at Winteringham Fields, Lincolnshire, which had two stars at the time. My travels took me to Canada for a year, working at one of the country's best hotels, a five-star Relais Chateaux, but it was after I returned to England that my eyes were really opened.

It happened while I was head chef at the Mirabelle in Eastbourne's Grand Hotel. I took a trip to Paris to eat at Pierre Gagnaire. The experience blew me away! I know a restaurant has been good if, when I come out and I'm walking down the street, I've got flavour memories in my head. I had a sole dish at Pierre Gagnaire and wow! I can still taste it. That was 2000 – the year I woke up – and the beginning of the next big change in my life. Since then, my cooking has been evolving into the modern cuisine that I do now.

The thing about Gagnaire is, he pushes the boundaries of cooking. He became a mentor for me and made me start questioning everything. Up to that point, I did things because that's the way they were done. After Gagnaire, I wanted to understand *why*. So, I began to read a lot more on the science of food, by authors such as Peter Barham, and Harold McGee. I was intrigued. I started studying the work of the brilliant French scientist, Hervé This, who wrote *Molecular Gastronomy: Exploring the Science of Flavour*. He has worked with a number of chefs, including Gagnaire, and is one of the founding fathers of molecular gastronomy.

It's all about breaking things down so you understand them – simple things like crème anglaise. Traditionally, you would split a vanilla pod, put it in the milk and heat, not realising that there is an enzyme in milk which works against vanilla and mutes the flavour. But, if you heat the milk up to 80°C first and *then* add the vanilla, the enzyme is killed by the heat, and this allows the vanilla to be absorbed better. It's such a simple little thing – but only when you know!

Take eggs. We poach eggs in a water bath. Egg white sets at a different temperature to egg yolk, hence you can hold a poached egg hot for hours without it setting – providing you know what temperature egg yolk sets at. So, if you hold the egg at 64° C, the yolk won't set.

This kind of knowledge is the key to improving your cooking techniques. However, as I've said, I was trained in the classical French tradition – it was drilled into me! If you look at those chefs around my age group who are cooking well now, nearly all of us have solid classical French backgrounds. It induces such a firm foundation to build on.

The only worry now is that the next generation of cooks, who want to do the foams and all the high-tech modern cooking, won't have that solid foundation. They want to do this all-singing and dancing cooking but lack the basic building blocks. If you ask them can they make puff pastry, they just look blank. I asked one young chef, who had done three years at college, if he could make crème anglaise. He replied, 'No, can you show me?' I said, 'You've done three years at

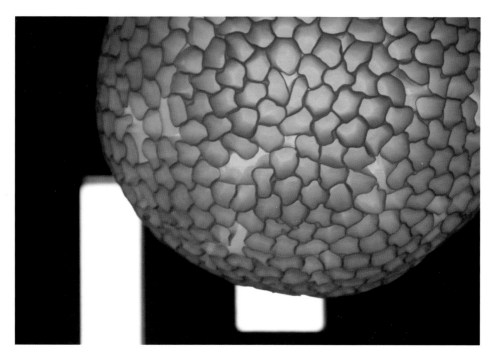

college and you don't know how to make custard?' 'No, we didn't do that. I can make a rose out of marzipan.' Really good functional stuff that!

We make everything here – except cheese biscuits. I buy those in – decent ones, like Duchy, charcoal, lavender oatcakes. We make our own breads – I love bread, you see. Of course, there's no point in doing it just for the sake of putting 'handmade' on a menu. If a local baker can make a superior product, and save you time, buy it in – there's no stigma attached. To get bread right, I think, is a bit more difficult than people say. I've spent many an hour, studying and experimenting and working it. Because bread is not something you can just take from a book. It's something about the texture, the feel – and I know when it feels right.

I'm a thorn in the side of suppliers because I always want something a bit better! 'It's only you ever moans, Marc', they tell me, 'nobody else does.' When I opened Fraiche, in April 2004, it was difficult to get the produce I needed. I had been working as head chef of the Latymer restaurant at Pennyhill Park hotel in Surrey. I was on the hub of London there, so produce and suppliers were thick and fast. I never had to worry about getting anything. I'd just ring up and it would be there the next day. My cheeses came twice a week from Rungis in Paris, the biggest wholesale food market in the world. Premier Cheeses would have two hundred of them in the back of the van, all proper cheeses – it was just heaven! But they don't deliver up here – too far away.

For ten years I used Pascal Beillevaire butter, which for me is the best in the world. If you go to Gordon Ramsay's restaurant in Hospital Road, or the Manoir aux Quat'Saisons, that's what you get and it is fantastic – but Pascal Beillevaire doesn't deliver here either! Salads were another problem. If I asked for woodruff, verbena, purple basil, bulls blood leaves, or peashoots my suppliers would say, 'What d'ya want that for? Nobody else asks for them.' It was like Paul Heathcote all over again, a generation later!

Like him, I was coming back to my roots, coming home to my family. I like the Wirral, and Oxton is particularly attractive. In the centre, where Fraiche is, there are quite a few restaurants, cafés and pubs. There's strong community spirit too, with village events, which are good for Oxton – and good for business! But once here, I had to rethink quite a few things on the supply front.

Whenever possible I use local produce, but because we're a French restaurant I have French products too. Cheeses, for instance, come from France and here. We use Mrs Bourne's Cheshire and Bourne's Blue Cheshire and we also use unsalted butter from their family farm, just outside Malpas. I tasted a number of local butters and Mrs Bourne's was the best.

Fresh produce is gaining momentum, and I really look forward to the asparagus season at Claremont Farm here on the Wirral. Their asparagus is great, their courgette flowers too. I like flowers, full stop. I use them in my cooking – nasturtiums, roses, courgette flowers. I use rose extract and the petals too, which I crystallize so you get a crunch from them which is rather nice. I even use dandelion leaves to give salad a bit of a kick, a little like woodruff. Now it's spring, I'm looking forward to local wild garlic too.

I try to get to local Farmers' Markets whenever I can, but I wish we had more really good, local, daily food markets in this country. It's so frustrating when you see all the amazing examples in other european countries. I've spent many an hour in La Boqueria in Barcelona – the fish alone, the sea cucumbers and urchins – it's brilliant. But it's not just Spain or France or Italy you find them. In Ireland, Cork has its excellent English Market. Every city needs one. They're great for everybody, fascinating for children and great for encouraging local produce.

When I first came here, meat was a problem, but it's sorted now thanks to a fantastic high-street butcher at New Ferry on the Wirral. His name is Callum Edge. Through him I source excellent, locally produced meat, like my Gloucester Old Spot pork. He supplies my lamb and beef too, and when they have a rare breed, they'll let me know and we'll talk about hanging and for how long.

For so many of us today the connection from beast to frying pan is broken. You go to the supermarket and it's some product in plastic. There's no sense that it was ever a beast. Some kids you speak to might never, ever, have seen a cow. They don't realise where their bacon, or any other meat they see in a packet, really comes from. It's very, very easy to switch off from the real relationship, but it's important that we don't – as the recent national debate about battery chickens has shown. At Fraiche we only buy free-range chickens and free-range eggs, organic as well. It's not that I'm an organic obsessive, but what I buy must taste good *and* it must be reared well. So I'm specially pleased I can choose Callum for this book. There's such a demand for his meat, I felt sure another chef would claim him before I got the chance!'

Collection of Rabbit

SERVES 4

1 rabbit (ask your butcher to cut into pieces and to keep the offal intact)

Booth's ventrèche bacon, sliced wafer thin

2 calamari with tentacles

3-4 tbsp chicken mousse (blend a cooked chicken breast with double cream until a smooth consistency)

2 tbsp carrots, finely chopped, (blanched in boiling water for 1 minute then plunged into ice cold)

2 tbsp celeriac, finely chopped, (blanched in boiling water for 1 minute then plunged into ice cold)

1 peeled onion (for the stock)

1 roughly chopped celery stick (for the stock)

Tarragon leaves

1 baby Gem lettuce

Duck fat

1 medium Maris Piper potato

Paprika

Kikkoman soy sauce

Thyme / Parsley / Rosemary / Bayleaf / Peppercorns

1 The day before salt the legs with lots of herbs (thyme, parsley and rosemary). **2** Bone the loins, wrap tightly in cling film into a torpedo shape. **3** Trim and clean the offal – clean the liver and make sure that any green bile residue has been removed, cut out the white sinews, soak the heart in water, remove the outer sinew from the kidneys and soak over night in milk. **4** Use the rabbit carcass to make the stock – place the carcass in a saucepan with 1 chopped celery stick and 1 peeled onion, add thyme, parsley, bayleaf and some peppercorns. Cover with water and simmer for two to three hours until reduced by half. This will be used later to braise the lettuce.

Cannelloni **1** Next day, confit the legs with the duck fat at 80°C for 3 hours. Then leave to cool. Break down once cold – do not flake meat while still warm. **2** Mix the chicken mousse with the confit rabbit and add the chopped vegetables, pre-blanched and refreshed. **3** Blanch the tarragon to remove bitterness, chop finely and fold into the mix. Leave in the fridge to rest. **4** Clean the calamari, removing all the visible membrane and split lengthways. Pound with a meat cleaver until even and to ensure tenderness. Scrub the tentacles of grit and soak for 5 minutes in water. **5** Build the 'cannelloni' using the flesh of the calamari as the pasta with the rabbit confit mix rolled inside. **6** Once you have created your cigar shape, wrap in finely sliced ventrèche bacon to cover the calamari. Wrap tightly in cling film and rest. **7** Cook for 8 minutes in a simmering pan of water, rest, then roast in butter to finish – just to give a good colour. **8** Pan fry the loin meat of the rabbit for a couple of minutes each side in a hot frying pan. **9** Dust the tentacles with flour, salt and paprika before deep frying at 180°C until crisp.

Garnish **1** Peel the potato and grate coarsely, season, form into rounds and brush with butter. Bake in the oven for around 8-10 minutes at 150°C / gas mark 2 or longer until crisp. **2** Cut the baby Gem lettuce in half, braise in the rabbit stock for about 10 to 15 minutes. Test they are cooked by inserting a skewer to check they are soft all the way through. **3** Dry the offal, brush with Kikkoman soy sauce, and then quickly roast on the stove and rest.

To Serve **1** Slice the cannelloni into 4 even pieces, top with the crisp tentacles. **2** Build the tiers of loin and offal between the rosti, layering in the braised baby Gem lettuce leaves.

Marinated Pork Belly with Cocoa Roasted Shallots and Apple Cream

SERVES 4

For the Pork Belly
1 half Neston Gloucester Old Spot pork belly, salted for 24 hours with sea salt and hard herbs (rosemary, thyme, tarragon)
Fat for roasting
1 chopped onion
2 carrots

For the Marinade
200ml Kikkoman soy sauce
250ml sweet white wine
50ml white wine vinegar
2 heaped tbsp tomato puree
3 tbsp honey
3 star anise
Crushed coriander seeds

Pork Belly **1** Wash the pork belly to remove the salt. Lay it on the onions and rough chopped carrots to keep the meat out of the fat in the roasting tin. **2** Slow roast for 2-3 hours in the oven at 150°C / gas mark 2 until cooked through and tender. **3** Allow to cool then press by putting them in a terrine dish, placing a plate on top that is weighted down with weights (or tins of food could be used). Place in the fridge for 4 to 6 hours until the meat feels firm to the touch, cut into 4 generous portions and drop in the marinade and leave for 8 hours.

For the Apple Cream
1 Granny Smith apple
Olive oil
5 tbsp apple juice

For the Cocoa Shallots
16 baby shallots
Cocoa powder
Thyme
Knob of butter

Cocoa Roasted Shallots Peel and blanch whole shallots. Dust with a sprinkling of cocoa powder and cook in butter and thyme in a microwave on full power, covered for 3 to 4 minutes until soft.

Apple Cream Peel and cook the apple in the juice and olive oil until tender, then purée.

To Serve We serve with pickled girolles and wild rocket, together with a black pudding tian, which is a layered tower of potato with thinly sliced black pudding.

Taste of Carrot

SERVES 4

For the Carrot Cake
250g plain flour
1 tbsp baking powder
1 tbsp bicarbonate of soda
1 tsp ground cinnamon
Fresh grated nutmeg
200g unrefined sugar
200ml ground nut oil
3 eggs
350g carrots, peeled and grated
50g raisins
50g sultanas

For the Carrot and Orange Jelly
200ml fresh orange juice
50ml fresh carrot juice
10g passion fruit juice
40ml water
40g sugar
$^1/_3$ leaf bronze gelatine
2g agar agar (available from health food shops)

Carrot Cake [1] Sieve flour with baking powder and bicarbonate of soda. [2] Whisk the eggs well with the sugar and slowly add the oil. [3] Make a well in the flour mixture and pour in the egg mix, mix slowly until well combined. [4] Add the rest of the ingredients, stirring in well, so everything is evenly distributed. Place in a greased standard loaf tin. [5] Bake at 150°C / gas mark 2 for 20 minutes. Test with a prong or toothpick after 20 minutes – if it comes out clean the cake is cooked.

Carrot and Orange Jelly [1] Pre-soak the gelatine in cold water. [2] Place all ingredients into a pan and heat, adding the drained gelatine, and whisk gently as you bring it to the boil. [3] Take off the heat and pass through a fine sieve into a deep dish to allow to set. [4] It should take about 20 minutes to become jelly.

For the Sesame Biscuit
65g caster sugar
20g toasted sesame seeds
30g butter
35g flour
25ml orange juice

For the Carrot Sorbet
250ml carrot juice
180ml orange juice
65ml still mineral water
70g caster sugar
1 tbsp glucose

Sesame Biscuit [1] Cream the sugar with softened butter, add the juice and, as it mixes, start to add the flour to stop the mix from splitting. Finally add the seeds. [2] Place in a sealed container, in the fridge, for at least 4 hours. [3] Either shape before baking using a cutter and place on a non-stick sheet or to give a more rustic look spread out on the sheet and break into pieces after cooking. Cook at 160°C / gas mark 3 for 15 to 20 minutes.

Carrot Sorbet [1] Place all the ingredients into a pan and heat gradually to dissolve all the sugar then allow to cool. [2] Churn in an ice cream maker or freeze in a flat dish, stirring every 30 minutes and store in the freezer.

For the Carrot Slices
2 carrots
Stock syrup
100ml water
80g caster sugar
20g grenadine

Carrot Slices [1] Peel the carrots, remove top and bottom, peel thinly and blanch in boiling water to soften. [2] Make the stock syrup by adding the sugar and grenadine to the water. Boil until it starts to thicken but don't let it change colour. [3] Place the carrot slices in the stock syrup and store in the fridge

To Serve Slice the carrot cake thinly, place on a plate, shape the sorbet into an even egg shape (quenelle) and sit in a small piece of cake to hold in place, add orange jelly and hibiscus sauce, which can be bought, ready made, from Lakeland Ltd. [2] Dry the carrot slices on a piece of kitchen paper and roll into a tube shapes, to which you can add more sorbet or fill with a vanilla mousse as we do in the restaurant. [3] Finish with a piece of sesame biscuit and, if possible, dust with citric acid over the sorbet.

Callum Edge
Meat like it used to be
New Ferry, Wirral

A JOLLY BUTCHER. THAT'S CALLUM EDGE. The expression could have been coined for him, he's such a sunny personality. He looks it too: open face, rosy cheeks, lively eyes and fair hair that sports an engagingly Tintin-like tendency. He bouys you up with his friendly way and the infectious enthusiasm he has for his calling. And with Callum, it *is* a calling.

He's the fifth generation of his family to run this remarkable butcher's shop. Built by John Edge in 1844 as a first-rate enterprise, it has never wavered. 'Throughout the generations, we've always tried to have the best of stocks', says Callum. 'We're very passionate about our business here.'

You can see that passion – and pride – from the moment you arrive. The whole place gleams: from the shop-window to the chiller cabinets; from the counter to the white-tiled walls. Edge and Son are the way good butchers used to be. Fine matured carcasses hang whole from polished steel racks. Smart young men are cutting customers' meat to order, or wrapping up Edge's home-cured bacon, home-made sausages, mince and burgers, all produced from the rare and traditional native breeds which are the speciality of the business.

On blackboards, suspended from the ceiling, they chalk up their current stock. And what a roll-call of Britain's best is here: Gloucester Old Spot pork; Southdown and Suffolk lamb; Hebridean mutton. As for beef, today you can take your pick from Shorthorn, Longhorn, Hereford, Highland and Aberdeen Angus. It's meat with that rare quality in the 21st century – real flavour.

This is why customers beat a path to the shop. Whether they're young or old, from the immediate neighbourhood or much farther afield, they all have one thing in common: discerning tastebuds. This meat is unlike your average supermarket offering. You can tell just by looking. The colour is different, the flesh firmer, un-wet. That's partly because Callum hangs his pork and lamb to mature for at least one week and up to two; his beef from three to five weeks.

Then there's the provenance. He buys direct from small farms in the vicinity, from people who share his commitment to the endangered native breeds, who treat their animals well and practise good hands-on husbandry. Callum has no truck with unnatural foodstuffs, growth-promoters or anything else he thinks inimical to a healthy diet and a healthy animal. 'We're only interested in the best bred, the best fed and the best kept stock we can find.'

Once upon a time, Callum could find much of that stock at cattle markets. He went to two a week, like his father and grandfather before him. But a decade or so ago, things altered. 'I was looking for Traditional Herefords or Dexters or Shorthorn beef, and I'd want them to be two-and-a-half to three years of age. But all that was available were twelve-month old continental breeds, all extremely lean. It just wasn't the type or standard of beef we wanted.'

Then he was approached by the meat marketing operation of the Rare Breeds Survival Trust. 'They're called the Traditional Breeds Meat Marketing Company and they told us about their scheme to link around fifty butchers in the UK with farmers who were breeding just the sort of stock we were looking for. It was was like a breath of fresh air! They accredited us as the butcher in the Northwest and that put us in touch with the specialist farmers.'

The accredition scheme requires butchers to work to exacting standards, and encourages shoppers to check for product authenticity. Individually signed certificates guarantee that the meat you're buying is what it claims to be. They also provide information on an animal's life history.

'Traceability – it's a bit vague at times isn't it?' Callum muses. 'It's hard to believe all the supermarkets know where every ounce of their meat comes from when they go through so many thousands of tons. Here traceability is easy, simple and assured. We can tell you about every animal we buy, from birth right through to the shop-counter. We can tell you how and where it's been reared and what it's been eating.'

They can also tell you where the animal was slaughtered. In most instances, the answer is: 'Here'. Because Edge and Son have their own slaughterhouse – a common feature of butchers' shops until the 1930s, but most unusual now. They have just completed a major refurbishment of their small facility, making it, and the associated boning and preparation areas, as ultra, ultra modern as the shop and meat are traditional. It is an investment that bucks the trend. In recent years, roughly three-quarters of Britain's small local slaughterhouses have been forced out of business by a deluge of government regulations and rocketing inspection costs. Less than 300 are left.

'I asked one of the guys from the licensing authority, Defra (Department for Environment Food and Rural Affairs), if he thought I was crackers to renovate. Financially it doesn't make any sense at all because we could contract our slaughtering out. But I knew, in my heart of hearts, if we did that our food miles would shoot up and the quality would drop down. Everything we stand for, we'd lose. Controlling your own destiny is very important, and you can't put a price on your reputation.

'It's quality we're looking for, not speed, which is unusual to say in this day and

age. When the licensing officer comes here and sees a lamb carcass we've just dressed he says, 'Gosh, I wish everybody did them like you.' But we do 10 an hour, whereas some slaughterhouses are doing more than 550. Once you up the numbers in any activity, you lose that individual attention.

'Then there are the farmers to think of. If we didn't carry on with the slaughterhouse we'd be leaving them on their own without any support. Many would be forced to give up.'

This is exactly the situation in large areas of the country. The steep decline in small slaughterhouses has created great difficulties for the nation's farmers, and there are serious welfare issues with animals having to be transported longer and longer distances. The big industrial abattoirs and cutting plants, which supply meat to the supermarkets, often don't want to deal with farmers producing small numbers, however good they may be.

Most of Callum's farmers are in Cheshire, where his own family farmed livestock during the 1700s, in the hamlet of Edge. From there, they would walk them to the 'new ferry' and cross the River Mersey to sell them wholesale in the up-and-coming new town of Liverpool. When ship-owners and prosperous merchants began to settle around rural New Ferry (then part of Cheshire), road and rail connections followed, along with John Edge to cater to the carriage-trade.

Over the years, the area has altered with the arrival of industry, commerce, suburbia and supermarkets. Edge's fortunes have fluctuated with the changes, but in recent times the business has flourished, more than doubling its turnover in the last few years. A big factor has been Callum's decision to diversify into supplying farmshops and fine dining restaurants. 'We have to sell a carcass from nose to tail, so if you have a restaurant that only takes fillet steak, they're not much use to us. The fine dining restaurants may well have fillet steak on the menu, but they have so much else as well. They use a wide variety of cuts because they have such culinary skill and do so much work with them.

'Nobody can put more effort in than Marc Wilkinson. I don't think we've ever had a restaurant here like Fraiche in Oxton, which is going to such high levels that it could be Michelin starred. We never would have had that ten years ago.

'It's my job to understand what the chefs are trying to do. And just as Marc Wilkinson comes here and tells me what he wants and how he wants it, I do the same with our farmers. It's important to get things straight with the people who are supplying you, and with the people you are serving.'

In the shop they serve a wide social mix of families and individuals. Callum says the average age has dropped over the last fifteen years ('a lot are much younger than me') and they are much more knowledgable too, often asking for beef, in particular, by breed. He reckons half come because he is selling good products; the other half because they want something different – and better. They like the fact that it's all raised locally as well, whether it's Cheshire-bred Hebridean mutton from Norley and venison in season from Beeston Castle, or Gary Pratt's Longhorns from Barnston and, at Christmas, Sally Hawkins turkeys from Childer Thornton on the Wirral.

But don't a lot of people feel nervous coming into a proper butcher for the first time, after the anonymity of shopping for packets off the supermarket shelf? 'Without a doubt', Callum agrees. 'We haven't got everything all packaged up – we'll cut it for you, then and there. Some might say that's intimidating but you've a far better chance of getting the right thing, compared to picking up something with a vague description on it. When you see a label that says 'rump steak' in the supermarket, some of it will be just that, but some may be topside, some top rump – you'd have to be a butcher to know exactly what you're buying!

'Tell us what you're cooking and we'll guide you so you get the cut you need for your dish. Chefs are always saying, ask your butcher, and all of us here are happy to help. We have a training scheme for staff and they become very knowledgeable about meat and how cuts should be cooked – and very passionate about food in general. I'm very lucky that my wife, Debbie, loves cooking and has been a great help. There is a thirst for knowledge about meat out there, and if I was recommending one book it would be Hugh Fearnley-Whittingstall's *River Cottage Meat Book*. I learnt a lot from that. And where values and beliefs are concerned, his *Meat Manifesto* says it all for me.'

As we speak, a wonderful aroma of cooking wafts into Callum's tiny office. 'Ah, that's a piece of roast Shorthorn beef, and two Gloucester Old Spot gammons which we've cured ourselves and honey-glazed. The hams are from Nigel Jones who we're going to see this afternoon. We don't do a lot of cooked meats, but what we do, we do ourselves. We don't buy anything in.'

It's the same with their sausages. They make about 20 varieties. 'That's what the guys are doing at the moment. The biggest seller is what we call our '1844'. It's just a traditional pork sausage, but it's my great-great grandfather's recipe – very simple, very nice. This morning we did one of my favourites, which is a gluten-free pork sausage using Basmati rice instead of rusk. I think the rice really takes in the flavour of the meat. We sell more sausages than we ever have and I think we make them better than we ever have – though I don't suppose my father would agree!'

Mr Edge senior retired about sixteen years ago, but there's at least one member of the eight-strong all-male team, besides his son, who worked with him. That's Stan who started here at 16 in 1963. He reckons he's stayed so long because he's a

perfectionist and Edge's is a place where he can make the most of that characteristic. He's not alone as a long-stayer. John's put in eleven years, and it's ten years since Callum's nephew Graham Edge joined the firm. 'It was his choice, there was no pressure on him', says his uncle. 'I don't have any children and it would be nice if the business went down another generation. We'll have to see what he wants to do.'

Callum reflects: 'We do have an amazingly slow turnover of staff. 'It's funny, I think it's a bit about belonging. We have a dress standard here about wearing a tie, and when I asked a couple of the younger ones about having polo shirts for the summer they were dead against it. "Oh no", they said, "we're so different from everybody else!" My father and grandfather always wore a straw boater. I tried one in my early twenties, but I couldn't get on with it. Butchers' boaters are rigid and if you touch against anything in one, it's like hitting your head with a hammer! I'm the first Edge not to have worn one – so you can see how standards are falling away!'

> "Tell us what you're cooking and we'll guide you so you get the cut you need for your dish."

Would he ever have considered *not* coming into the family business? 'I never wanted to do anything else. Though, if I wasn't a butcher, I'd love to have been a mountain guide or professional yachtsman – skiing and sailing are my other passions. If this was a normal butcher's shop, I don't think I'd be so interested. I love the rare breeds, the variety of the work, and I like dealing direct with people – the farmers, the chefs and the customers in the shop, helping them and advising them.'

Like the traditional native livestock breeds, highly skilled craft butchers like Callum Edge are rare in Britain. Their average age is 57. That, fortunately, gives Callum more than ten years leeway, but at present the broader picture is less promising for his ilk. Side by side with the public's increasing interest in quality meat, is a serious staff shortage in high street butchers and a dearth of young people interested in training. Some, though keen on eating meat, are not prepared to handle it raw, or recognise the reality of where it comes from – a case of what Joanna Blythman calls 'the yuk factor'. Callum Edge believes in honesty in the food business and sells fully traceable, real meat from properly dressed carcasses, properly hung and cut with skill. Without him and butchers like him, many small local livestock farmers, and native breeds, would soon fade from Britain's fields, and a rich diversity of taste from its tables.

Nigel Jones
Gloucester Old Spots
Ness Heath Farm, Cheshire

WE'VE COME ABOUT SIX MILES DOWN THE ROAD on the Wirral peninsula from Edge and Son Butchers to Ness Heath Farm, where Nigel Jones rears his Gloucester Old Spot pigs. The journey has taken us across the local government border from Merseyside into Cheshire and from an urban to a rural landscape. In a further demarcation twist, we're now on land belonging to the University of Liverpool, on the extensive site of their world-class Veterinary School, Leahurst. There are two teaching farms here: Wood Park, specialising in dairy cows, and this one which Nigel manages, concentrating on beef cattle, sheep and pigs.

'The students come to learn about animal husbandry and best practice', he explains, as the three of us stand in a barn, deep in straw, looking at an enormous Gloucester Old Spot sow with her piglets scampering around her. There are nine of them, in coats like silk velvet, pink and white and black polka-dotted, taking terrible liberties with their weighty mother. We're wreathed in smiles, riveted by their antics, but what they're really after is a drink off mum, and she doesn't seem to be co-operating

Nigel explains: 'They suckle when she let's them know she's ready. Usually, it's after she's eaten. She seems to signal to them, then they gather round her and she lies down – hopefully without crushing any of them. It can take up to four or five minutes before she lets the milk down. She'll grunt nineteen to the dozen when it starts to flow and the look of concentration on the piglets' faces is incredible! Of course, they're all trying to get the best teat, you see.' A good sow will have fourteen teats – but not all may be functional.

As we talk, the sow's mood changes and she prepares to lie down. It's a dangerous moment for the eagerly clustering piglets and they show an instinctive wariness. Even though these are not newborns (who weigh little more than a kilo), but sturdy little chaps (a couple of weeks old and about the size of a Jack Russell terrier) they have no chance of withstanding the full 420 kilo impact of their immense dam. Three people watch transfixed. Thump! Three deep intakes of breath, then urgent counting: five … seven … nine. Relief. 'They're all there, Nigel, and nine's a good litter.' 'Yes, but we had 11 last week until she laid on two. It's heartbreaking, but we nearly always lose one or two.'

Although Old Spot sows are known for being devoted mothers, they have a terrible habit of laying on their piglets. From that point of view, it might seem a wonder that this, the oldest spotted pedigree breed in the world, has survived at all. Indeed, it nearly didn't: in 1970 there were only 100 left. But the cause was human, not porcine. After World War Two, pigs with black pigmentation fell from public favour. Intensive, indoor farming began and outdoor rearing declined (the Old Spot is a hardy, free-foraging, open-air pig); people wanted lean breeds (the Old Spot is famed for its tasty fat and crackling); and the big commercial breeders wanted fast growers (the Old Spot is slower to mature).

As for the rich flavour and succulence of the meat, everyone forgot about that, except for a few Gloucestershire folk, especially those in the Vale of Berkeley where this so called 'orchard pig' originated. A few Old Spots survived, a fine sight with their portly frames, lop-ears and snub-noses, flourishing on windfalls from the fruit trees, as they had done for centuries.

The decisive factor in saving this delightful pig from extinction was an initiative, taken by the Rare Breeds Survival Trust in the 1990s, to develop a speciality market for Old Spot pork and bacon. As a result the population grew, proving the adage that rare breeds are only rare because people stopped eating them. Today there are some 600 pedigree breeding sows – not sufficient for complacency but enough to lift the Gloucester (or perhaps more properly, Gloucestershire) Old Spot off the danger list. Asked to name a rare breed of pig today, this is the one which most of us will cite.

'I think we were one of the first farms round here to have them', Nigel recalls. 'We started about six or seven years ago. We hadn't had pigs before, because the students used to go off site for them. Once we decided to have them here, I began looking for a placid breed because we do the first-year handling class and, understandably, many of the students are quite frightened to begin with. I was always interested in traditional breeds, so I took advice from the Survival Trust and they recommended Gloucester Old Spots for their easy-going nature.'

We leave the sow and her quiet, contented piglets for a group of vociferous 'fatteners' next door. They are bouncing around, rooting in straw, the picture of health and vigour. At six months old, with the biggest weighing between 72 and 75 kilos, eighty to ninety per cent of these pigs will go to Edge's by the end of the week. They are reared two or three months longer than a commercial breed. 'But if you let them get to over 90 kilos', says Nigel, 'they'll start to lay down a lot of fat'.

'You'd end up with chops like T-bone steaks!' points out Callum. 'They'd simply be commercially unviable.' 'And', Nigel adds, 'although I'm part of the University, I've got to make a profit on each enterprise: sheep, cattle and the pigs.'

How do a farmer and butcher manage to sustain a successful business relationship in the uncertain world of animal rearing and the volatile livestock market? Callum answers: 'My grandfather would have said you can't buy direct from farmers because you'd have to feel every animal in the pen to make sure it's good quality, and even then you'd never be able to agree a price. Two things have changed since his time. One is the quality. It's consistently high and that's a great testimony to the farmers. With someone like Nigel, I'm very confident in what I'm selling. He's very passionate, but also very professional. I couldn't wish for better farm management.

Nigel Jones, Ness Heath Farm, Marc Wilkinson's supplier 331

'The other change is that buyers and farmers have become much better business people. Dealing in livestock is not the easiest thing. Prices might rocket one week and come down the next. What we have to do is hit a happy medium and roll through it. Nigel is producing a premium product and I agree to pay him a premium price for it, throughout the year. That way we can work together in a stable and secure environment to produce high quality, out-of-the ordinary products.'

Nigel nods in agreement as he steers us towards the Landrover. It's a beautiful afternoon and we're off to see the dry sows in pig who will farrow later on. They live on the other side of this 100-acre farm and, as he drives, Nigel interprets the topography for us, from flatland to ridge to the Dee Estuary. 'We're on sandstone bedrock here, water goes straight through it. So rain suits this farm, we can hardly get enough of it. But here', he says, pulling up, 'there's a bit of clay.'

Before us are a quartet of sows, wallowing gloriously in mud and grunting with pleasure. The spa is scrupulously maintained – by hose when necessary – for the welfare of these shapely bathing beauties. 'They don't sweat, do they? So it's their only way of cooling down. They love it!' says Nigel. And with that, he's in among them, fondly patting a great hairy back.

'It's a cracking little paddock for them', he observes with a happy smile. And so it is: a long, narrow, tree-shaded stretch of lush grass. One hardy loner is grazing in the distance, a few nap in their spacious shed, out of the sun's glare.

In separate quarters is Betwys Gerald, pedigree boar to these pedigree sows, and a fine figure of a pig in every way. 'We have twelve breeding sows and they have two litters a year. When they go to the boar they mustn't be too fat or the conception rate is lower', Nigel explains. 'When a sow is ready to give birth, usually in 120 days, she comes down to the farm. I'll put her in a pen so I can supervise the farrowing and I'll have a heat lamp set up to keep the piglets warm. We'll wean them in seven weeks, about a month longer than commercial ones.'

'I always wanted to keep pigs', says Nigel reflectively. 'They're fascinating creatures, so intelligent. I've worked on several farms since I did my degree at Aberdeen University, but this has been my first opportunity to have any. As a student I worked on big intensive pig units. Horrible! If people knew what went on, a lot more of them would become vegetarian.

'There are 61 million people in the UK. Could we all eat this traditional kind of pork? I don't know, probably not. But I do think, as a nation, we eat too much rubbish meat and processed meat that has turned it into a factory industry. If we all ate a bit less but better quality, we could make a big difference – and be healthier.' Callum agrees: 'I think we have a moral obligation to give animals respect and treat the meat we get from them properly. We should also remember, there's an awful lot of energy involved in intensive rearing and in processed meat.'

But if none of those arguments carry weight, just savour the difference in taste. In the words of Derek Cooper, founder of BBC Radio 4's Food Programme and doughty campaigner for Britain's regional food: 'Once you try Gloucester Old Spot pork, you'll turn your back on the tasteless, dried up, intensively reared pork forever.' It's equally true of the bacon, dry-cured and sold loose. Eat that and you'll find it hard to return to the watery, vacuum-packed stuff that shrinks, dries up and exudes a white, salty residue on pan or grill.

'We're told we've got more choice of food than ever before, but a lot of it's not worth eating. When you've tasted the real thing, you'd rather do without the rest. This is the thing about food now', Callum notes, 'there's such a vast gap between good food and poor food.'

And some food pretends to be better than it is and costs top whack on the strength of it. Meat may be labelled with the name of a rare breed, but look more closely and it turns out the mothers were commercial livestock and only the father was pedigree. Some meat may say it has been hung, without mentioning that means deboned, divided into the various cuts and left to mature in an oxygen-free vacuum-pack, rather than hung on the bone to age naturally.

Both men think we are all becoming better informed about our food, but both wonder why we have valued our native breeds and distinctive local produce so little in the recent past, especially in comparison to the rest of Europe. Well now the Gloucester Old Spot is fighting back. During 2008, a consortium that includes Defra and the Rare Breeds Survival Trust, hopes to secure Traditional Speciality Guaranteed status from the European Union to protect Gloucester Old Spot pork and bacon that is produced from pedigree stock. It could be the start of a trend.

Trading Places
Traditional Markets

'OH LOOK, LOOK LOOK! LOOK AT THOSE LOBSTERS – and the scallops – and the crabs!'

'Yeh, but look at the sea bass on the next stall, all fresh and firm, like it just swam in …'

'What'll we have then? Oh I can't choose, you choose.'

'Just walk along a bit, I think I can see some lovely looking monkfish down there …'

They sounded like tourists at La Pescheria market in Venice, but of course they weren't. This couple were tourists in Bury, just outside Manchester. They'd come, like a lot of other visitors do, to mingle with the lucky locals at the town's award-winning market. It's a huge, modern, bustling place that sells all sorts – 50,000 product lines from pot-scourers to hand-raised pork pies – across 370 stalls, in three separate areas, indoors and out. Every week, 250,000 shoppers pour in. That's right: a quarter of a million. Because people love a good traditional market.

There's a real thrill to shopping in a place like this. You don't know what you might see, who you might meet – or what you'll come home with. It's full of energy, colour and individuality. Instead of the supermarket's one monopolistic fish counter, and meat counter, and cheese counter, and fruit and vegetable selection there's a whole competing clutch of them, and lots of independent market-traders, up close and personal, ready to advise, befriend – even flirt a little – while we make a real choice between their varied wares.

In the Fish and Meat Hall, undoubtedly the centrepiece of Bury Market, you have the feel of an authentic, valued food culture, the sort of thing that people are so impressed by in markets abroad. The glorious variety, the pungent smells, the possibilities on offer, all make you want to collect up these ingredients and cook them. Shopping here is a tonic.

It's an experience which contrasts sharply with the monoculture of the supermarket, where the big weekend shop is so dull, so impersonal, so mechanical, it seems like an ordeal.

We're not predestined to be food-industry automatons, condemned to meals in cardboard boxes, to shrink wrapped brassicas or to fish so limp and wall-eyed it would seem only decent to dispose of them. So why do we put up with it?

Partly because a lot of us don't have much option. Retail markets like Bury's are few and far between, although the Northwest is luckier than a lot of areas. Bolton, which has four markets, has even managed to retained its spectacular glass-roofed, cast-iron market hall – and fully refurbished it. Birkenhead and Chester have lost their Victorian equivalents, but still run popular traditional retail markets – and there are others. But UK-wide the traditional markets are in decline. All around the country, the city centre sites which they once occupied have fallen prey to strangulating traffic schemes and shopping malls, while

supermarkets have lured us in with the promise of convenience and free parking.

The First National Survey of Retail Markets, undertaken four years ago, found that average stall occupancy rates were 75% and falling. However, there are signs of a reverse in the trend, in no small part due to the traders themselves; people with exceptional products and the drive and determination to use markets to sell them.

Andrew Sharp is one of them. He decided to take his meat to market. When he set out, a decade ago, it was a step in the dark, and a long step too – all the way from Lindal-in-Furness to a run-down part of London where a failing food market was trying to pull itself up by the bootstraps. Eventually, it succeeded so well that it has now become the country's most important retail market for fine foods. Andrew succeeded with it. Let's look at how he did it.

Farmer Sharp

The man who went to market
Cumbria

ANDREW SHARP HAS THE GIFT OF THE GAB. In broad Cumbrian, when he chooses. He's a spieler, a showman, a cheeky chappie, a real character who can hold an audience in the palm of his hand. That's one reason why his butcher's stall at London's famous Borough Market is so popular. Another, even more compelling, is the sheer quality of the Cumbrian meat that he sells there.

And, when it comes to meat, master-butcher Andrew knows his stuff. He can advise his customers with precision on which cut they need and how to cook it. Witty, pithy *and* wise. Pretty passionate about it all too. But how come a chap who lives in rugged Cumbria and loves it to the bedrock, can be found in the sprauncy Big Smoke half the week? It's a tale worth telling.

First, the bare facts. The business goes by the name of Farmer Sharp, and in that persona Andrew represents a co-operating network of fifty Lake District farmers. They specialise in rearing grass-fed Herdwick sheep and Galloway cattle – ancient, hardy breeds, traditional to the area – which produce meat of tight-grained texture and moreish flavour. Andrew specialises in selling it for them: properly hung and matured mutton, lamb, and beef; naturally reared pink veal, and a range of charcuterie products, including his award-winning air-dried mutton. His customers are wholesale and retail, internet and personal shoppers. They range from an array of top chefs to the elderly lady who dubbed him 'Farmer Sharp' – an inspired monicker if ever there was one.

It happened like this. Borough Market, the capital's longest-running wholesale food market, was haemorrhaging business badly when its trustees hatched an inspired plan. They would start a retail food market on the centuries-old site, which lies in Southwark, just over London Bridge, a stone's throw from Shakespeare's Globe Theatre.

Their venture opened in 1998, with half a dozen pioneering stall-holders who sensed potential in the place. Among the first were three Cumbrians, looking to boost their regionally-challenged fortunes. They hitched up their wagon – a shared one-ton van – and clubbed together to try their luck in London. As well as Andrew Sharp, were Peter Gott of Sillfield Farm, with his wild boar and rare-breeds pork, and Les Salisbury of Furness Fish, Poultry and Game. The trio are well to the fore in British food today, but at the time they had no idea that Borough would become such a runaway success story – *the* place to buy food in London.

'At first we slept in the van, then Peter got a walk-in fridge on his stand and we slept in a room at the back, like the bunkhouse in Bonanza – Hoss Cartwright and the team! In fact, it was a lot like the Wild West – a wing-and-a-prayer job. We had to keep our outlay down to the minimum because we were a long way away from home and costs are a fortune in London. For a while, we stopped in a backpackers' hostel – a tenner a night for a bed. Later, *twelve* of us rented one three-bedroom flat and it felt like we were back in the bunkhouse again!

'In those days, a great old lass used to come in to Borough Market – she was like the Emmeline Pankhurst of the Countryside Alliance', Andrew recalls, his voice full of affection. 'She used to say', and he enunciates in cut-glass vowels and a commanding alto: ' 'We must support the countryside!'

'And she would come to me for one lamb chop, because she lived on her own. She'd buy a small fillet of seabass from Les, and something off each trader – just to support everybody. She had these Toytown names for us all – and mine was Farmer Sharp.

'All my buddies in the Market thought it was fun to take the mickey and call me Farmer Sharp, and soon everyone was at it, until the customers didn't know me by anything else. The name was a gift, a great gift – and *it* picked me, not the other way round!'

But Andrew knew how to use it, so it's his face – the face of Farmer Sharp – under his trademark flat hat, that appears as the business logo. That natural talent for marketing and communication is what his farming colleagues in Cumbria rely on. While they employ their expertise and effort to raise fine beasts, he uses his to make the connections and do the deals that will give them a decent return for their labours.

'It's dead simple in a co-operative group', he explains. 'You either pick a winner to represent you and pay him a percentage to get a better price for your product, or share the work among yourselves. You've got to make a choice. Now farmers', his voice rises to an emphatic crescendo, ' farmers are *notoriously* bad at working together. The way we've managed it is I do that job, I take those risks, and they get an extra margin. In the long run, success is all about brand and marketing. There's meat everywhere, but not meat of the same quality, provenance or marketability. Breed, husbandry, animal welfare; proper slaughter, maturing and butchering – those are the elements that combine together to make great quality.'

Nowhere is that more evident than in Farmer Sharp's mutton. Rich-tasting, meltingly tender and succulent, it's doing a roaring trade. Yet, for generations, top-quality mutton had been lost to us. The rear-'em-fast, kill-'em-quick, sell-'em-now practices of the post-war years rendered this superb meat virtually unobtainable. That is because mutton is a slow food. It takes at least two years (five for Farmer Sharp) to rear ewes and wethers for mutton, instead of the usual four to six months for lamb. Then it takes at least two weeks to mature the meat after slaughter. And time means money. So mutton disappeared from the mainstream. People forgot its rich taste; forgot how good the best could be.

Andrew remembers the stirrings of change: 'It started when Prince Charles said we should be helping our hill farmers and doin' summat better with ewes in this

country at the same time. So 'e asked the Academy of Culinary Arts to have a look at it and find people who were selling mutton. I was one of the few at the time. Me and Bob Kennard of Graig Farm Organics in Wales, we were the first two advisers to the Mutton Renaissance campaign.' They also supplied mutton for the dinner which launched the Campaign at The Ritz in 2004.

Since then obligatory standards have been laid down for producers of what is called 'Renaissance quality'. Even so, mutton is still a misunderstood meat. Few people today have ever eaten it, but they equate it with something old and undesirable – in culinary terms, fit only for a very slow pot. Renaissance quality mutton is very different. 'The biggest fallacy', explodes Andrew, 'is that mutton has to be stewed to death. It frustrates the hell out of me! You can take *our* mutton – loin, fillet or French-trimmed best end – and cook it as pink as our lamb. That's because it's been hung and matured properly – the right sheep, raised in the right way and finished in the right way.'

Those sheep are Herdwicks, native to Cumbria for at least a thousand years. Their keepers cleared the trees and built the dry-stone walls; the sheep close-cropped the fells. Between them, they have shaped the landscape into that stark grandeur which is unique to the region. The small, sweet-faced Herdwicks grow slowly, feeding on grass, heather and lichens, a diet which imparts a distinctive flavour to their flesh. They roam at will, and forage expertly, because they are hefted to the fell – in Cumbrian, 'heafed'. This means they instinctively know the land their mothers trod.

The outbreak of foot and mouth disease in 2001, and the government's policy of mass slaughter, brought this small miracle of evolution under severe threat, and with it the livelihoods of the upland farmers, as heafed to the land as their sheep. Andrew Sharp was among them. His own ancestors have farmed here for hundreds of years. More recently, his great-uncle, Tom Storey, was shepherd to Beatrix Potter who did so much to safeguard the survival of the Herdwick breed.

Andrew was determined to stand up for the traditional livestock farming of Cumbria: 'I represent farmers. I fight their corner and I fight it vociferously. Artisan food will never make you a millionaire but it should make you a living wage. Anyone who works hard seven days a week and fifty-odd weeks of the year – and produces an excellent product into the bargain – deserves that.'

He has been outstandingly successful in reaching his goal. Could he have done it without coming to the capital and Borough market? 'Unfortunately, and much to my dismay, this country is London-centric. But, really, this whole food phenomenon is stopped by the lack of market places for traders to vend their products – places that don't demand massively high rents. Borough Market is unique because it has charitable status. It's there for the benefit of the public, not to make a profit per se.

"The biggest fallacy is that mutton has to be stewed to death. It frustrates the hell out of me! You can take our mutton – loin, fillet or French-trimmed best end – and cook it as pink as our lamb. That's because it's been hung and matured properly – the right sheep, raised in the right way and finished in the right way."

'The powers-that-be talk about city-centre regeneration. Put a market in the centre, make it not for profit, not high cost, and the centre will regenerate itself. Borough Market has revived that whole area of Southwark. When I first went there the shops were closed, buildings were boarded up. Now they've been renovated, and businesses are trading profitably again because the Market draws people in.

'It's not rocket science. It's simple. But there's got to be a will on the part of local councils to create food markets like that for the good of the community. Then people like me, Reggie Johnson, or anybody else, wouldn't have to go to London.'

But tomorrow, as usual, that's where he'll be, leaving behind the Lindal-in-

Furness field, where the preparation plant and his spartan office stand, for the eager bustle of Borough. Think of him there, selling his wares, advising the customers who've brought in 'recipe off t'internet' – and giving lessons too: 'Every Friday evening I run Mastering Meat classes on the stall. I got the idea because people would stand by my block whilst I was working, watching me boning out or butterflying a leg of lamb. So I'd turn the knife round and say, 'Y' wanna' ave a gaw?'

'Ooo, I couldn't do that!'

'Course y'can. Anyone can do that. My careers' teacher always said all you need is a strong arm.'

He assumes a challenging, teacherly tone: 'What yer gonna do when yer leave school Sharp?'

(Deferentially) 'I'm gonna be a butcher, Mr Smith.'

(Loftily) 'All yer need is a strong arm, lad. On yer way.'

When our laughter dies down, he says laconically, 'Well, I've got a strongish arm, but I think it might just have a bit more to it than that.'

And there he is, in Borough's glazed, pillared and porticoed Victorian market hall, providing people with a touch of the northwest's idyllic Lake District as they do their shopping, and giving everybody a bit of fun at the same time. 'It's just talking isn't it?' says Andrew. 'Anyone can do that.'

Mutton is the meat I love.
On the dresser see it lie;
Oh, the charming white and red;
Finer meat ne'er met the eye,
On the sweetest grass it fed:
Let the jack go swiftly round,
Let me have it nice and brown'd.
On the table spread the cloth,
Let the knives be sharp and clean,
Pickles get and salad both,
Let them each be fresh and green.
With small beer, good ale and wine,
Oh ye gods! how I shall dine.

From *A Receipt to Roast Mutton*
by Jonathan Swift, 1667-1745

Farmers' Markets

THE FIRST FARMERS' MARKET IN BRITAIN in modern times was held in Bath in 1997. Since then the growth has been phenomenal. Today there are about 580 nationwide, with 10,000 stallholders selling to the public on approximately 9,800 market days. Their soaring popularity springs from their unique selling point: the person you are buying your produce from is the person who grew it, reared it, caught it, brewed, baked, preserved or otherwise processed it – and all within a tightly prescribed radius, usually thirty to fifty miles.

The advantages are clear: on a regular basis in your own town centre, you can buy food that is very fresh and little travelled, often organic. And you buy direct from the producers. You can ask them anything you want to know about their product and, if you've a mind to, come back after you've eaten it and give them your opinion.

Go to the farmers' market in city centre Manchester's Piccadilly Gardens and you can buy Mrs Kirkham's Lancashire cheese straight from the hands of her son, Graham, who made it. You'll find Michelle Partington there too, with her Savin Hill beef and pork. Encouragement from chefs and the public, has freed them, and so many like them, from the constraints of scale and uniformity imposed by supermarkets. Diversity has reappeared – rare-breed meat, more flavoursome varieties of fruit and vegetables, traditional farmhouse cheese – and with it, better tasting food.

The Northwest of England is well favoured for farmers' markets, with more than fifty in the region. But one has a particular distinction. In 2007, the tenth anniversary year of the first farmers' market in this country, Wirral Farmers' Market was named Best in Britain. They were the first winners of a new award in the food 'Oscars' – the BBC's prestigious Food and Farming Awards.

Wirral Farmers' Market is held in New Ferry, Merseyside monthly on a Saturday morning. It's a vibrant affair, colourful and crowded. Unlike most farmers' markets it does not take place in the street but indoors, in the urban village hall. There are thirty-five stalls that, between them, have got the lot: top quality meat, free range eggs and chickens, fresh fruit and vegetables, fish, bread, cheese – even locally brewed beer and locally grown chillies. If you need a little something to revive you before you take your shopping home, try the café, which is run by volunteers from the neighbouring primary school.

In fact, the entire market is run by local volunteers. New Ferry is not a particularly affluent spot, and it was the drive and enthusiasm of a group of locals who wanted to regenerate the area which started the ball rolling. At a public meeting they asked for ideas and a farmers' market was proposed. Market chairwoman, Anne Benson takes up the story: 'The idea came from a lady called Amy Brady. People were very sceptical at first and said the idea would never work – people wouldn't come to New Ferry to shop – but Amy was undaunted. She quickly pulled in helpers and producers.'

That was in 2000. In the subsequent eight years, Wirral Farmers Market has won the support of the local council, tripled its stalls and brought in the crowds.

What's the secret of their success? Anne Benson: 'People often ask us that. On reflection, we have come to realise that the most important factor is the team behind the market. Our volunteers are a resourceful bunch, constantly coming up with ideas for improvements.'

There's a real community feel to the whole enterprise. The money raised in the café is used to help improve the school, and all the profits from the market are invested back into New Ferry via grants to local voluntary and community organisations. In the last five years they've contributed £16,000. As well as receiving an award from Wirral Metropolitan Borough Council for their work, in 2005 their beneficial impact on the area was recognised with an award from the British Urban Regeneration Association.

Good food, good value, good people and a sense of place: those are prime ingredients in the success of Wirral Farmers' Market and its counterparts. Farmers' markets, reborn in the USA in the 1970s, imported here in the nineties, have revolutionised the way producers and consumers interact. For years, food retailing in Britain has largely been concerned with buying goods from producers and selling them on to the shopper at an added margin. Farmers' Markets cut out the middleman. They have started to loosen the stranglehold of the giant supermarkets, ushered in new standards of quality for the shopper, and lifted many a small producer out of penury and into profit. At least 50,000 rural jobs are directly supported by them and, indirectly, tens of thousands more.

At a time when we are producing so little food in these islands and becoming more and more dependent on other countries to feed us, we not only need to keep our dwindling band of growers, but attract a new generation with the assurance of a decent living to be made. According to Lantra, the Skills Council for environmental and land-based industries, we are losing 15,900 workers a year in this sector, and the British farmer could be extinct by 2035.

Meanwhile, an estimated twenty million of us are spending £2bn a year at Farmers' Markets, and local authorities are keen to see more set up. They value their ability to revive local neighbourhoods – economically and socially – to promote local identity, and help local people gain access to fresh, healthy, affordable food.

But how can you be sure a farmers' market is the genuine article? In 2002 a certification scheme was launched by the National Farmers' Retail and Markets Association (FARMA). This imposes stringent criteria, and markets are individually inspected by independent assessors to ensure standards are maintained. To date, over half of all farmers' markets have the right to display the FARMA logo of certification.

Once a month, sometimes once a week, Farmers' Markets bring new life and colour to our towns and cities. But don't let's forget their more occasional cousins – the local annual food festivals. These joyful events have spread throughout the country. The Northwest loves them – when you're googling 'farmers' markets' try 'food festivals' too and you'll see. It is people-power that has brought about both these phenomena. A fact worth remembering.

Farm Shops

LIKE FARMERS' MARKETS, the upsurge of farm shops is another sign that consumers and farmers want to do things differently. Just a few short years ago, if you managed to find a farm to sell you anything at all, you would probably have been limited to buying a few eggs or potatoes at the farmhouse door. Nowadays, head off anywhere in the Northwest and you can't help coming across plenty of fully-fledged free-standing – even purpose-built – farm shops. Large or small, fancy or simple, they come in all guises. Many have such an impressive range of products you could do your entire week's food shopping in them. Others may have a particular speciality that is simply too good to miss.

In this section we take you to a small selection of farm shops. Abbey Leys Farm, in Cheshire, puts a particular emphasis on organic products. Organic eggs – hen, goose, duck – along with organic potatoes and seasonal vegetables, organic milk and honey are their specialities, though by no means all they sell. Willington Fruit Farm, as the name suggests, specializes in soft fruit, apples and home-pressed apple juice, as an important part of their range. Yew Tree Farm in Merseyside, offers a wide choice of seasonal produce, plus meat prepared on site. All three are small, straightforward shops, which concentrate on selling their own and other local products.

Low Sizergh Barn, in Cumbria, has gone one step further and has managed to create an entire visitor attraction, including an extensive farm trail, around its shop, which combines shopping for food with a craft gallery and a tea room. There is even a kind of bucolic cabaret, provided every afternoon by the cows, which visitors can watch being milked from a bird's eye vantage point in the café.

Sometimes farm shops will even move out of their natural setting and head to where the customers are. Tebay Services, on the M6 motorway, now has two farm shops on its site, drawing in commuters and holidaymakers alike. Other motorway services, having watched Tebay go from strength to strength, are following suit and copying the idea of selling local produce.

Wherever you find them, farm shops offer a delightfully different shopping experience: different from one another, and definitely different from the mainstream. If you are fed up with stock fare, these are the places for you. There's no telling what seasonal, home-produced or homemade discoveries lie in-store. As someone once said: they're a sort of farmers' market, but seven days a week.

At the end of the section we have added a supermarket, a special sort that features food from a plethora of small-scale producers. Following on from that, just in case you are wondering who shops for busy chefs, we introduce you to Anthony McGrath who spends his days doing just that.

Abbey Leys Farm
High Legh, Cheshire

AS YOU MAKE YOUR WAY DOWN THE SERENDIPITOUSLY NAMED Peacock Lane in the late afternoon, you can hear the conversational cluckings, quackings and honkings of hens, ducks and geese long before you actually see them. Eventually, they come into view, waddling across a huge field at Abbey Leys Farm, heading for their roosts in sheds dotted around the perimeter. The hens go in without any fuss, quite content to settle down for the night, but before the ducks will oblige, they insist on seeing their food being brought. The M56 motorway roars away in the background but it doesn't seem to detract from this timeless rural scene.

Keeping poultry is the driving force behind this place, which specializes in producing organic, free-range eggs, with a special emphasis on pure bred hens. The farm was founded in 1934 by Ernest Harrison. Originally a tailor, he started keeping chickens in the unlikeliest of circumstances – while serving his country in Egypt during the First World War. On his return, he transformed his new-found interest into his livelihood, eventually setting up here, at High Legh, near Knutsford in Cheshire. In due course, the farm passed to his three sons, Tom, Ernie and John, and now rests in the hands of grandson Tim Harrison and his wife Janet, who both share Ernest's passion for poultry.

It is nearly ten years since Tim and Janet decided to make Abbey Leys fully organic and free-range in a bid to provide a premium product which, they recognized, was becoming an increasingly important selling point in a highly competitive market. 'It was all doom and gloom in farming', remembers Janet, 'so we took the decision to go organic. It was a way to make the business more sustainable.' They are now accredited by the Soil Association. This requires adherence to extremely stringent standards: no artificial fertilisers or chemicals on the land; they must use only approved feed. The poultry must also be kept in smaller flocks and have ample space indoors and out: a provision which reduces aggressive behaviour and makes for happier, healthier hens, which live longer and lay a better tasting egg.

In the main, the chickens roost in the traditional wooden henhouses that Tim's grandfather put up in the 1930s. This generous and sturdy accommodation, with its roosting perches and cosy, straw-lined nest boxes, has more than stood the test of time, keeping the birds warm, comfortable and well protected from nocturnal predators. By day the chickens roam at will, free to scratch the earth and forage as nature intended.

By keeping pure bred chickens as well as their hybrids, the Harrisons are able to produce more interesting and unusual eggs – always popular at farmers' markets. For example, their dusky Welsummers – friendly hens and Janet's favourite – produce a lovely, large, dark brown egg with a particularly strong shell. The showy but placid Araucanas produce spectacular green eggs. The more excitable and aloof

White Leghorns produce a delicate pearl-white egg with an almost translucent shell.

People are often surprised that the yolks from such breeds, organically kept, are sometimes pale in colour, rather than the deep golden yellow they have come to expect. What they don't realise is that darker yolks are often achieved by the use of additives. The Harrisons are convinced you can taste a qualitative difference in *their* eggs (Rick Stein, for one, seems to agree, listing them in his *Guide to the Food Heroes of Britain*). Janet certainly draws the line at baking with them. 'These are not eggs you would use for making cakes', she insists, 'they're far too good for that!' Many a cake-maker might disagree – the better the ingredients, the better the cake! The eggs are particularly popular with vegetarians, who are reassured to know that the pure bred hens live out their lives naturally, even when their laying days are over.

Abbey Leys also produces organic, free-range eggs from hybrid hens, like the docile, homely-sounding Speckledy, a cross between Rhode Island Reds and Marans. The resulting hens lay chestnut brown speckled eggs, so popular that they disappear off the farm shop's shelves at great speed. There are now two thousand chickens, as well as ducks and geese at Abbey Leys, with the flocks spread across several fields in the area. 'We used to have guinea fowl too, but they flew away', laughs Janet.

The eggs on sale are very fresh. Those in the farm shop will be a day or two

old, the ones they take to farmers' markets, less than a day. Duck and goose eggs are also sold in season. In addition to a range of foods from other local producers on sale in the shop, the Harrisons are branching out themselves. Tim has started growing organic vegetables, with around ten different varieties of potato, including the rarely seen pink fir apple. They sell their own honey, and a bakery has been set up, where Janet creates delectable home-made cakes. They plan to bring in a baker next to make their own breads.

At present, Tim and Janet are working on a project to bring school groups on to the farm to see the whole egg production process. Children will see eggs being laid, chicks being hatched, and later they will make egg sandwiches in the kitchen. The Harrisons already support their local school, providing incubators so pupils can experience that fascinating moment when a chick emerges from the egg. Urban schools are next on their list, where they hope to help a whole new group of youngsters appreciate ethical farming and good quality, local food.

Tim and Janet are clearly devoted to what they do, but it doesn't make for an easy life. 'It is hard', admits Janet, who also holds down an outside job. 'As well as the day to day running of the farm we are at farmers' markets each weekend, and we have one here on the first Sunday of every month too. You lose your social life.' 'But', adds Tim, 'it's in your blood, so you keep right on going!'

Low Sizergh Barn
Kendal, Cumbria

EVERYTHING AT LOW SIZERGH BARN, from the entrancing wildflower meadow in the car park, to the farm shop full of sumptuous local produce, exemplifies the Park family's philosophy that a properly run farm can enrich the lives of the whole community. It was in 1980 that Alison Park, her mother Marjorie, father John and brother Richard, began renting the 250-acre dairy farm, which is part of the National Trust's Sizergh Castle estate, on the outskirts of Kendal. They quickly realised that they would have to diversify if they wanted to survive and, taking advantage of our renewed interest in how food is grown, they began by selling pick-your-own strawberries.

The venture was a success and prompted them to open their own farm shop, in 1991, in the picturesque setting of their eighteenth century stone barn. At the time, farm shops selling local produce were not that common. 'It looks like we were a bit entrepreneurial, but really we were doing what our family had always done – selling directly to the customer, the way my grandfather used to sell at market,' explains Alison. The award-winning shop has gradually increased the range of its products, now offering an impressive variety of excellent foods. On the cheese counter alone you will find around sixty specially selected cheeses, many of them from local makers.

The entire farm is maintained in the traditional way, becoming completely organic in 2002. Everything which happens on the farm is carried out according to organic farming principles which include: maintaining healthy fertile soil; recycling natural waste; creating wildlife habitats; protecting the environment and achieving high standards of animal welfare. Alison readily admits that it was primarily a business decision to go organic, though both she and her brother – who runs the dairy herd – had been interested in the concept for a long time. 'We're certain you can taste the difference in our milk. Farming success depends on the health of your soil. You have to have good soil to grow good crops, which you use to feed the cows, so they produce good milk', she explains.

The lush pastureland is bordered by traditionally managed hedges, many of which are over four hundred years old. They are just one feature among many which would have been found on an old-fashioned mixed farm. In addition, there are two hundred and fifty laying hens and twenty sheep, a pond teeming with wildlife, and a restored orchard, stocked with traditional varieties of damsons, plums, apples and pears.

One of the most imaginative innovations at Low Sizergh is a six-acre horticultural project called Growing Well. Managed by the inspirational Beren Aldridge, this social enterprise combines an operation growing organic vegetables for the shop with a therapeutic route back into work for people recovering from mental health problems. Growing Well has been a great success on both fronts.

What is more, in these days when we are all aware of the importance of food miles, they can boast that all their produce is delivered to the shop by wheelbarrow. You can't get much greener than that!

The eighteenth century stone barn, which forms the hub of the farm, contains many surprises for the visitor, not least the tearoom with its massive plate glass wall of windows looking straight into the milking parlour. At a quarter to four in the afternoon, when the Parks' herd of cows comes home, a major attraction begins. Customers vie with each other to secure tables which afford the best view, neglecting cups of tea and home-made cakes, to watch the cows being milked.

This milk, from the 120-strong dairy herd, is at the heart of the Parks' work: it provides all the milk and cream for the tearoom, as well as supplying the shop. In the 1990s, they tried to sell their milk more widely, but there was little interest. Now, however, as the public and chefs become more interested in local produce, Lower Sizergh is able to market its organic milk and cream much more readily. Chefs now visit the farm to see production for themselves and appreciate the extra effort that farming organically entails.

Currently, the bulk of the milk is sent to Chris Sandham at J.J. Sandham's dairy at Barton, near Preston, where it is turned into cheese. This famous maker of cheese produces three delicious varieties with it: Kendal Creamy, Kendal Crumbly

and Kendal Crumbly with Red Onion – all of which are sold in the shop. The cream is sent to Windermere to make luxurious Windermere ice cream, which is also sold in the shop and throughout the region.

Like its produce, the farm has grown organically, now employing sixty people, both full and part-time. 'We never had a master-plan', says Alison, 'we just wanted to have more control over our market by selling direct to the public.' The shop has given an important boost to the local economy too, by stocking as many products as possible from the area. There are also craft galleries beneath the barn, in the old shippons where the animals were once over-wintered. The gnarled beams and slate dividers (called boskins) are still in place, but nowadays they display the wares of local potters, painters and craftspeople.

Many visitors also enjoy walking the two-mile trail around the farm. As you traverse this ancient farmland, in the possession of Sizergh Castle since 1239, it is easy to make the connection between our food and the way it is grown. In these days, when most of us have become totally divorced from that process, Low Sizergh Farm is like a breath of fresh air, reconnecting us with reality in a charming yet down to earth way. It all adds up to a winning formula, and both shop and tearoom remain packed throughout the year.

Westmorland Farm Shops
Tebay Services, Cumbria

MOTORWAY SERVICE STATIONS SEEM AN UNLIKELY SPOT, to find farm shops, but Cumbria's Tebay Services are very different from other motorway service stations. For a start, they are the only ones to be built and operated by a local, family company. They also have a strong reputation for excellent home-made food in their cafés, coffee shops and outdoor barbecues, as well as in the award-winning farm shops. If all motorway services were like the those at Tebay, taking a break from driving would be transformed – from something we resort to out of a necessity – into a real pleasure.

Tebay Northbound, which opened in 1972, and Tebay Southbound, which followed in 1993, are just north of Junction 38 on the M6. They are set against the spectacular backdrop of Howgill Fell, in the Lune Gorge, in England's beautiful Lake District, on what used to be secluded farmland until the coming of the motorway. But instead of bemoaning the great road's invasion of their rural tranquillity, John and Barbara Dunning decided to take advantage of the situation and applied to run the services themselves. This was a brave move in an industry dominated by large and powerful chains. However, Tebay Services not only made it but were recently voted the best motorway services in Britain by *Which Holiday* magazine.

Barbara and John and their daughter Sarah, who is now Chief Executive of the company, Westmorland Limited, have continued to expand their business activities. These now encompass an hotel, caravan park, truck stop, and Europe's largest grass-covered building which houses the rich and varied Rheged Visitor Centre near Penrith. But it was in 2003 that John Dunning, who still farms on land adjoining Tebay north and south, introduced his surprising new concept of the farm shop to British motorway service stations. The Westmorland Farmshops were installed in two attractive log cabins on both north and southbound areas and HRH Prince Charles opened them.

Today, some sixty local producers supply an impressive range and quality of foods. Some bear well-known names; some, like Lynn Ballantine-Dykes' Wardhall Blue goats cheese, are wonderful new discoveries. All are very, very tempting – everywhere you look in these shops. There's bacon from Slacks of Cumbria, salami made from Peter Gott's wild boar; yoghurt and freshly-made soups from Jeremy's; home-made herb jellies, chutneys, sauces, cakes, biscuits, bread and puddings; over forty farmhouse cheeses, mostly straight from the farms.

Aficionados of the hand-raised pie are in their element here with an irresistible selection from John Lomas at the Upper Crust Pie Company. In 2007 alone, Westmorland Farm Shops sold best part of forty thousand of his variously topped Gloucester Old Spot pork pies.

Alex Evans, who brings with him sixteen years' experience in Harrods' Food Hall, is manager. 'The idea', he says, 'is to source local first. But we're lucky – our location lets us look to the north and south, as well as to east and west for our suppliers.' Some of their most local products come from the Dunnings' own High Chapel Farm where they rear Galloway and Blue Grey beef cattle, Herdwick sheep and other hardy breeds, which are best suited to the unforgiving fells. Both their beef and lamb are sold from the fresh meat counter.

At the beginning of 2008, Westmorland Farm Shops went a step further, and opened a traditional butchery on the southbound side. 'This allows us to do our own cutting and hanging of meat', says Alex. 'Customers can order exactly what they want, rather than simply having a choice of pre-packed cuts, and staff are on hand to offer advice too.' The beef is hung on the bone in the maturing room to develop flavour and tenderness, but as well as supplying the usual cuts, Westmorland Farm Shops also stock their own Galloway burgers and beef olives. Their own marinated meats are on sale too, together with sweetbreads, local Saddleback pork, chicken, venison and other game.

In 2004 Westmorland Farm Shops won Best Local Retailer in the BBC's Food and Farming Awards; in 2006 Tebay Services were named Breakfast Champion of the North West. The whole enterprise is undoubtedly a real boon to travellers looking for a break with good food, in beautiful surroundings. The intriguing questions is: what imaginative new developments will have transpired by the time any of us get there?

Yew Tree Farm
Halewood, Merseyside

DRIVING THROUGH THE INDUSTRIAL AREA OF HALEWOOD and Speke in southern Liverpool, passing by huge car plants and pharmaceutical factories, the last thing you would expect to come across is a farm shop. But duck off the major bypass and within minutes you are surrounded by flat, rich, agricultural land, intersected by hedges, containing fields of crops and livestock. Soon, the little settlement of Halewood Village comes into view, with its early nineteenth-century church and old rectory, its later Victorian schools and schoolhouse. Just here, in Lower Road, is where you will find Yew Tree Farm.

In the fields cows, sheep, pigs and donkeys go about their animal affairs. A faithful old dog lies sprawled across the entrance and makes a token move to greet you as you walk in. His younger companion, a Border Collie by the name of Moss, who is being trained to gather the sheep, is livelier but, all in all, it's a relaxed atmosphere at Yew Tree. It is a place where children can come and get to know the animals and find out what farming is really like.

Since the millennium Yew Tree, which is still very much a working farm, has been part of the government-run Countryside Stewardship Scheme. The initiative is designed to encourage wildlife back onto farms, especially nesting birds and insects, by providing them with suitable breeding grounds and a protected environment. At Yew Tree Farm this has taken the form of two new ponds, an orchard with fifteen varieties of traditional English apples, plums and pears, plus a lengthy network of hedgerows and footpaths. As part of the brief to safeguard wildlife, there is no wholesale spraying or spreading with pesticides or fertilizers on the farm either.

A seventeenth-century hay-barn is home to the farm shop. It has been very attractively converted and is full of first class foods, from just-picked fruit and vegetables, to quality local meats, including home-reared lamb and Wirral White turkeys in season, plus ready meals, ice cream and, of course, Robbie Wood's local Halewood Honey. A garden section offers hanging baskets and bedding plants in spring and summer and plants and shrubs all year round.

The whole enterprise is run by Ann and Graham Lund who have been farming together for twenty-seven years in total, all but six of those at Yew Tree Farm. Theirs is not one of those big, all-singing, all-dancing farm shops, with any number of different attractions. It is down to earth, a good place to browse in the knowledge that there's always a wide selection of seasonal produce and that the Lunds always look for suppliers locally before they look anywhere else. Another plus is their emphasis on low food-miles. This applies particularly in respect of their own meat: their sheep travel only four miles to slaughter; their turkeys are reared and slaughtered on the farm; the beef sold in the shop is also produced and slaughtered on Merseyside.

For people in the neighbouring community and those prepared to travel a little bit further who want to get away from supermarket shopping and find good, local food, Yew Tree Farm is a blessing on the southern edge of the Liverpool conurbation. It is small local outlets such as this which are helping to transform the nation's food buying habits – and for the better.

Willington Fruit Farm
Willington, Cheshire

IT IS MAY AND THE APPLE TREES ARE IN BLOOM, pink and white and oh so delicately scented. A rosy froth of flowers crowns the farm-shop roof, clematis alpina in all its rampant vigour. Sitting in the office are brother and sister John Winsor and Ella Wood, conferring over their crops and dealing with a steady stream of telephone calls and visitors. Theirs is a hard-working, down-to-earth partnership, fully focussed on growing top quality fruit and continuing the successful management of the family business.

Willington Fruit Farm was set up by their father, Phil in 1950. At the time, he was working for Shell as a chemist, but he had always loved growing things, even as a child. His dream was to own his own farm. Eventually he found this one at Willington, in an outstandingly beautiful part of Cheshire, just south of Kelsall and close to Delamere Forest. Charmed by the tranquil setting and convinced by the fertility of the land, he bought it. As well as growing apples in a small orchard, he also grew soft fruits: raspberries, gooseberries, blackcurrants and strawberries. Soon he began supplying local markets. Each morning he would get up in the early hours, load up and make his deliveries to Liverpool, Ellesmere Port and other local centres. Then he'd be off to Shell and back to being a chemist for the rest of the day.

Unlike their father, Ella and John are able to devote themselves to the farm full-time. They now have 300 acres in total, spread out over several different farms in Cheshire. Their oldest trees, which are around fifty-four years old, testify to the fact that a goodly number of varieties have long been grown here. Today they comprise no less than sixteen. When other growers, urged on by government initiatives, were grubbing up their orchards and the old varieties were disappearing, the Winsors persevered. 'Put it down to dad's enthusiasm!' says Ella. 'Yes', John agrees, 'but there are other reasons why we've ended up with different types – like the time we ordered Bramleys and something else turned up! So we just stuck with them.'

Sticking out against the trend paid off. The tide turned against perpetual offerings of Gala and Golden Delicious. People rediscovered diversity, began valuing it and found there was a multitude of different taste sensations to be had in apples. Many of the old varieties proved to be far superior for texture, appearance and flavour. Willington can offer a bevy of such beauties. Belle de Boskoop, of 1856, is a red and russeted, dual-purpose apple, sharp and slightly sweet to eat, which cooks to a golden yellow fluff. Then there's the inimitable Egremont Russet, an eating apple first recorded in 1872, crisp, sweet and nutty-flavoured. Or try the golden-orange Chivers' Delight. Raised by Mr Chivers in 1920, you can cook or eat this sweet, juicy, tangy, apple.

'There was a time when it was becoming quite hard to sell them', John recalls. 'Now I can't grow enough. And there's no doubt, people want all sorts of different kinds.' The recent resurgence of interest in apple varieties has helped the Winsors enormously. Of the sixteen sorts they grow, three are early croppers, ready to enjoy before any of the rest, but not recommended for winter storage. The thirteen types of keeping apple start coming ready from September. Some will store until Christmas, others until January or February, while juicy green Crispin (dessert apple and cooker) can stay the course till March. How you store them is important. You don't need to wrap each one, but coolness, darkness and ventilation are essential, plus regular inspection to remove the rotten ones.

What is John's favourite apple? 'They are all my favourites', he laughs, 'every apple has its season.' What goes into making a good one then? 'A lot of love and a lot of care', he asserts. It certainly does take diligence to keep the orchards going. At one point, when they were buying land to expand, the Winsors were warned that it was too far north and far too cold for an orchard. Early frosts can damage both flowers and fruit. But Ella and John knew they had a natural advantage. This area of Cheshire has its own microclimate, protected as it is by the gentle ring of hills which form the Sandstone Trail, running from Frodsham to Whitchurch. As they point out, 'Willington Fruit Farm is widely renowned as one of the most northerly commercial producers in the United Kingdom.'

In the old days the Winsor family used to pile boxes of apples and soft fruit in their porch and people would pop along to buy what they needed. Now there is a farm shop where you can buy apples, pears and rhubarb, as well as raspberries, gooseberries, blackcurrants and strawberries – and there's Pick Your Own too in season. 'Rhubarb is an exciting thing at the moment, for some reason', says John. 'We can't provide enough!' They also sell salads, vegetables, local preserves, cheese, herbs and flowers, as well as their own pumpkins, beans and home-pressed apple juice and pasteurised pure juice. Eggs are available from their modest flock of twenty-five chickens, which Ella and John are planning to increase.

'You should be able to take a bite of any apple with your eyes closed and tell what variety it is.'

After fruit picking finishes in the autumn, thoughts turn to next year's crop. From December to February the apple trees are pruned. Then in spring, when the buds start to burst, there must be careful spraying to prevent disease. When the apples start to form, the numbers growing on each tree must be checked. Too many, and you produce apples that are too small; too few and the apples will grow too large. The skill is in the judgement: get it just right and you will produce perfect fruit. Touring the orchards on a sunny afternoon, you imagine Indian summers, with pickers languidly plucking ripe fruit from the trees.

However, this Cider with Rosie vision is far from reality. It is labour intensive work which takes a lot of dedication, great attention to detail and unending battles against inimical weather, pests and diseases.

By late August, if the fruit looks good you've probably succeeded, but the ultimate test is the taste. Says John: 'You should be able to take a bite of any apple with your eyes closed and tell what variety it is.' At Willington you have sixteen to try.

Supermarket
Booths

THE FIRST TIME YOU GO INTO A BOOTH'S SUPERMARKET, you wander wide-eyed, like a child let loose in Willie Wonka's chocolate factory, finding delectable discoveries at every turn. But this is real food, like Herdwick lamb from the Lake District and Eskdale Saddleback pork; fine quality fish from Chris Neve in Fleetwood, Cheshire apples from the Winsors at Willington, caulis from Peter Ascroft, banana shallots, artisan breads, charcuterie, and an amazing selection of cheeses – from Britain, continental Europe and England's Northwest – and on a proper cheese counter too, where they'll cut exactly the amount you want and let you taste before you buy. It's all top-notch stuff, all beautifully presented, all very inviting and competitively priced – food that isn't easy to find elsewhere.

If you haven't spent some time in this part of the country, you probably won't know about Booths. It is a family-owned firm, established since 1847, which has 26 stores, mainly in Lancashire, but also in Cumbria, Yorkshire and Cheshire. Apart from their astonishing range and the sheer quality of what they sell, the hallmark of the stores is their remarkable, long-time attachment to using local producers in the counties which they serve. From Lytham St Annes in the west to Settle in the east, and from Keswick in the north to Knutsford in the south, the access which Booths provide to top quality regional food is quite phenomenal.

About 25% of everything they sell is locally sourced, which means it is fresher too – vital for retaining flavour, texture and nutrients. There can scarcely be a better example than their 'dug today' potatoes, a great favourite with chef Steven Doherty at the First Floor Café in Windermere. Typically, these potatoes will be lifted in Lancashire, loaded and on their way in the early hours; delivered to all the stores and on display by the time their doors open at 8.30 am – and flying off the shelves even quicker than they came. They are hugely popular with customers.

A striking characteristic of Booths is the way they take note of their customers preferences. When a lot said they liked their potatoes with the dirt left on, Booths obliged. When others said they wanted to buy their fruit and vegetables loose, Booths obliged. But for those who don't, there's still a choice. Interestingly, the customers are a pretty loyal bunch. So are the staff, many of who have been with the company for decades and are notable, not just for friendliness, but for the enthusiasm and knowledge they display about the products they sell. As long ago as 1920, staff were invited to become shareholders, and many of Booths 3,000 employees own shares in this private company today.

The ethos of Booths can be traced straight back to its founder, Edwin Henry Booth who set out the firm's philosophy over one hundred and sixty years ago: 'To sell the best goods available, in attractive stores, staffed with first class assistants.' The fifth generation of the Booth family are now running the company, chaired by

another Edwin, and they are firmly wedded to that approach. The new stores which they have built in recent years are also conspicuously well designed. At the Windermere branch, where we took our pictures, they have refurbished the fine Victorian Gothic railway terminus where the Lake District's first tourists would have alighted. Then they have added a modern extension, paying tribute to the architectural vernacular by using Westmorland stone and slate. The interior is no less attractive, with island units displaying their goods under gentle down-lighters, and sinuous counters of frest meat, cheese and delicatessen running against a background of tiled and mosaic walls.

Here you'll find Cumberland sausage and bacon from Richard Woodall, air-dried Cumbrian ham, Andy Holt's excellent black pudding, Morecambe Bay Potted Shrimps from Les Furness, Aidan Monks' bread and Anne Forshaw's range of irresistible yoghurts. On the meat counter there are seasonal delights to be had like the Herdwick lamb, at its best between January and May, and Saltmarsh lamb from the Cumbrian coast, which takes over between July and November. In the pre-packed range you might find venison, guinea fowl and Gressingham duck. All the beef, lamb and pork is from the northwest region and farm-assured, as it is in all Booths stores.

For people who like to buy organic, there is a wide choice of products. In fact it is now possible to eat well and entirely organically by shopping at Booths. People looking for ready meals are handsomely catered for, too. At Windermere these are popular with holiday-makers, and include traditional British dishes by Cranstons of Penrith, made with their own meats and without additives or preservatives. All shoppers are keen on the café. Like those in other Booth's stores, especially the 'Artisan' cafés at Kendal and Lytham St Annes, it is definitely a cut above.

On the Windermere store's cheese counter, apart from all the continental cheeses and the Wensleydales and Cheddars, the Stiltons and Red Leicesters, the Sage Derby, there are about twenty varieties of Lancashire on sale, with at least three different kinds from the Sandhams alone, not to mention Mrs Kirkham's, or Dew-Lay's, including their fabled Garstang Blue. Then there are even rarer treasures, like Allerdale Goats Cheese, Bowland, and Cobble Tasty ... Naturally, a National Cheese Retailer of the Year Award is among the many Booths have won.

The company is a prize-winner for its beers and wines too, as CAMRA's Real Ale in a Bottle Retailer Award testified in 2005. In 2008 the company scooped North West England Regional Merchant of the Year at the International Wine Challenge Awards, the biggest annual event in the wine world. On a local note, damson gin, made from Lyth Valley damsons, is also on sale.

Clearly Booths is no ordinary supermarket. The ambience and the offer lie more between a large, specialist food shop and a top department-store food hall. How do they manage to be so innovative and so varied in their content? The answer lies partly in their ethos, partly in their size. This is buying and selling on a human scale. They get the plethora of marvellous products because they go looking for them; and they are receptive when some simply arrive at their door, brought by small local producers. They don't buy in huge volumes so small numbers don't faze them, and they are prepared to be flexible with small enterprise. If a grower, like Peter Ascroft, has a glut of cauliflowers, they'll like as not run a special promotion to help him out. If production dips with, say, an artisan cheesemaker, they're prepared to wait until stocks recover. It is all remarkably personal.

Playwright and author, Alan Bennett, captures the Booths dimension perfectly in *Untold Stories*. Describing a shopping trip to his local Yorkshire branch, he comments, with characteristic humour: 'We had to buy some Parmesan from the local supermarket, Booths ... The man reeled off this list of about six and then he said, "And now, finally, the Reggiani – the Rolls Royce of Parmesans". And I thought, well, you don't get that in Sainsbury's Camden Town.'

Caterers Supplier
Catering Connection
Manchester

CHEFS ARE NOTORIOUSLY BUSY PEOPLE and those who single-handedly try to source their products direct from local growers, often find that, although it has its rewards, it is also a time-consuming and laborious process. Step forward Anthony McGrath and his company Catering Connection, which works behind the scenes, researching and preparing produce – even encouraging the development of new produce – in order to serve chefs, as efficiently as possible, with what they are seeking.

Before taking over the company, Anthony spent eighteen years working alongside his father who founded it, learning the business inside and out. In 2003, he decided it was time to shift the premises and the focus of the undertaking. Accordingly, Catering Connection moved into the New Smithfield Market in Manchester, to get closer to the producers and the produce, and started to specialize in sourcing and promoting local produce for the restaurant trade.

In the main, it's fresh fruit and vegetables that Andrew runs to earth for his customers, as well as farmhouse and continental cheeses, plus other choice food products, which staff at Catering Connection prepare personally before delivering them in optimum condition to the chefs. Anthony puts a lot of time into talking to farmers and horticulturalists; working with them and giving them the encouragement to be more adventurous in what they grow. Planting a new crop is risky: it represents significant investment and your return on the first year is unlikely to produce a profit. And if you have no experience growing it, a lot else can go wrong and scupper your efforts completely.

These were among the principal considerations that prompted Anthony to start an allotment two years ago. He wanted to discover for himself the problems involved in growing different vegetables and fruit. He's every inch the pragmatic businessman, but the kernel of his passion for local food is detectable just below the surface. Get him on the subject of his allotment and his eyes light up. He's got the growing bug – no question – and it's plain to see how proud he is of the results he has achieved. 'I have brought in seeds from Italy and organic seeds too, and I've managed to grow quite a lot of things– plants you would not normally find in this country.'

He has even been able to provide produce from his own allotment to help out a chef or two on occasion. 'A few times, where a chef has had a special event and only needed small quantities, I have provided them with my produce. For example, when they are doing competitions I have provided courgette flowers, which don't last long once they are picked, and also Swiss Chard, Ruby Chard and Cavolo Nero cabbage, all of which had only travelled about two miles to the table.'

Anthony's business acumen becomes apparent when he talks about key decisions, such as joining North West Fine Foods in the first year that he took over the company. He has used his membership to full advantage and by tapping into their resources and list of contacts, has been able to forge a network for the promotion of local food. He's found it a very satisfying experience: 'It's nice to work with local produce; with something that has been grown only twenty or thirty miles away, rather than ringing someone in a big company in another country. It means that what you are buying is fresh. Another bonus is, you're also supporting the local economy.' He is particularly excited by farmers like Peter Ascroft in Lancashire and Andrew Pimbley from Claremont Farm on the Wirral, both of whom, he feels, are breaking the mould by being receptive to new ideas. He wishes that more farmers were prepared to do the same.

Not all the produce on offer at Catering Connection is local. There are also seasonal products from abroad for example, in summer, truffles from Perigord, in south west France. Much of the charcuterie is also from the continent, as are some of the specialist regional cheeses. This is all part of a comprehensive policy to ensure that chefs are able to get what they need, precisely when they need it. To this end he offers an emergency call-out service, customer helpline and free delivery.

In recent years, Anthony has started to work more closely with chefs across England's Northwest, who are now recognising the value of good local food. 'They are changing. Years ago they competed to have the most obscure things on their menu, using new ingredients in order to draw people in. But more and more they are asking for local products and naming their sources on the menu.' Catering Connection now supplies a variety of prestigious establishments in Manchester, such as The City Inn, The Lowry Hotel and Malmaison.

Anthony McGrath is convinced that demand for local produce will continue to grow – and he wants to be at the forefront of that movement.

Contact details

Paul Askew
The London Carriage Works
40 Hope Street
Liverpool
Merseyside L1 9DA
www.hopestreethotel.co.uk
0151 705 2222

Andrew Pimbley
Claremont Farm
Old Clatterbridge Road
Bebington, Wirral
Merseyside CH63 4JB
www.claremontfarm.co.uk
0151 334 1906

Peter Jones
Wirral Watercress
Woodside Nurseries
New School Lane
Childer Thornton
Cheshire CH66 1NG
07779 019348

Paddy Byrne & Tom Gill
Everyman Bistro
5-9 Hope Street
Liverpool
Merseyside L1 9BH
www.everyman.co.uk
0151 708 9545

Mick Evans at L Rice
Fruit & Vegetable Wholesale Market
Edge Lane
Old Swan
Liverpool L13 2EP
0151 254 2929

George Wright Brewing Company
Unit 11, Diamond Business Park
Sandwash Close
Rainford
Merseyside WA11 8LY
www.georgewrightbrewing.co.uk
01744 886 686

Ward's Fish
CP27 Birkenhead Market
Wirral
Merseyside CH41 2YW
www.wardsfish.co.uk
0151 666 1842

Warrick Dodds
previously at **Cassis**
Stanley House
Mellor
Lancashire BB2 7NP
www.stanleyhouse.co.uk
01254 769 200
currently at **The Sparling**
807 Garstang Road
Barton, Preston
Lancashire PR2 5AA
www.thesparling.co.uk
01772 863789

Ian Banks
Eaves Green Game Farm
Banksfield
Eaves Green Lane
Goosnargh
Preston
Lancashire PR3 2FE
01772 865300

Eddie Cowpe
Huntleys
Huntley Gate Farm
Whalley Road
Samlesbury
Lancashire PR5 0UN
www.huntleys.co.uk
01772 877123

Steven Doherty
The First Floor Café
Lakeland
Alexandra Buildings
Station Precinct, Windermere
Cumbria LA23 1BQ
www.lakeland.co.uk
01539 447116

377

Chris Neve
C & G Neve
19 Copse Road
Fleetwood
Lancashire FY7 6RP
www.cgneve.co.uk
01253 774100

Aidan Monks
Munx Lakeland Bakery
9-11 Mill Yard
Staveley
Kendal
Cumbria LA8 9LR
www.munx.co.uk
01539 822102

Nigel Haworth
Northcote Manor
Northcote Road
Langho
Blackburn
Lancashire BB6 8BE
www.northcotemanor.com
01254 240555

Peter Ascroft
H & P Ascroft
Worthington's Farm
Tarleton
Preston
Lancashire PR4 6JN
01772 814465

Michael Price
Port of Lancaster Smokehouse
West Quay
Glasson Dock
Nr Lancaster
Lancashire LA2 0DB
www.polsco.co.uk
01524 751493

Paul Heathcote
The Longridge Restaurant
104-106 Higher Road
Longridge
Preston
Lancashire PR3 3SY
www.heathcotes.co.uk
01772 784969

Reg Johnson
Johnson & Swarbrick
Swainson House Farm
Goosnargh
Preston
Lancashire PR3 2JU
www.jandsgoosnargh.co.uk
01772 865251

Graham Kirkham
Mrs Kirkham's Lancashire Cheese
Beesley Farm
Goosnargh
Preston
Lancashire PR3 2FL
www.mrskirkhams.com
01772 865335

Robert Kisby
Cock O'Barton
Barton Road
Barton, Malpas
Cheshire SY14 7HU
www.thecockobarton.co.uk
01829 782277

Elaine Von Dinther
Deemster House
Wirswall, Nr Whitchurch
Cheshire SY13 4LF

Anne Connolly
Larkton Hall Farm
Hampton Heath, Malpas
Cheshire SY14 8LR
peter.clayton@claytonpartnership.co.uk
01948 820520

Gary Manning
60 Hope Street
Liverpool
Merseyside L1 9BZ
www.60hopestreet.com
0151 707 6060

Paul Hevey & Dan Weston
Lakes Speciality Foods
5 Bankside Barn
Crook Road
Staveley
Cumbria LA8 9NH
www.lakesspecialityfoods.co.uk
01539 822713

Bob Day
High Chapel Farm
Orton
Cumbria CA10 3RE
07771 534194

Robbie Woods
Halewood
Merseyside
0151 487 9650

Simon Radley
The Arkle Restaurant
The Chester Grosvenor & Spa
Eastgate, Chester
Cheshire CH1 1LT
www.chestergrosvenor.com
01244 324024

Barry & Gillian Pugh
Pugh's Piglets
Bowgreave House Farm
Garstang Road
Bowgreave, Garstang
Lancashire PR3 1YE
www.pughspiglets.co.uk
01995 601728

Michael Dykes
Eddisbury Fruit Farm
Yield Lane
Kelsall
Cheshire CW6 0TE
www.eddisbury.co.uk
0845 0941023

Simon Rimmer
The Earle Restaurant
4 Cecil Road
Hale
Altrincham
Cheshire WA15 9PA
see www.onionring.co.uk
0161 929 8869

Andrew Holt
The Real Lancashire
Black Pudding Company
Unit 4, Waterside Industrial Estate
Haslingden
Lancashire BB4 5EN
www.rsireland.co.uk
01706 231029

Michelle Partington
Savin Hill Farm
The Barn
Savin Hill
Lyth Valley, Kendal
Cumbria LA8 8DJ
www.savin-hill.co.uk
01539 568410

Marc Verité
The Warehouse Brasserie
30 West Street
Southport
Merseyside PR8 1QN
www.warehousebrasserie.co.uk
01704 544662

Christian Peet
Southport Seafoods
11 Shellfield Road
Marshside
Southport
Merseyside PR9 9US
www.pottedshrimps.co.uk
01704 505822

Marc Wilkinson
Fraiche
11 Rose Mount
Oxton, Wirral
Merseyside CH43 5SG
www.restaurantfraiche.com
0151 652 2914

Callum Edge
Edge Butchers
61 New Chester Road
New Ferry, Wirral
Merseyside CH62 1AB
www.traditionalmeat.com
0151 645 3044

Nigel Jones
University of Liverpool
Faculty of Veterinary Science
Ness Heath Farm
Leahurst, Neston
Cheshire CH64 7TE
www.liverpool.ac.uk/vets
The pork is not available for
sale to the general public

Trading Places

Bolton Market
Office 7
Ashburner Street
Bolton
Lancashire BL1 1TJ
Telephone: (01204) 336825
Fax: (01204) 336829
Email: business@bolton.gov.uk

Bury Market
c/o Bury Markets Management
1 Murray Road
Bury
Lancashire BL9 0BJ
www.burymarket.com
0161 253 6520

Piccadilly Market
Held at Piccadilly Gardens,
Manchester M1 1LZ
for further information on Manchester's
Specialist Markets
Manchester Markets Head Office
New Smithfield Market
Whitworth Street East
Openshaw
Manchester M11 2WJ
Phone: 0161 234 7356
Email: specialist@manchestermarkets.com

Andrew Sharp
Farmersharp
Diamond Buildings
Pennington Lane
Lindal-in-Furness
Cumbria LA12 0LA
www.farmersharp.co.uk
01229 588299

Wirral Farmers Market
The Village Hall
New Ferry, Wirral
Merseyside CH62 5AX
www.wirralfarmersmarket.co.uk
second Saturday of the month

Tim and Janet Harrison
Abbey Leys Farm
Peacock Lane
High Legh, Nr Knutsford
Cheshire WA16 6NS
www.abbeyleys.co.uk
01925 753465

Alison Park
Low Sizergh Barn
Sizergh
Kendal
Cumbria LA8 8AE
www.lowsizerghbarn.co.uk
01539 560426

Westmorland Limited
Westmorland Place
Orton, Penrith
Cumbria CA10 3SB
www.westmorland.com
01539 624511

Ann & Graham Lund
Yew Tree Farm
Lower Road
Halewood
Liverpool
Merseyside L26 3UA
www.yew-tree-farm.org
0151 487 5165

John Winsor & Ella Wood
Willington Fruit Farm
Hillside Farm Chapel Lane
Willington, Tarporley
Cheshire CW6 0PH
www.willingtonfruitfarm.co.uk
01829 751216

Booths Supermarket
The Old Station
Victoria Street
Windermere
Cumbria LA23 1QA
www.booths-supermarkets.co.uk
015394 46114

Anthony McGrath
Catering Connection
Unit A15 New Smithfield Market
Openshaw
Manchester M11 2WJ
www.cateringconnection.co.uk
0161 223 8811

Contacts for Further Information

Food Northwest
The Heath Business & Technical Park
Runcorn
Cheshire WA7 4QX
Tel: 01928 511011
Fax: 01928 581330
Email: info@foodnw.co.uk
www.foodnw.co.uk

Details of food festivals, food events and local and regional producers can be found on the web sites of the following food agencies.

Made in Cheshire
Reaseheath College
Reaseheath
Nantwich
Cheshire CW5 6DF
Tel: 01270 613195
Mob: 07969 780886
Email: jane.casson@reaseheath.ac.uk
www.madeincheshire.com

Made in Cumbria
County Offices
Busher Walk
Kendal
Cumbria LA9 4RQ
Tel: 01539 732736
Fax: 01539 729480
Email: food@madeincumbria.co.uk
www.madeincumbria.co.uk

Made in Lancashire
Myerscough Rural Business Centre
Myerscough College
Myerscough Hall
Bilsborrow
Preston PR3 0RY
Tel: 01995 642255
Fax: 01995 642245
Email: info@madeinlancs.co.uk
www.madeinlancs.co.uk

Contacts for the Tourist Boards in England's Northwest

Further information about places to visit and stay can be found on the following web sites or by phoning the relevant number.

Lancashire & Blackpool Tourist Board
St George's House
St George's Street
Chorley
Lancashire PR7 2AA
Tel: 01257 226600
Fax: 01257 469016
Email: info@visitlancashire.com
www.visitlancashire.com

Marketing Manchester
Carver's Warehouse
77 Dale Street
Manchester M1 2HG
Tel : 0161 237 1010
Fax : 0161 238 2960
Email : mm@marketing-manchester.co.uk
www.visitmanchester.com

Visit Chester and Cheshire
Chester Railway Station
1st Floor, West Wing Offices
Station Road
Chester CH1 3NT
Tel: 01244 405600
Fax: 01244 405601
Email: info@visitchesterandcheshire.co.uk
www.visitchester.com

The Mersey Partnership
12 Princess Parade
Liverpool L3 1BG
Tel: 0151 227 2727
Fax: 0151 227 2325
Email: info@visitliverpool.com
www.visitliverpool.com

Cumbria Tourism
Windermere Road
Staveley
Kendal LA8 9PL
Tel: 01539 822222
Fax: 01539 825079
Email: info@golakes.co.uk
www.golakes.co.uk